Please remember that this is a library book,
and that it belongs only temporarily to each
person who uses it. Be considerate. Do
not write in this, or any, library book.

Challenging
the
Boundaries
of Reform

Conflicts in Urban and Regional Development,
a series edited by John Logan and Todd Swanstrom

Challenging the Boundaries of Reform

Socialism in Burlington

W. J. CONROY

Temple University Press
Philadelphia

For Mary Liguori,
my wife and lifetime partner

Temple University Press, Philadelphia 19122
Copyright © 1990 by Temple University. All rights reserved
Published 1990
Printed in the United States of America

The paper used in this publication meets the minimum
requirements of American National Standard for Information
Sciences—Permanence of Paper for Printed Library Materials,
ANSI Z39.48-1984

Library of Congress Cataloging-in-Publication Data
Conroy, W. J.
    Challenging the boundaries of reform : socialism in Burlington /
W. J. Conroy.
        p.   cm. — (Conflicts in urban and regional development)
    ISBN 0-87722-702-0 (alk. paper)
    1. Burlington (Vt.)—Politics and government.   2. Sanders,
Bernard.   3. Socialism—Vermont.   I. Title.   II. Series.
F59.B9C66   1990
974.3'17—dc20   89-28771
                                                      CIP

Contents

Acknowledgments

This book could not have been written without the help of many individuals. As with all pieces of scholarship, the work of others has created guideposts. I truly want to thank the mostly unmet individuals whose works have been cited.

On a more personal level, I am grateful to Mary Liguori, my wife, who typed, retyped, and edited both my dissertation and much of the early stage of this book. Her unflagging emotional support kept me going during some very frustrating moments.

I would like to thank my dissertation mentors at Fordham University, Professor Martin C. Fergus and his predecessor, the late Professor Stephen David. Professors Bruce Andrews and Mark Naison also aided me through this journey. The Graduate School of Arts and Sciences at Fordham made not only this project but my graduate education possible with three successive fellowships.

Librarians at Fordham University, Fairfield University, the University of Vermont, and Burlington's own public library all aided in small but most consequential ways. At Fordham, Sara Gross deserves special mention for making the *Burlington Free Press* available to me through interlibrary loan.

In Burlington, Greg Guma and Marsha Marshall befriended me in that wintry city and also offered research assistance. Also, many political actors, including Mayor Bernard Sanders himself, allowed me to interview them despite their hectic schedules.

At Cornell University, both Pierre Clavel and Renée Jacobs

opened their files on Burlington to me. Their generosity moved me further toward my goal.

At Temple University Press, my series editor, Todd Swanstrom, carefully guided me in pruning an overly long dissertation by one-third and reorganizing it into a coherent book. Michael Ames, editor-in-chief, also furthered the editorial process in countless ways, but I am most especially thankful to him for his willingness to consider this topic initially. I would also like to thank Jennifer French, my production editor at Temple, and Debby Stuart, my copyeditor.

At Mercy College, Provost Peter French and the Faculty Development Committee aided my writing by granting me course reductions. Peter Slater, chair of the Department of History and Government, carefully arranged my schedule to give me large blocks of invaluable writing time. Eileen Callan and Rosemarie Farella aided me in photocopying.

I must also thank Elisabeth F. S. Solomon, who graciously allowed the unlimited use of her office and its facilities to me. Without her help this work would certainly never have been completed.

Above all, I would like to thank my mother, June M. Conroy, who instilled in me a sense of intellectual curiosity and, more important, refused my request to drop out of high school.

Kentucky Wesleyan College
Owensboro, Kentucky

Challenging the Boundaries of Reform

1
Burlington's Vibrant Politics

Four months after President Ronald Reagan's first electoral triumph, in 1980, the city of Burlington, Vermont, elected its chief executive. Bernard Sanders, running as an independent against a Democratic incumbent, won by the razor-thin margin of ten votes. Unlike Ronald Reagan, Sanders was a self-proclaimed socialist, a fact widely known throughout the community. The election was a concrete example of local resistance to national trends: while America was shifting to basic conservative principles, Burlington was nurturing the seeds of radicalism. Eight years later, America's voters stayed the course by electing as Reagan's successor George Bush, while Burlington's voters had reelected Sanders the year before with equal faith. In fact, the November 1988 election, which put Vermont in Bush's column, placed Sanders within 3 percentage points of being elected to the United States House of Representatives. In March 1989, after Sanders chose not to run again for mayor, his closest political ally, Peter Clavelle, kept the office in radical hands by winning 54 percent of the vote.[1] The radical experiment, running parallel to the conservative one, had endured beyond its most prominent standard bearer.

This book is in part a description and an analysis of the reforms that Burlington's radicals attempted. It is a story of few triumphs and great frustration. The efforts of Burlington's radical community cannot be placed into neat categories of failure and success. Any final determination must reflect both what these self-labeled progressives accomplished, however modest, and what they prevented in the face

3

of unrelenting hostility. The impact of their experience resonated far beyond the city's boundaries and raised some important questions.

Four questions about Burlington's experience are addressed in this book. First, how much autonomy did local government possess? The basic assumption was that radicals demanded reforms that were the maximum possible or even impossible. Second, were the needs and constraints of the business community the primary forces that circumscribed local autonomy? Third, did the noneconomic demands of the new social movements (Burlington's ecologists, peace activists, and gays and lesbians) face different constraints than did the economic reforms and did they thus have a greater chance for enactment? Fourth, what lessons could be drawn from Burlington that would aid the American left in its struggle to capture both government and civil society? Burlington's successes and its failures together point the way to a fruitful strategy based upon electorally capturing state and local government.

SANDERS BECOMES MAYOR

The central character in Burlington's left local government is Mayor Bernard Sanders. Sanders was born in Brooklyn, New York, in 1941; he grew up in a "solid, lower-middle class" Jewish household.[2] Sanders has noted: "Being Jewish has greatly influenced my intellectual and emotional development. I was very conscious as a kid that my father's whole family was killed by Hitler. The understanding of what went on in Germany made me sensitive to the fact of activites like that."[3]

Sanders' modest family finances were further strained by the deaths of both of his parents before he finished his undergraduate degree, which he started at Brooklyn College and completed at the University of Chicago. After changing his major several times, he finally was graduated in 1964 with a degree in political science. While he was in Chicago Sanders became politicized by both his extensive reading and the spectre of racism that pervaded that city. He became a civil rights activist and joined the Congress of Racial Equality. Sanders married upon graduation and returned to the East, fatefully buying eighty-five acres in Middlesex, Vermont, while maintaining his residence in New York City. In 1968, Sanders, now divorced, moved to Vermont and took a position with the state of Vermont. With a change of administration, Sanders lost his job.[4]

Shortly thereafter Sanders became a free-lance reporter living a penurious existence. In 1971, he joined the Liberty Union party, a third party that has vacillated between left and libertarian politics. That same year, Sanders attended the Liberty Union party convention and put forth his own name in nomination as a candidate for the United States Senate in a special election held in January. He won the nomination but received only 2.2 percent of the vote in this informational campaign. Later that year he ran for governor on the Liberty Union ticket with the same abysmal results. Sanders became the party chair in 1973 and with great effort increased his share of the Senate contest vote to 4.1 percent in 1974. Finally, in 1976 Sanders again ran for governor on the Liberty Union ticket and this time broke into the double-digit category with 12 percent of the vote.[5]

Sanders left the Liberty Union party in 1977, complaining that it was not remaining "active on a year-round basis in the struggles of working people against the banks and corporations which own and control Vermont and the nation."[6] After his exit, Sanders became director of a historical society and made some independent films. During this period, Sanders remained outside electoral politics.[7]

In 1981, Burlington was ripe for electoral change. The incumbent, five-term mayor, Gordon Paquette, had aroused the ire of many Burlingtonians. Paquette's Democratic machine was proposing a 31 percent increase in the property tax (the main source of revenue for Burlington and all other Vermont local governments). The incumbent had held the line for several years on taxes by successfully soliciting federal funds and directing city policy toward federal program opportunities. There were numerous complaints that basic city services were both neglected and underfunded. With discontent at such a high level, the opposition Republicans squandered their chance to capitalize on the situation by failing to nominate a candidate to run against Paquette.[8]

If Sanders had dreams of becoming Burlington's next mayor, he never publicly articulated them until one of his best friends, Richard Sugarman, broached the topic.[9] Once decided, Sanders ran an underfunded, grass-roots campaign. He spent many hours going door to door. His campaign organization, a dedicated group of local activists, registered new voters and spread the word. Sanders ran on the issues. He opposed a waterfront development plan that called for the construction of two eighteen-story skyscrapers that would block the waterfront. In fact, he made the incumbent appear to be a supporter of this plan, though Paquette had specifically protested that he was "not with the big money men."[10] Sanders also opposed the property tax hike and the Southern Connector, a proposed four-lane highway through the South End to downtown Burlington that was a pet project of the incumbent mayor's. On the positive side, Sanders supported new sources of taxation, housing for low- and moderate-income groups, and the efforts of the police department to upgrade pay. This moderate platform helped to give Sanders credibility with the citizens of Burlington, the majority of whom are no more "radical" than most Americans.

Despite the moderate nature of Sanders' platform, virtually no one predicted that he would actually win. All elections are a jumbled mess of individual decisions informed by larger factors; this election was no different.[11] One of the major reasons that Sanders eked out his narrow victory was that Paquette and the other Democratic party officeholders in Burlington had become estranged from their reelection constituency. The Democrats under Paquette's leadership implemented an urban renewal program that had the dual effects of destroying an ethnic neighborhood (French-Canadian) and reducing the supply of low-income housing. Such a double blow to the working class, the Democrats' traditional constituency, is a feature common to urban renewal programs in older cities.[12] Consequently, Paquette was seen as being an ally of "the banks, big real estate owners, big businesses and wealthy individuals" even before Sanders accused him of such complicity.[13]

In addition, Paquette ignored the new social movements that were making their appearance all over town. Since the 1970s Burlington had been the focus of organizing efforts patterned on those of the pioneering radical organizer from Chicago Saul D. Alinsky.[14] One early group, PACT (People Acting for Change Together), was interested in class-based issues such as welfare and tenant rights, as well as youth and health issues. Although PACT virtually collapsed before the 1981 election, a panoply of other neighborhood groups arose all over town from the richest to the poorest neighborhoods. These local groups made numerous demands on Paquette's City Hall only to be ignored.[15] In fact, when Paquette debated Sanders at the behest of these groups, the mayor made a clumsy remark demonstrating his isolation: "Some of these organizations I didn't know existed until three weeks ago."[16] In addition to the profusion of neighborhood groups, Burlington was experiencing the growth of tenant organizing. A combination of public housing in ill repair and rising rents throughout the city caused by a tremendous shortage of apartments had aroused Burlington's tenants. Shortly before the election, Paquette, who had once backed a fair-housing board to regulate tenant/landlord disputes, repudiated a referendum to establish such a board.

Paquette's arrogant disdain toward tenants and neighborhood groups was also extended to his challenger. Paquette consistently dismissed Sanders as no threat and ignored the many obvious signs of political turbulence. Everyone knew the city was changing demographically. A walk down any city street demonstrated that Burlington was losing the traditional two-parent/two-child household to the suburbs while the elderly and poor remained behind.[17] The area's booming economy was drawing young technocrats, urban professionals, and paraprofessionals to the city. In addition, the remnants of the 1960s left (which included the future mayor) were attracted by Vermont's reputation for tolerance and its scenic countryside. Contrary to national trends, the overall student population had been increasing or at least remaining steady at Burlington's four institutions of higher learning. By 1981, the majority of people living in Burlington were not natives, and they had no loyalty to the local Democratic organization based on past performance.

Another major factor that made Sanders' independent candidacy credible was the endorsement of the Burlington Patrolmen's Association, which had been through many labor disputes (especially over salary) with the Paquette regime. Rank-and-file police support made the radical Sanders seem far less threatening. One reporter from a local weekly commented that police support "gave Bernie [Sanders' nickname] an endorsement from a very credible source that in and of itself negated all the possible . . . redbaiting that would have gone Bernie's way. . . . I mean, how can you be a communist if the police are for [you]?"[18]

Sanders' credibility was further boosted when the local media gave him access and reported on his campaign activities. A local television station, WCAX-TV, played a key role, since its broadcaster and editor disliked Gordon Paquette. As the campaign got rolling, even the local newspaper, whose editors would prove to be almost unremittingly hostile to Sanders, had reporters who covered the challenger fairly. The local weekly, edited by a left sympathizer, actually endorsed Sanders for mayor.[19]

Two other Democrats correctly perceived that Paquette, although a five-term incumbent, was vulnerable. A local restaurant owner and another dissident Democrat, who ran virtually no campaign, siphoned off a total of 1,128 votes. If only 11 of those votes had been switched to Paquette, he would have won.[20]

A SHORT POLITICAL HISTORY OF BURLINGTON

Beginning in 1981, an ad hoc, partisan group of activists who elected and campaigned for left candidates in Burlington continuously controlled the mayor's office under the auspices of Bernard Sanders.[21] Nevertheless, this Progressive Coalition, as they called themselves, never won control of the aldermanic council or a majority on any but a few of the city's commissions.

During Mayor Paquette's five successive two-year terms the Democrats had consistently controlled the thirteen-member Board of Aldermen and appointed a majority of the commissioners. This political machine, as it was frequently referred to by the *Vermont Vanguard Press* (a Burlington-based reformist weekly newspaper) and Mayor Paquette's political opponents, was short-circuited by the election of the independent candidate Sanders.[22] It was a diverse combination of liberals, tenant groups, young adults, the elderly, blue-collar workers, disaffected Democrats, and other residents who were not native Vermonters—a group much larger than those who later attended the Progressive Coalition meetings—that elected Sanders.[23]

To this day, the Progressive Coalition remains an amorphous body run more like an ad hoc committee than a political party, which it formally became in 1986. In fact, the Coalition did not establish itself as a formal political party during the first half of the decade. Unlike other radical parties, the Coalition was a democratic body that had no formal organization, no codified rules, and no professional elite other than those of its candidates elected or appointed to city offices. The Coalition's lack of structure was a strength and a weakness. On the positive side, all groups and individuals in the community who identified with the Coalition were welcome to attend meetings. Burlington's feminists, gays, environmentalists, socialists, anarchists, elderly, Rainbow Coalition Democrats, and poor could all articulate their demands and help choose new candidates for office. On the negative side, the Coalition's elected officials had almost no worry of internal challenges to their incumbency. Since there were no codified democratic rules and no "Progressive" designation on the ballot before 1987, most Coalition incumbents ran as independents and others as

Citizen party candidates. This prevented the building of third-party name recognition.

In 1981, when the Coalition elected Sanders, two other supporters were elected with him.[24] Terrill Bouricius, a Citizens' party candidate, and Sadie White, a maverick Democrat running as an independent, won seats as aldermen. The Republicans won three seats, while the Democrats kept the remaining eight seats (five of which were not up for election that year) on the aldermanic council.[25] Sanders was therefore faced by a Board of Aldermen dominated overwhelmingly by the opposition.

Upon taking office, the mayor and his two aldermanic supporters were met immediately with hostile opposition. Using a procedural hiring technicality, the Board of Aldermen fired the mayor's personal aide, though after some public skirmishing she was rehired.[26] The aldermen rejected most of Sanders' other appointees, forcing him to retain the former regime's incumbent officers. Inside City Hall covert efforts to sabotage the new mayor's administration included those of Frank Wagner, a Paquette-appointed city clerk, who was caught stealing the mayor's mail. In addition, employees loyal to the old regime started their own City Hall underground newspaper lampooning the new administration.

Compounding the harassment from within City Hall, the Federal Bureau of Investigation conspicuously sent several agents to question local citizens about Sanders because of his previous affiliation with the Socialist Workers' party, the target of an FBI investigation.[27] Even the Republican-dominated Editorial Board of the daily newspaper the *Burlington Free Press* called the FBI's public investigation a McCarthy-like tactic.[28] The almost constant hostility of opposition aldermen, the local newspaper, and local businessmen to Sanders' proposals was not overlooked by the voters in the following year's elections.

The elections of March 1982 were for seven of the thirteen aldermanic seats. The initial results were three seats for the Progressive Coalition, two for the Republicans. In two wards, runoff elections were scheduled between the two highest vote-getters, since no candidate in either three-way race was able to capture 40 percent of the vote. A Republican and a Democrat won the contested seats, defeating Progressive candidates. Democrats had now lost their majority position on the Board of Aldermen. The final distribution of seats was: Progressive Coalition, five; Republicans, four; and Democrats, four.[29] The significance of a five-vote minority on the board was that it strengthened Mayor Sanders' institutional mechanism of negative power, the veto. Since it takes nine votes to overturn a mayoral veto, Sanders now had the opportunity, as long as the Progressive Coalition voted as a bloc, to frustrate the will of the aldermanic majority as they had previously blocked his initiatives. With such overt anti-left hostility emanating from the two opposing parties, the Coalition's aldermen did vote consistently together. The 1982 election results changed the aldermanic playing field by destroying Democratic/Republican control and creating a stalemate. This impressive shift of partisan strength in one year belied the opposition claim that the previous year's election of a "socialist" mayor had been a fluke.

The election of March 1983 demonstrated the left's continued electoral strength when Bernard Sanders was reelected mayor by a majority of voters (52 percent) over his two major party challengers, Judith Stephany, the Democrat, and James Gilson, the Republican. The campaign was marked by the Democratic candidate's trying to co-opt Sanders' progressive initiatives on development and yet embrace the business community, whose hostility to Sanders was manifest. Stephany did not address the inherent contradiction in her position.

James Gilson, an unabashedly pro-business Republican, ran a campaign that vacillated between pledging more spending on social services and portraying Sanders as a nemesis to business. The Republican mayoral candidate and his supporters took out a full-page advertisement in the Burlington Free Press that proclaimed:

If Sanders is re-elected this could happen: higher phone bills * higher electric bills * more delays on the northern & southern connectors * rent control * city rooms & meals tax * an anti-business Mayor * more unemployment * higher tuitions * a Mayor more concerned about foreign policy & making national headlines than running a city.[30]

The stop-Sanders campaign was escalated in the daily newspaper a few days later. Another full-page advertisement appeared (this one sponsored by the business community) that pictured fourteen conspicuously empty business locations. The accompanying captions included the following:

Burlington business provides: 21,442 jobs in Burlington . . . 50.3% of Burlington's taxes. . . . Where will these jobs go? What will happen to these tax dollars? . . . Bernard Sanders does not believe in free enterprise. We need a sensible mayor who will respect the principles on which our country was founded. Burlington needs new leadership.

The advertisement asked voters to cast their ballots for either Stephany or Gilson.[31] Interestingly, most of these buildings were vacant before Sanders' 1981 victory; four years later, most were occupied. Despite a well-organized, well-funded opposition, that March Burlington's voters chose the left alternative. Unfortunately for the Progressives, however, Sanders' victory did not sweep his supporters into lower offices. The aldermanic composition after the 1983 elections changed only slightly: Progressive Coalition, five; Republicans, five; Democrats, three. The Coalition had failed to gain an additional seat.

Despite Sanders' impressive victory over two mayoral challengers, there was no letup in harassment by the opposition-dominated Board of Aldermen. Just one month after the election, Allen Gear, the Republican president of the board (elected by Democratic and Republican aldermen), ruled that the city charter did not allow the mayor to speak at the meetings of the Board of Aldermen.[32] Sanders had attended and spoken at aldermanic meetings for the preceding two years; his effective and vituperative rhetorical style had earned him the enmity of the opposition. Throughout the political year March 1983–March 1984, the board sidetracked major Progressive proposals such as redesign of the proposed Southern Connector highway and efforts to assess street excavation fees on utilities. The electoral victory did, however, give the Progressive Coalition some bargaining power over the opposition and cooperation on the more routine issues of city governance. During June 1983, all of the mayor's top aides were reappointed (in contrast to Sanders' first year in office).[33] Also that same month, when Sanders' annual budget was passed by a nine-to-four vote, the mayor received most of what he had proposed.[34]

In the election of March 1984 the Progressive Coalition managed to pick up one additional seat on the board. Although the new alignment was: Progressive Coalition, six; Republicans, five; and Democrats, two, it left the Coalition one short of an absolute majority. Still, the win put Sanders significantly closer to electoral control.[35] An unexpected opportunity arose barely a week after the March 6 election. Linda Burns, a conservative Democratic alderman, resigned from her seat on the board for personal reasons.[36] Within days the board passed a long-stalled Progressive Coalition proposal for a street excavation fee to be paid by utilities.[37] On April 2, Terrill Bouricius, a

Progressive Coalition alderman, was elected president of the Board of Aldermen; however, it took thirty-one ballots before the Democratic/Republican bloc relented and gave their support to break the tie. Although the board president has little authority, he or she can recognize (or more important, not recognize) other aldermen to speak and can rule upon procedural questions. Republican President Gear had abused these powers by gagging the mayor at previous meetings. Unfortunately, in May 1983 the Coalition's hopes for a board majority were undermined when a Democrat soundly defeated the Progressive Coalition's candidate for the vacant seat in a special election.[38] After the reinstitution of the slim Democratic/Republican majority on the board, it alternated between tentative cooperation and the usual rejection of the Progressive Coalition's major proposals.

With progress on the Progressive Coalition's proposals being three steps forward and two backward since the 1984 election, a January 1985 *Burlington Free Press* article reporting on a University of Vermont poll showed Sanders to be significantly ahead of his Democratic opponent for mayor, Brian Burns, for the upcoming March election.[39] In addition to Burns, Republican Alderman Diane Gallagher chose to run for mayor as an independent after influential Republicans unsuccessfully tried to talk her into withdrawing from the race. The failure of Democrats and Republicans to field a fusion ticket and the early polls that showed Sanders way ahead of his opponents encouraged the Progressives to believe that the mayor's coattails would finally pull in a Coalition majority on the board. The polls accurately predicted Sanders' victory; he received 55 percent of the vote.[40] Nevertheless, the board remained in a potential deadlock with six Progressives, five Republicans, and two Democrats.

In April, the Democrats and Republicans elected William Skelton, a Republican, president of the Board of Aldermen, denying the post to the Progressives even though they had a plurality of seats.[41] Eventually the Coalition plurality did translate into more seats on key commissions; in fact, the Progressives gained a majority position on the Electric Commission.[42] Still, most commissions and the Board of Aldermen remained under Democratic/Republican control; only the mayor's office was firmly held by the Progressive Coalition.

The aldermanic elections of 1986 posed a threat to the Coalition. Of their six aldermen, four were up for reelection, and three of those four were retiring. If the Coalition lost just two seats, it would lose the ability to sustain the mayor's veto, and the de facto Democratic/Republican coalition on the board would rule much the way it had during the first year of the Sanders administration. The Republicans saw the elections as an opportunity to expand their representation and fielded candidates in all but one ward. Two Progressives won comfortably and one lost. The fourth, Erhard Mahnke, was forced into a runoff with a very conservative Republican, Walter Simendinger. The two parties put in maximum effort. Comments by both Simendinger and Mayor Sanders kept the debate centered on Sanders' radicalism.[43] In the end, Mahnke won by the thin majority of thirty-one votes. The Progressive Coalition had been challenged and wounded, but it survived.

After the March 1986 Board of Aldermen elections, Bernard Sanders finally announced that he was running for governor as an independent candidate. Even though a 1985 poll had given him a favorable response rating by 50 percent of Vermonters, Sanders' bid was a long shot.[44] Madeleine Kunin, the incumbent, was a quasi-liberal Democrat and the first woman governor of Vermont. It was suggested that if Sanders had any success at all, it would be to elect the Republican candidate by drawing off Kunin's left support. Sanders sought Vermont Rainbow Coalition support and even hired Ellen David-Friedman, a former chair of the state Rainbow Coalition, as a top campaign aide. Finally, despite some dissent, the Vermont Rainbow Coalition voted an endorsement of Sanders' quest.

As the campaign got under way, it faltered. Sanders raised only one dollar for every ten that his two challengers did.[45] He tried at first to run a grass-roots campaign with little mass media advertising but later switched to a media campaign. Despite the grass-roots emphasis, the campaign was governed under Sanders' autocratic tutelage. One member of the Rainbow Coalition called it a "one-man show."[46] Soon the campaign collapsed; the Sanders' state capital campaign office closed and Ellen David-Friedman recommended withdrawal from the race. Although Sanders proved to be an excellent debater in front of television cameras, he was buried in the election, garnering 15 percent of the vote. This was barely 3 percentage points better than Sanders' 1976 run, which had been only an informational campaign. Since Kunin was just short of 50 percent of the vote, she was duly elected by the Vermont legislature. When no candidate receives a majority of the popular vote, such a procedure is specified by the state constitution.

Despite the trouncing, Sanders claimed he was "revitalized" by the run for the governorship.[47] In December 1986, he accepted the mayoral nomination endorsement from the Progressive Coalition.

The Democrats in their largest caucus in years chose Paul Lafayette, a blue-collar native Burlingtonian and popular Democratic alderman, who retained lines of friendship with the old Democratic regime. There was speculation that Lafayette could attract both the former Democratic partisans and some of the newly arrived professionals.[48] The Republicans decided not to field a candidate, thus making it impossible for Sanders to win with less than a majority of the vote cast.

The race began poorly for Sanders. The blue-collar, unionized constituency he so often championed was courted by Lafayette. Both the municipal workers' union and General Electric's largest union endorsed Lafayette. City fire and police unions, former bastions of support for Sanders, declined to endorse anyone. As the race progressed, however, the tables turned.

Lafayette's policy positions were similar to Sanders', little reason for voters to change leadership. Also, unlike Sanders, Lafayette was not a skilled debater. Even the notoriously conservative *Burlington Free Press* Editorial Board found Lafayette's performance lacking and, to the shock of the community, endorsed Sanders for mayor.[49] On election day, Sanders won by an impressive eleven-point margin and even took Lafayette's own ward. The Coalition picked up one more seat but still remained one short of a working majority.

The 1987 aldermanic races had little effect on the electoral power struggle on the Board of Aldermen. The Progressives kept their six representatives although one newcomer glided through by only seven votes. A more interesting development than the election was the Hatch Act investigation by the United States Merit Systems Protection Board of the Progressive Coalition alderman Erhard Mahnke. Mahnke had a job in the nearby town of Winooski that was funded in large part by the national government. Under the Hatch Act, an employee of this status cannot run for any "partisan" election. Assistant City Attorney John Franco, a Progressive, gave Mahnke a legal opinion that the elections in Burlington are not "partisan" and that therefore Mahnke could run. Eventually, the Protection Board found the opposite and Mahnke was barred from running again. For a short time the Democratic/Republican majority refused to seat Mahnke.[50]

At the end of 1988, the Progressive Coalition was facing its greatest challenge. Mayor Bernard Sanders was making a bid for the United States House of Representatives and, win or lose, he would not be a candidate for mayor in the March 1989 elections. Apparently learning from his gubernatorial run in 1986, Sanders almost won this bid for statewide election. In a three-way race with no incumbent,

Sanders garnered 38 percent of the vote by running a hard-hitting populist campaign. The winning Republican, Peter Smith, eked out a 41 percent victory. He chose to beat back Sanders' late surge with negative advertising, something Sanders refrained from using. Paul Poirer, the Democrat, ran a poor third.[51] True to his promise, Sanders, upon losing, did not seek the support of the Progressive Coalition for the next mayoral race even though he would have received it.

Many local commentators believed that the Progressive Coalition owed its success to the popularity of the abrasive but charismatic Sanders. Steven Soifer, a chronicler of and an activist within the Progressive Coalition, concluded, "After Sanders is gone, the prognosis is clear. It's hard to imagine the Progressive Coalition lasting much beyond the involvement of the man who was an inspiration for it all."[52] Many on the left both within and outside the Progressive Coalition were critical of Sanders' authoritarian style.[53] Some even accused him of fostering a "cult of personality."[54] Progressive Alderman Peter Lackowski called Sanders a "social democrat." By this Lackowski meant that instead of authority flowing up from the rank and file, in the Progressive Coalition "the elected officials are basically the leadership."[55] Without the Coalition's foremost leader, a political vacuum was likely.

The best empirical study of the "identity crisis" of the Progressive Coalition was done by Tom Rice, a University of Vermont professor of political science. Using a feelings thermometer, ranging from 0 to 100, Rice found that Burlington's voters rated the Democrats at 58.7, the Republicans at 48.6, and the Progressive Coalition at 39.5 degrees. Sanders rated 57.4 degrees, dramatic proof that his support crossed party lines. Within the sample, 17.5 respondents gave the Coalition 0 degrees; another 30 percent did not rate it at all. Only 10.8 percent of the respondents "identified" with the Progressive Coalition. Rice concluded that "when Sanders does exit, the Progressive Coalition will probably not be far behind."[56]

During a June 1988 meeting, the Progressives began to grapple with the coming post-Sanders period. At that meeting a rule was adopted by the group forbidding any Progressive Coalition candidate from accepting the endorsement of the Republican or the Democratic party. Only one potential 1989 mayoral candidate unequivocally supported the resolution—Alderman Terrill Bouricius, a committed socialist.[57]

At a December 1988 meeting, the Progressive Coalition endorsed Peter Clavelle, head of the local Community and Economic Development Office and a Sanders' appointee, over his two rivals, Alderman Bouricius and Treasurer Jonathan Leopold (another Sanders' appointee). Bouricius gave his support to Clavelle, but with little enthusiasm: "He is very open to socialist ideas, even though he isn't schooled in Marxist analysis." Leopold, however, not only declined to endorse Clavelle but said he might support a Democrat or Republican candidate. He went on to say: "I have a real problem with leftist politics because of its holier-than-thou attitude." Outside of the Coalition, Sandy Baird was planning a run for mayor on the Green ticket; such a move would surely divide Burlington's left-voting constituency. She complained that the Progressive Coalition was "hooked into a trickledown theory of economics, which will inevitably mean more development for Burlington."[58]

The results of the March 1989 mayoral elections confounded the pessimistic political wisdom of these local observers. Despite the absence of both Sanders and a Republican challenger and despite the addition of the Green party candidate, Baird, Peter Clavelle won with 54 percent of the vote, 1 percentage point less than Sanders' winning percentage in 1987. Baird took a paltry 370 votes, while Nancy Chioffi, the runner-up Democratic candidate, lagged behind Clavelle's total by 1,293 votes.[59] The program (not Sanders and not the party) provided the margin of Progressive Coalition victory. Thus, Republican President George Bush and Progressive Conservative Mayor Peter Clavelle spin in parallel orbits around their mentors whose programs they embrace at the opposite ends of the American political universe.

The case studies that follow in Chapters 5–8 will show the frustration that the Coalition endured as one policy proposal after another was stifled. Some of this frustration was due to or at least paralleled by the electoral stalemate. Nevertheless, whenever the Progressive Coalition could marshall a majority vote either by the absence of opposition members or with the aid of the occasional defector, it was still very likely that the new policy would not reach the implementation stage. The community power picture of democracy at work painted by the pluralist theorists of the 1950s and 1960s was mocked by the experiences in Burlington in the 1980s.[60]

The next chapter will summarize and critique the existing theories of political economy as they relate to the experience of Burlington. In their place, a new theoretical framework will be offered.

2

Theory and Method

A key issue for both urban analysts and political activists is the degree of authority possessed by the local level of government. To assess the success of attempts at radical reform in Burlington, Vermont, the previous work on the boundaries of local government authority must be reviewed and critiqued. While most theorists have dealt with the question in an oblique fashion, a few have approached it directly, and the most important of these approaches will be evaluated. The contributions of the two contending schools of urban political economy, public choice and neo-Marxist, and Paul Peterson's analysis of this issue will be analyzed. The potential benefits of post-Marxist theorizing on the issue of local autonomy will also be addressed.

Within the discipline of political science there has been a prominent debate on the degree of autonomy possessed by the State.[1] For this book, city "autonomy" is defined as the elected leadership's capacity to enact and implement policy without the obstruction or direction of any societal structure, class, institution, group, or actor. Such a definition leaves some ambiguity about the relationship of democracy to autonomy. For example, assuming that referenda are a fair reflection of what the majority wants, Burlington's majority sometimes effectively blocked policies proposed by its elected officials (frequently, those emanating from the Progressive Coalition). To be consistent with the norms of democracy, a caveat must be added to our definition: when known, the majority's will supersedes that of the elected leaders', and city autonomy is then defined as the majority's capacity to enact and implement policy over any of the aforementioned obstructions.

Although this debate about autonomy has been argued mostly within the confines of neo-Marxist thought, increasingly the mainstream of the profession has joined the argument. As interesting as this debate is, it only sheds a dim, indirect light on our central issue: the extent of local autonomy. Debate about the autonomy of the State has been largely focused on the nation-state; local government is in quite a different position. As a narrower part of the larger State whole, local government has some of the characteristics of the whole but lacks many of the most important sources of authority that the nation-state has. For example, nation-states can regulate the flow of capital and people across their borders.[2] Cities have this power in only a truncated form, such as in the right to regulate land use, and even that is limited. Nation-states also have most authority over import and export laws, the creation and control of money, and foreign and defense policy.[3] Despite these differences between the nation-state and the "local state,"[4] one of the generalizations established in this debate has a measure of utility. The notion that when the left captures a part of the State, authority migrates to another sector, which in turn frustrates democratic reform, will be explored in Chapter 4.

Because of the extent of scholarly attention to the question of State autonomy, there has been a spillover effect that has meant that both left and mainstream scholars have provided analyses of the limits of the local state's sovereignty.

PETERSON'S CONTRIBUTION

The most important contribution, from the mainstream perspective, on the issue of local autonomy has come from Paul E. Peterson.[5] Because Peterson's book, *City Limits*, has caused such an uproar in the field of urban studies, it will be critiqued at some length. In the book Peterson takes a decidedly pessimistic approach. As a non-Marxist economic determinist, he argues that cities have almost no sovereignty. Elected urban political elites shape their policies within a very narrow spectrum of alternatives that favor economic growth because local economic prosperity is tantamount to reelection. To explain local policy choice, Peterson posits three policy arenas: developmental, redistributive, and allocational. Developmental policies are those that "enhance the economic position of a community in its competition with others."[6] These are most favored by local political elites since they provide more benefits than costs to a local community. Redistributive policies take resources from the wealthier members of the community and give them to the poorer members. Since such policies provide more costs than benefits, they tend to retard economic development. Elected officials oppose redistributive programs because of their negative cost/benefit ratio. Allocational policies involve basic services, such as fire and police protection, from which all members of any given community benefit and therefore have no clear effect on development. In Peterson's book all economically important policy choices fit into one of these three categories.

These categories are of limited use in determining the limits to reform, which is the object of this book. A primary problem is that Peterson's policy framework, which is explicitly economistic, cannot address local issues such as ecology, foreign policy concerns, and equality between the sexes, all agenda issues in Burlington. Also, except for in the redistributive arena, the question of who benefits and who loses from particular policies remains unanalyzed.[7] For example, was the formation of police teams to combat radicals and militant blacks in the late 1960s a neutral allocational policy decision? Peterson sidesteps the issue of who won and who lost by arguing that economic development and prosperity are approved by the majority because the positive benefits of growth reach most people (though necessarily unequally). According to this reasoning, almost the entire community benefits from economic growth.

Even if we were to accept Peterson's framework, however, we would find little analysis of those in the community who seek redistributive policies. In fact, Peterson summarily dismisses as wholly ineffective those opposition groups who resist policies that allocate city resources to aid business development and who make counterdemands for the redistribution of city funds to poorer citizens. Instead of redistributing resources to those who are the dominated in our society, city political elites merely manage class conflict or other resistance-group conflict with effective strategies, such as delaying a response to demands, studying the problem until the crisis ends, enacting token reforms, co-opting resistance leaders, or actually devolving political authority to resistance groups but with little or no change in the unequal proportions of resources.[8] Peterson is not arguing that elected municipal leaders are callous or cynical, but he is arguing that cities do not have sufficient money or authority to redistribute resources without causing a combined exodus of business and productive people, that is, the middle and upper classes.

Peterson's universe of possible city leaders and decision opportunities is so narrow that, according to his definition the radical city regimes recently elected in Santa Monica, Santa Cruz, and Berkeley, California, and Burlington, Vermont, cannot possibly exist. People espousing and attempting the redistribution of wealth could never capture city hall! Peterson seems to be unaware of the historical presence of a popular Socialist party that had hundreds of elected officials in cities in the first third of this century and controlled the mayor's office in middle-sized industrial cities such as Bridgeport, Connecticut; Reading, Pennsylvania; and Milwaukee, Wisconsin.[9] The existence of these past and present radical regimes contradicts Peterson's assumptions that city political elites are invariably probusiness and try to contain class or other types of group conflict.

Peterson developed his conservative economic determinism by walking a line between the public choice school, a political offshoot of the Chicago school of conservative political economy, and the structural variant of the neo-Marxist school.[10] He leans heavily toward the former. The Chicago school has focused on the problem of local autonomy in an oblique manner. Charles M. Tiebout, using the familiar Chicago School, neoclassical economic framework, has argued that mobile, well-informed consumers make deliberate, rational choices about where they will live based on the array of services offered by a particular municipality. Thus the fragmentation of government authority inherent in the federalist structure provides increased possibilities for decision-making to discerning consumers.[11] By implication, local government autonomy is lacking since a community cannot juridically control the flow of citizens and capital across its borders, although it tries to enact policies to keep and attract them. The byproduct of decreased city autonomy, however, is increased residential consumer autonomy; in this analysis, the market delivers in an optimal, noncoercive, invisible fashion.

Tiebout knows that all players in the market do not have equal resources, but he identifies that fact merely as a given, much as it is in other classical economic analyses. In this type of analysis, the inequality of consumers is excluded by narrowing the factors under analysis to a chosen few and dismissing all others under the unstated but always implied qualifying condition "all other things being equal." But equal they are not. Ever since the scholarship of an earlier Chicago school of city ecology, we have known that areas that contain central cities are markedly and systematically different as one travels outward from the core. These physical differences translate into class and other differences. Instead of being unconstrained consumers, most residents are confined to certain neighborhoods because of their incomes and can move only laterally to other similar sections. The existence of class walls, not mobility, is the salient factor to be considered. Today the central city is dominated by the alternating neighborhood extremes of wealth and poverty and is the most diverse place for class mixing. By contrast, the concentric circles of suburbs that surround core cities are largely segregated by class and race. By failing to factor in the formidable constraints of spatial class segregation, Tiebout fails to emphasize that the ability to shop for municipal services is almost strictly an upper-class prerogative.

With the emphasis on efficiency, cost/benefit analysis, and growth maximization, public choice theorists deemphasize those factors that are inherently political. In particular, the degree of inequality and the political conflict caused by such inequality are consistently played down or ignored despite a past decade of racial strife and burning cities.[12] It is no wonder that most of the necessarily economistic public choice literature remained of little import until Peterson's book appeared.[13] Peterson tried to put the "political" back into political economy.

While the neoclassical school of political economics has ignored the issue of local autonomy, the neo-Marxists have been more fruitful. An examination of constraints on city policy by the economic system is common to almost all neo-Marxist analyses. The factors that are key to such analyses are the needs of the capitalist economy, the demands of the lower classes (though race, ethnicity, and other noneconomic factors are examined, they usually remain subsidiary to the economic), and the inherently contradictory role of government, which must be responsive to this antithetical set of demands. By and large, most neo-Marxist urban theorizing is an elaboration or variation on James O'Connor's influential work on the theory of the State, *The Fiscal Crisis of the State*.[14] This analysis has significantly furthered the understanding of the limits of local autonomy. Some neo-Marxist urban studies virtually ignore the "class struggle" aspect; these studies unintentionally complement Peterson's conservative economic determinism.

The similarity of conclusions about economic constraints from a wide variety of cases demonstrates the consistency of the neo-Marxist line of analysis. Neo-Marxist studies in cities as diverse as New

Haven, Denver, New Orleans, New York, Cleveland, and Gary have all demonstrated persuasively that capitalism ubiquitously acts as both a major restraint and a major directive to local government's policy decisions, notwithstanding the context of community resistance, that is, when significant organized opposition exists.[15]

As useful as most neo-Marxist analyses are, they do fail to give adequate weight to the constraints and directives imposed by all levels of government on the local state. Neo-Marxists who have studied urban renewal have made superb analyses of the role of the national government in that policy area, but the pivotal role of state government remains underanalyzed.[16] Specifically, left urban analysts tend to ignore the limitations placed on the local state by Dillon's Rule, which allows state government the right to veto or mandate policy at the local level at the will of the state legislature.[17] In most of the neo-Marxist literature, the theoretical analyses of the limitations of the local state focus primarily on capitalism to the minimization of other limitations that emanate from within the federal system.

Another deficiency of neo-Marxist urban political economy is the paucity of prescriptions.[18] Paul Peterson off-handedly makes this case in *City Limits:* "Another school of thought, generally neo-Marxist in orientation, sees few alternatives other than the total redesign of western societies."[19] What neo-Marxists have not done is specify what kind of reform at the local level can both destabilize capitalism and further democratic socialism.[20] The final chapter of this book will present a strategy for left reform that is premised on a local approach. In Chapters 5, 6, 7, and 8 the reforms undertaken in Burlington will be evaluated for their radical content. Also, reasons why more radical reforms were not undertaken will be offered.

The strategy for radical reform has always been a point of contention for the American left. The lack of a successful socialist movement has bedeviled left political practitioners and academics alike. As far back as 1906, a German observer of American politics asked: "Why is there no Socialism in the United States?"[21] Historically the left has attempted two different strategies in the United States, both focused on constructing a mass movement. One strategy has been to mobilize within one of the two major political parties, that is, to create a party within a party in order to pull that larger party to the left. Some efforts to implement this strategy have been notable, even lasting, successes, while others have been abject failures. Among the more notable failures was the Populist capture of the Democratic party in 1896, which might also be interpreted as the Democrats' co-opting of the

Populists and which did not succeed in creating a viable mass labor-farmer party.[22] More successful were the Progressive Era social reforms that came from both the Republican and the Democratic parties, though the left progressives (symbolized by the settlement house movement) in each party were thoroughly diluted by the dominant business sector of the movement.[23] The left wing of the Democratic party continued this essentially Fabian-socialist tradition of reform in the 1930s and again in late 1960s. In each period of crisis the left made some impact, but almost all the reforms they introduced were watered down. As each crisis passed, the left's influence became negligible and the forces of reaction attempted to nibble away at the left's legacy.

Today, the left still pursues this Fabian approach though its influence at the national level is close to its nadir. Democratic socialists who identify with the evolutionary bent of Michael Harrington and Irving Howe recommend radicalizing the existing Democratic party and pushing for left liberal reforms that resemble the Western European socialist party line.[24] Their prescriptions, ameliorative and incrementalist, are directed at the national level of government. These left attempts at inside-the-system reforms are ignored by a Democratic party intent on keeping the allegiance of liberal business supporters.

An alternative to the incrementalist, work-within-the-two-major-party strategy has been the left's efforts to create a third party. This third-party strategy has been to create a mass movement that would radicalize and unite the working class throughout the entire nation. The Socialist party established in 1901 came closest to realizing this dream. When the party was at its height in 1912, Socialists had elected twelve hundred state and local candidates, seventy-nine of whom were mayors; Socialists had elected officers in one-half of the states. This state and local success was not duplicated in elections to the national government. By total percentage of the vote garnered, the Socialists' best year was also 1912, when Eugene V. Debs, their presidential candidate, took 6 percent of the vote.[25] Putting aside the contentious issues of the reasons for the decline of the Socialist party after 1912, we must conclude that the 6 percent figure is embarrassingly low. Since American elections are winner-take-all contests, 6 percent of the vote offers no hope for influence, let alone victory.

Efforts by the left to use a third party to stimulate a nation-wide mass movement have consistently failed. However, local victories of Socialist candidates (encumbered by the same winner-take-all laws) demonstrated the success of the third-party strategy. Not only were

Socialist mayors elected in the first three decades of this century, but in Bridgeport and Milwaukee, they were reelected through the 1950s, decades after the mass movement collapsed.

Similarly, by viewing the fortunes of the contemporary left, we find that local radicals have had some success, despite a national climate that is so intensely anti-left that it parallels the McCarthy years in its rhetoric. Besides the small universe of radical cities already mentioned, there are other communities, including New York City; Madison, Wisconsin; Ann Arbor, Michigan; and Cambridge, Massachusetts, that have radical representatives sitting on local legislative bodies. As proved in Burlington, at the local level, left third-party candidates can mobilize voters and win offices despite the well-documented bias that American election laws have against alternative parties. It is on the state and local level that the left should focus its meager resources for victory. As the analysis of Burlington's attempt at radical reform unfolds, it will become apparent that capturing the state level of government is the only probable route to both electoral success and radical reform.

Neo-Marxist urban theorizing, which offers too few left prescriptions underanalyzes the role of state government constraints, can also be faulted for overemphasizing the imposition by the capitalist class (usually developers) of its priorities on the community while minimalizing the support of the rank and file in the community for the same policies. Although developers or other investors are overwhelmingly following their self-interest, local support for capital investment is not limited only to those who will materially benefit. Left political economists have made a strategic and theoretical error in assuming that both the impetus for and sustenance of local policies that favor economic growth are primarily external phenomena. Because Marxian theory is heavily dependent on the ruling class/working class theory of domination, it is logical for neo-Marxist urban theorists to take as a starting point that city policies are directed to a large degree by the external structure of capitalism through its agents and the State. What is insufficiently explored and often ignored by such analysis is that pro-growth attitudes are widely spread throughout American society. Since growth is believed to be synonomous with progress, the impetus for economic development can come from within the community, and support for policies that promote development can exist in classes other than the bourgeoisie.

One prominent urban radical scholar, John H. Mollenkopf, has distanced himself from the traditional Marxist ruling-class subjugated-majority model. In his study of pro-growth coalitions in Boston and San Francisco, Mollenkopf found that business neither created nor dominated these groupings. He concluded that the political realm had its own independent causal effect with power springing from many sources:

> Few of the actors involved were aware of the systemic consequences of their actions, and when they were, it was political consequences they most often had in mind. They were searching for concrete solutions to pressing problems. They developed a progrowth programmatic framework with a jumbled character because they had to accommodate and logroll among many different interests none of whom—even the most powerful corporate chieftains—could control the entire process or even assume that its interests would be taken fully into account.
>
> Public actors, not private actors, generally possessed the critical initiative, and the results of their actions shaped private interests just as much as private interests shaped public action. A power structure, power bloc, or capitalist class model must be rejected because each draws the causal arrow in the wrong direction, or, at any rate, in only one direction, and because even capitalists must achieve popular support for measures government takes to benefit them.[26]

Until recently, support for growth, while qualified, has been nearly ubiquitous.

Throughout both the Paquette and Sanders eras, the argument from most of Burlington's political actors, including those who opposed developers' plans, was not about whether there should be a cessation of economic development; instead, there were several questions about the nature of growth: Where should it be? What should it look like? Who should pay for it? Who should benefit from it? Could the city guide or even initiate its own economic development? The question of whether growth should actually be severely limited was voiced by only a small group of ecologists who opposed virtually all economic development as it is commonly conceived.

Unlike ecologists, neo-Marxists along with most other Americans favor economic growth. In fact, socialist regimes, like capitalist regimes throughout the world, are preoccupied with bolstering economic growth. Capitalists would likely not dispute the charge that they are guilty of economism, but socialists, and neo-Marxists in particular, heatedly dispute this charge.

The argument that Marxism is an economically reductionist school of thought is far from new. The best evidence we have that

Karl Marx and Friedrich Engels were knowingly culpable is in a letter Engels wrote in confidence to an associate:

According to the materialist conception of history, the *ultimately* determining element in history is the production and reproduction of real life. . . . If some-one twists this into saying that the economic element is the *only* determining one, he transforms that proposition into a meaningless, abstract, senseless phrase. The economic situation is the basis, but the various elements of the superstructure . . . also exercise their influence upon the course of the histor-ical struggles and in many cases preponderate in determining their *form*.

Marx and I are ourselves partly to blame for the fact that the younger people sometimes lay more stress on the economic side than is due it. We had to emphasize the main principle vis-à-vis our adversaries who denied it, and we had not always the time, the place or the opportunity to give their due to the other elements involved in the interaction.[27]

Notice how Engels wants it both ways. The economic is "the ulti-mately determining element in history" but other "elements of the superstructure" can "preponderate."[28]

The problem of economic reductionism has plagued Marxist studies since the original writings. Many Marxist scholars have devi-ated from economic reductionism to include noneconomic factors. By doing so, however, they violate a fundamental tenet of Marxism, ap-tly phrased by Louis Althusser, that all social formation "in the last instance [is] determined by the economy,"[29] that is, all relations in society are fundamentally shaped by the form of organized produc-tion. For Althusser, other areas of organization, such as politics and ideology, are relatively autonomous and have their own effects. Even these semi-autonomous realms, no matter how far removed, can ulti-mately be traced to the mode of production. By going back to Marx's original texts, Althusser hoped to retrieve the real Marx; if Engels' letter is accurate about his partner's thinking, Althusser succeeded.

In the United States, neo-Marxists have struggled with this prob-lem of economism. Michael Albert and Robin Hahnel made an impor-tant theoretical breakthrough with their *Unorthodox Marxism*.[30] Elab-orating on a now familiar critique of Marxist economism, Albert and Hahnel describe other core characteristics of American society that are not class-determined: race and sex. Although a step forward, this work has two drawbacks. First, "unorthodox Marxism" is really a de-nial of Marxism since it theorizes that economics is not the final deter-minant but only one of three. Second, if there is more than one key system of social relations in society, why single out race and sex as the only other systems of domination? Can ageism, militarism, or the instrumental domination of the environment be reduced to one or more of these categories, or are these struggles inferior to those of sex, race, and class?

Similar problems with neo-Marxist theorizing can be found in the urban literature. William K. Tabb's *The Political Economy of the Black Ghetto*, an early, perceptive neo-Marxist study of the problems of the black slums, published in 1970, fails to treat race as even a coequal determinant of economic deprivation of blacks.[31] Tabb focuses on how blacks fill a need for capitalism. Race as an independent factor that explains black deprivation is ancillary to Tabb's argument. The ghetto may well function as an internal colony, as Tabb claims, but this does not explain why blacks are the colonized.

Other neo-Marxist urban studies, published since 1970, deal with struggles of race or sex by recognizing them as separate from class relations. Some neo-Marxist theorists push the class aspects into the background and emphasize other factors, such as the role of professions or the stultifying effects of bureaucracy.[32] Some of these useful studies lose their Marxist character altogether. However, other, more popular studies, such as those by Frances Fox Piven and Richard A. Cloward, are explicitly class-grounded explanations of the successes and failures of urban (predominantly black) social movements.[33] All of these studies are worthwhile since they elucidate the relationship of race (and other salient factors) to class. However, racial relations as a system of domination irrespective of the economic organization of society has by and large been ignored by most neo-Marxists.

A neo-Marxist study of the autonomy of the local state can be hampered in two specific ways by the tendency of neo-Marxism to be ambiguous about economism. From the neo-Marxist academic's perspective, either the issues analyzed are explicitly economic, or the economic aspects of the issue dominate the analysis. A study on urban racism, for example, is more likely to center on economic exploitation than racist cultural practices.[34] Also from the neo-Marxist activist's perspective, the demands by social movements that are not economic are treated as subordinate to the economic. In Burlington, this was certainly true. It took the Sanders administration six weeks to find a meeting room for the autonomous Task Force on Women. In contrast, to manage economic development the administration set up an independent office with a director and a staff. Such internal division is another limitation on the extent and direction of the reforms that can be taken by a radical city regime.

In sum, the neo-Marxists have greatly furthered the study of the limits to reform in the city by examining how class relations both guide and limit policy in the city. Neo-Marxists, who have strayed from the purely economic, have elucidated the relationship of capital and class to other forms of domination, and some have gone on to explore other modes of domination. Nevertheless, as with all theoretical advances, there are some drawbacks. Four problems, three specific to urban theorizing, have been identified. One, neo-Marxists have not paid enough attention to the role of federalism, in particular, state government's stewardship over the city. Two, there has been a notable lack of prescriptions offered in the neo-Marxist urban literature. What should be done and what can be done have been left unanswered; the emphasis has been on what has been done. With the election of radicals in several communities throughout the nation, the first two questions demand practical answers. Three, the top/down model of unequal relations in which the business community imposes its will on a dependent community needs to be supplemented by a model that integrates the support for economic growth that is widespread (but qualified) among Americans. Four, the role of economism, particularly the ways it sets the agenda while causing strain within the left of the 1980s, needs to be examined in the context of the city under study, Burlington.

THE POST-MARXIST ALTERNATIVE

The remedy to Marxism's shortcomings remains in a state of becoming. Post-Marxism is an emerging paradigm that retains the radical critique of society characteristic of Marxism. However, the new paradigm recognizes that there are systems of domination other than, and as important as, class. This paradigm is now in the process of evolving through two sets of scholars. One set is comprised of those Marxists who realize that economism is endemic to the Marxist paradigm; for them there is a point at which valid analyses recognize systems of domination other than class. This realization is a direct refutation of Marxism as universal theory.[35] Nevertheless, although many doubt that class is the ultimate determinant, most do not make a total break with Marxist theory. Hence we have "hyphenated" theorists such as socialist-feminists, who recognize two independent systems of oppression in society of equal weight: patriarchy and capitalism.[36]

A second set of scholars is deeply influencing the first: left radical non-Marxists who have never been aligned with or have completely broken with Marxism. Left Hegelians, radical feminists, and ecologists have made significant radical critiques of bureaucracy, patriarchy, and the domination of the natural world, respectively; many of their contributions have found their way into neo-Marxist thinking.[37] In addition to these non-Marxists, ex-Marxist radicals who broke with Marxism before the rise of neo-Marxism in the 1960s have made their impression. Michel Foucault, among other French thinkers, has been important.[38] In particular, Foucault's histories of the way the professions have ordered the relations of sex, mental illness, and punishment reveal the construction of systems of domination not in any way reducible to class.[39] In particular, Foucault's thesis that unequal power relations are produced individually throughout society challenges the ruling class/working class Marxist model. In sum, non-Marxist radical critics have challenged the fundamentals of Marxism while remaining faithful to one of Marx's most important goals: revealing the unequal relations that are characteristic of the organization of this society.

The events that shaped the rise of neo-Marxism can be traced to the struggles of the 1960s and 1970s. Demands made by gays, feminists, ecologists, senior citizens, and oppressed ethnic groups cannot be reduced to class demands. Homosexuality cannot credibly be traced to the mode of production. Hence the rise of the non-Marxist radical theorists.

New scholarship is not the only challenge to Marxist theorizing. The decline of the traditional working class made Marx's prediction that the proletariat would unite and overthrow the working class irrelevant. As Erik Olin Wright has empirically demonstrated, the traditional working class (those who are a part of the manufacturing process yet have no supervisory responsibilities) is less than 20 percent of the American workforce and diminishing.[40] Even if we lay aside their functional incorporation into the capitalist system through collective bargaining as a reason that the proletariat has failed in its revolutionary mission, today the numbers are insufficient for any kind of successful revolution. One could even question whether this one-fifth of the workforce has the right to reorder class relations and reappropriate all surplus value for itself, at least without the active consent of the rest of society. The traditional working class as the basis for a revolutionary movement is therefore now a moot issue for all but the most orthodox Marxists.[41]

Changes in the traditional working class have also meant that the

Marxist two-class model is not an accurate description of postindustrial capitalist society. The rise of a managerial-professional class that is neither working class nor bourgeois has created a "crisis" for neo-Marxist theory. All of the many solutions to this problem involve identifying factors other than the relationship to the mode of production that determine class.[42] Such solutions are missing the salient point. The importance of the new class, as neoconservatives call it (or new middle class as neo-Marxists label it), is in their nonclass demands, which do not emanate from the social relations of production.

Important to the study of Burlington, many of the members of the new social movements are from this new class. Mainstream as well as radical social scientists have documented the privileged positions, both material and educational, that characterize most members of the new social movements.[43] Unlike the bourgeoisie and the working class, the new middle class is usually remote from the daily workings of the mode of production. Those members of the new middle class who have jobs associated with actual production of commodities are neither producing those items nor directly receiving the surplus value accrued from their manufacture and sale. Most members of the new middle class are not involved with production in any tangible way. Large numbers of managers and professionals work either for the State or for the burgeoning not-for-profit service sector. Because this "class," if indeed it can be called that, is not primarily shaped by the mode of production, any attempt to define its actions or consciousness by its relation to the shop floor is an example of a theoretical non sequitur.

Interestingly, by being distanced from the actual mode of production, this stratum tends to make demands that are not class specific. Some demands are universal (for example, civil libertarians claim all individuals have equal rights); other demands, in contrast, are specific to one identifiable aggregation of people (for example, gays want protection for their unique lifestyle).[44] Either way these demands differ from class struggles, which tend to be zero-sum in nature. As most who work in society move farther away from the industrial mode of production, it becomes a residual category of employment; the number of people who are thus removed from that direct polarizing influence will greatly increase while the numbers of the traditional working class dwindle. In postindustrial cities like Burlington, there will be uneasy alliances subject to periodic ruptures between this emerging stratum and its atrophying partner.

Besides the new middle class, the new social movements attract those who are outside the class system as defined by the relationship to production: students, housewives, retirees, and members of the counterculture. It is because these groups are removed from the production process that they can make demands that are primarily non-class. In essence, the new social movements are composed of people who define their needs irrespective of class, such as homosexual activists who argue for the right of "sexual preference." Members of the new social movements to a greater extent than workers choose their struggles rather than having them thrust upon them by an external material structure.[45]

Post-Marxists recognize the importance of these new social movements and their non-class demands, though they continue to claim that class issues are important. This reordering of theoretical priorities suggests that left premises of the substance of reform and the limits to reform must be reassessed.

An examination of the new-social-movement demands often overlooked by both neo-Marxist and post-Marxist schools of political economy provides a new perspective on the issue of the limit of local autonomy. On this essential issue, the post-Marxists have no clearly stated position; neither school has given sufficient attention to the limits to new-social-movement reforms. Nonetheless, Burlington's experiments with radical reform suggest that new-social-movement reforms may have a greater possibility for successful adoption than do most class-based proposals. With little or no opposition from local business and its allies, new-social-movement demands, which either had no economic component or had economic components that did not directly challenge capital accumulation, were more likely to be achieved in Burlington. This does not mean that there are no boundaries to noneconomic reforms at the local level; instead, it demonstrates that certain kinds of issues have not even been on the local agenda until recently. By refocusing the question of local autonomy away from the purely economic, the new social movements have enlarged the local scope of reform issues. Post-Marxist theory anticipates such new struggles and agenda items; neo-Marxist theory merely notes the significance of such phenomena.

Nevertheless, the demands of the new social movements are not the only salient concerns in any city. The relationship of class struggle remains a primary area of interest and the next chapter will focus on the relationship of capitalism to the city. In examining both the economic and the noneconomic limits and directions to reform in Burlington, I will use a post-Marxist approach.

3
Burlington and Capitalism

Urban observers of both mainstream and radical biases have noted that capitalism not only constrains local government policy choice but also encourages policies that promote private investment projects. The need to attract new capital and retain existing capital investment is a primary policy objective of most municipalities, with the exception of certain elite suburbs. Cities are in perpetual competition for a finite amount of investment dollars. To attract these dollars, the cities must provide an environment that offers potential investors a reasonable chance for profits. Most analysts of urban political economy agree that the city elites are usually willing partners in the capital accumulation process, even to the detriment of their constituents.[1] What happened in Burlington alternately affirmed and contradicted this academic generalization.

At one time Burlington, like other manufacturing centers, prospered by attracting the investment of industrial entrepreneurs and corporations. However, as capitalism matured into a postindustrial society, business began restructuring from a manufacturing-based to a service-oriented economy, and the population began to change from a two-class structure reminiscent of industrial capitalism to a society redefined by the emergence of growing professional and counter-cultural strata. The needs of both capital and the citizenry in the city have been reformulated. The terrain of local politics is totally new in the most advanced postindustrial cities, such as Burlington. The politics of prosperous postindustrial cities has provided a new opening for radical reform. These new possibilities for reform are affected nevertheless by the needs of capital.

CITIES IN COMPETITION

The best argument for the importance of private investment in communities is that cities have always competed for such capital. Since the early eighteenth century, cities and states have subsidized the construction of major means of transportation, beginning with canals and then railroads.[2] To be unconnected to major routes would have meant a leveling or an actual diminishment in growth. Cities are still preoccupied with providing transportation access. For example, ready access to air travel is now an important underpinning of local urban development. Not only did the city of Burlington establish an airport in the adjacent municipality of South Burlington, but through federal grants, this modern equivalent of the nineteenth-century railway station was upgraded to be a major Northeastern destination. The short-lived People's Express airline made Burlington a short hop from Boston and Newark. In turn, the easy access by air to regional centers of finance helped make Burlington the most likely candidate to be Vermont's financial center. However, not all forms of modern transportation equally enhance all types of capital investment.

Transportation routes to cities also lead away from cities; for certain types of capital investment the interstate highway system was the exit ramp to the suburbs. The enactment of the national Highway Act of 1956 accelerated the ever-increasing dispersal of American manufacturing from core cities, a trend that first became prominent with the rise of trucking in the 1920s. Although the intent of the 1956 law was not to impoverish the cities, it did so. Suburbs expanded geometrically with industrial parks and new tracts of single-family dwellings. Cheap land and low taxes encouraged Northern corporate planners to move to the suburbs (when not relocating in the South or Third World, havens for cheap labor). David Gordon makes the controversial argument that an even more important cause for the dispersal of American industry that preceded the growth of the trucking industry and new land-intensive single-story manufacturing architecture was the search for a more pliable, docile labor force.[3] Whatever the economic logic was for dispersal, the interstate highway system provided the necessary transportation infrastructure.

For Burlington the deindustrialization process was not a case of industry fleeing to adjoining suburbs; the textile and saw mills that were the original base of its economy had folded or relocated in the South long before the dispersal of industry from other cities began. The interstate highways that run through the suburbs adjoining Burlington (and not through the city's downtown) provided them with an edge to attract new manufacturing investment. The major plant investments of International Business Machines (IBM) and the Digital Equipment Corporation (DEC) in Burlington's suburbs lend evidence to the argument that these communities had a competitive advantage. In fact, Burlington's business community and the Paquette administration found it necessary to lobby for connector highways running from the central city to the interstate highway to protect retail and financial investment. Nevertheless, the same transportation system that attracted large-scale industrial capital to the suburbs helped facilitate office expansion in Burlington's downtown.

THE PARADOX OF THE DUBIOUS BENEFITS OF ECONOMIC GROWTH

Most community governments, with the important exception of those of wealthy suburbs, are seeking to promote growth. In this new era of quickening competition, what cities will do to attract new industry, encourage the expansion of existing industry, or maintain threatened industry ranges from positive inducements to attract new investment to belated responses to corporate threats of closing down shop. Tax rebates, state-assisted job training, subsidized site improvement, relaxed pollution controls, rezoning, and the creation of open land by destroying housing inhabited by low-income families comprise only a partial list of the strategies employed by state and local government officials to induce growth or at least forestall economic decline.[4] It is important to probe for reasons why so many local leaders are active promoters of business interests.

For elected leaders, success in office is usually equated by the electorate with economic prosperity; failure is associated with economic stagnation or decline. The publicly perceived notion of growth includes such benefits as increased tax revenue sources, lower taxes for homeowners, more jobs for the local entrepreneurs—in sum, a wealthier community. The rewards are indicative of an instrumentally positive power relationship; capital offers direct, tangible rewards for correct behavior and policies by local government.

The converse of the power relationship between capital and the community is evident in the negative consequences of disinvestment. The older industrial cities, such as Youngstown, Detroit, Gary, and Buffalo, offer the normative guidelines of possible consequences of a community's failure to prevent business decline. Unemployment, high crime, deteriorating housing, high taxes, and all the other characteristics that fall into that catchall phrase "urban blight" demonstrate to the surrounding publics the failure of a community to retain old industry or to attract new firms.

In some communities one neighborhood can act as the example for the whole community. In Burlington, the Old North End was, until the real estate boom of 1983, a poor neighborhood in decline. Active efforts by local community organizations may have stemmed the tide of decay but it is gentrification that is eliminating the Old North End's urban blight. In Burlington, as in most other cities, the poor will be displaced in direct proportion to the amount of private investment. Despite this negative consequence for the poor, the quest for growth remains strong. Political opponents of Mayor Sanders tried to use the presence of urban blight to discredit him, even though it was there when he took office. In the 1983 campaign, Sanders' opponents published pictures of vacant storefronts and suggested there would be more if he were reelected, a technique that was intended to associate the Brooklyn-born leader with the urban ills of his native turf. Burlington's incipient real estate investment boom undermined such crude efforts and Sanders won the election. Still, the fact that the failed effort was attempted demonstrates that it is widely known that capital disinvestment is a political liability.

Such simple cause and effect analyses do not explain the depth of the public's pro-growth sentiments. In fact, public perception of the effects of capital investment has proven to be much too complimentary to business when the costs and benefits are weighed.[5] Because of the additional costs that economic growth entails for a community, the added tax revenues and the new jobs created may result in a negative cost/benefit ratio for the community-at-large and almost certainly for those residents nearest to or displaced by an economic development project. Relocated factories, for example, particularly those from the oligopoly sector of the economy, may be capital rather than labor intensive and therefore provide few new jobs. Most often a relocated plant reduces its labor force significantly with the adoption of the latest manufacturing techniques. More jobs does not necessarily mean many more jobs.

Even if a labor-intensive plant or office is established and many more jobs are produced, the surrounding community may not benefit directly. One problem especially common to central cities is that jobs produced in their community are filled by citizens of the adjacent suburbs.[6] Burlington's high-rise downtown provides many jobs that are filled by residents of neighboring Shelburne, Wooster, and South Burlington as clogged city streets leading to and from those communities prove daily. Also, the new positions offered to city residents may be the lowest-paying deadend occupations. More hotels in Burlington translates into more housekeeping positions.

Besides the uncertainty of community benefits that come with simply more jobs, new strains are placed on existing public and private resources. The price of land near any large development project usually skyrockets. This increase pushes up costs for local businesses and those who are looking for new residences, and eventually rents will increase commensurately with the rising price of real estate. In Burlington, growth inflated the prices of housing in some neighborhoods over 100 percent in just three years. It also meant, as it does in other densely populated communities, the destruction of open space. When growth means more commuters in more cars and therefore traffic jams, highways will be built that will destroy both open space and available housing. In Burlington the Northern Connector did just this; if the Southern Connector is built, it will compound this environmental despoilation.

Other costs attributable to growth specific but not unique to Burlington included major investments in new infrastructure and expanded services. An increase in people equals more trash in a capitalist consumer society and an expensive disposal problem. Burlington was forced to make costly plans to rebuild the sewer system and close the city dump. More police, fire fighters, and educators (though the incredibly low birth rate among baby boomers may temper the need for greater educational expenditures) are on the agenda if condominium development continues unabated in Burlington. If the costs of capitalist development projects are compiled, the aggregate payoff to a community may not be positive. And the intangible costs of lost scenic vistas (such as the lakefront view in Burlington now threatened by high-rise development) and the loss of community caused by an influx of newcomers are impossible to calculate using quantitative techniques.

If economic growth is often of dubious benefit to a community's citizenry, in particular the poor, why do the overwhelming majority of state and local governments (including radical-led Burlington) vigorously compete for relocating and expanding businesses? A good part of the reason is the well-socialized pro-growth values of the populace at large. Until quite recently, the United States has been a nation of Babbitts when it comes to economic growth.[7] Americans all along the political spectrum, with the exception of radical ecologists, have long believed that economic growth equals progress, even though what kind of economic growth and where it will be located often give rise to conflict, and many want growth in someone else's neighborhood. In Burlington this pattern was affirmed. Neighborhood organizations in wards that would be untouched by the proposed Southern Connector highway did not protest its construction. Since the spillover benefits of growth are often idealized, the fear of negative effects is most often directly proportional to propinquity.

Political actors that one might think would be at the forefront of opposition to capitalist investment practices in Burlington were sometimes supportive of such growth-enhancing projects. Socialist Mayor Sanders was anticapitalist but absolutely not anti-growth (or opposed to working with local business). And Sanders was not being inconsistent, since socialism is an economic growth ideology. Alan Wolfe, a prominent socialist critic of capitalism has remarked: "Growth was a wonderful thing while it lasted, making possible all kinds of miracles (among them, the fact that the author of this book, a carpenter's son, became the author of this book)."[8]

Wolfe has analyzed how the Democrats became the dominant political party by forging a pro-growth coalition that sustained economic expansion (with periodic downturns) from the economic recovery after World War II to the faltering steps of the early 1970s. For programs such as Model Cities and Urban Renewal there were local chapters of the urban pro-growth coalition. During Mayor Gordon Paquette's ten-year reign, Burlington's Democratic party, along with prominent builders and the real estate business sector, implemented downtown urban renewal with federal largesse. For ten years the voters returned the Democrats to office under this pro-growth formula.

John Mollenkopf, a colleague of Wolfe's, has written a complementary urban study emphasizing the crucial growth coalition process necessary to implement urban renewal and its subsequent unraveling.[9] In Burlington, Sanders' election was a local version of the unraveling of this Democratic growth coalition. Sanders' election, in part, was a response to the neglect of city services by the Paquette regime, which placed urban renewal ahead of the neighborhoods.

Even so, economic growth did not disappear from the city's agenda. Bernard Sanders made one of his top priorities the creation of the Community Economic and Development Office, which offered low-interest loans (funds subsidized by taxpayers) to small businesses that wanted to expand in or relocate to Burlington. Socialists were not immune to pro-growth boosterism even though it furthered the nemesis, capitalism. In fact, the commitment by Sanders to economic development so provoked the Vermont Greens, an ecological group, that they accused the mayor of selling out to business by supporting a city-subsidized waterfront development plan that they opposed.[10] Notwithstanding ecological heretics, the myth of economic development as a positive good persists. This almost evangelical belief in economic growth is not a simple result of the aforementioned strategies that city leaders take to promote development; this belief is too widespread to be the result of actions by particular local decision makers.

In America, belief in economic growth can be traced to the relations established under capitalism since capitalism cannot sustain itself for long without growth. Yet despite these origins, the socialized belief that economic development is a positive good, precedes, surrounds, and informs large segments of the populace, those who actively promote and the larger group of those who passively approve of growth. There is a power relationship in which power cannot be reduced to an arrow pointing downward from a ruling class or elite to the mass below. Sometimes the people who are displaced by city-sponsored economic growth policies define such strategies as "progress." With respect to economic development, mass support, not merely elite, directs power flows laterally, horizontally, and every which way. Notwithstanding, elite support for economic development, particularly by the business community, is formidable. However, this pro-growth bias permeates almost all relationships between actors and institutions because its base of transmission (after the successful socialization of capitalist values) becomes inner-directed rather than imposed from without. In a capitalist society, prosperity and well-being are equated with economic growth in the private sector, and such beliefs have been ratified at the polls. Such a belief is consistent with capitalism's inherent need to grow.

BUSINESS CONFIDENCE

Although pervasive, the American public's belief in economic growth is not, in itself, enough to create an environment that is equally conducive to business in every city. Eagerness for growth is only one ingredient in a complex recipe, especially when capital is mobile and economic growth varies with the business cycle. It is still a goal of local government leaders to encourage "business confidence" in prospective developers and other investors. Business confidence is the belief by a significant part of the business community that a certain rate of return can be reasonably expected if they choose to invest. Business confidence results from a mixture of material and attitudinal characteristics that can be found within the domain of a particular community and is not established merely by local government's offering an agglomeration of business subsidies, direct and indirect.[11]

Unfortunately for purposes of analysis, business confidence is a nebulous concept. Different businesses require different environmental and other conditions to prosper. Large industrial manufacturers, for example, have no interest in Burlington. New England's high energy costs and Burlington's lack of large parcels of open space make it unattractive for investment. The discussion that follows will explain why factors that specifically attract industrial capital are irrelevant to contemporary Burlington.

Business confidence is built on conditions that relocating businesses consider important in their decision-making process: proximity to suppliers and customers, docility of labor, cost of labor, skills of labor, state labor laws, labor availability, transportation facilities, energy costs, climate, community livability, access to research facilities, availability of land, local prosperity, availability of private financing, taxes, and direct government aid.[12] These factors are a large part of the business confidence formula, but they are not exhaustive, and, as Edward Humberger has stated, many are not subject to local governmental influence.[13]

Burlington lacks the attraction of two conditions that are crucial for certain industries: proximity to suppliers and customers. In suburbs of Burlington, DEC and IBM have state-of-the-art factories and research facilities that are offshoots of the famous Route 128 high technology complex in Boston. Both companies have many specialty suppliers, any of whom, wishing to move closer to the markets, would be attracted by the cheap, nearby suburban sites complete with utilities

and additional state financing that are offered by the Greater Burlington Industrial Corporation, a private entity with state subsidies.

An important commercial agglomeration of suppliers and customers specific to Burlington is the banking industry. Burlington's banks,
sheltered from out-of-state competition by Vermont laws, are located
throughout the downtown. Burlington's advantage over other communities as a center for banking was enhanced by the expansion of
office space that was stimulated by urban renewal during the 1970s.
The original concentration of banking resulted from Burlington's former importance as an industrial center. During the 1800s this thriving
mill town was a center for industrial capital accumulation. Eventually
the original industry migrated or failed but the financial base remained. The development of the greater community as a high technology center, only indirectly because of the efforts of contemporary
Burlington political elites, solidified the city of Burlington as a home for
regional finance. In some ways, contemporary Burlington is more the
fortunate recipient than the active promoter of these capitalist assets.
Still, by utilizing urban renewal options, community leaders did facilitate this restructuring of Burlington from a manufacturing to a postindustrial office economy.

If Burlington has had only a limited measure of control over its
evolution into a center of finance surrounded by high technology suburbs, it has had even less control over its labor. The docility of labor,
the cost of labor, the availability of labor, and state labor laws are
beyond the city's ability to influence in any but a most marginal way.
International investment patterns, past relations between labor and
management, national government macro-economic policy, and national and state government legislation shape these labor factors with
little notice of Burlington's local needs.

One aspect of labor over which Burlington can have some influence is the skills of its labor force. Strong, well-financed schools can
provide the basic literacy needed for most jobs that are produced by
the capitalist service economy. Beyond meeting the demand for such
usually low-paying, boring service jobs, Burlington's ability to create
skilled workers depends on the type of skills needed by business.
Industrial jobs are disappearing in Vermont as in the rest of the
United States at a remarkable pace; these positions historically were
"the major source of high paying jobs in Vermont."[14] Thus, traditional vocational education at the secondary level with its industrial
bent is inappropriate for the postindustrial economy that is trans-
forming Vermont's employment needs, but Burlington also offers lo-

cal educational options beyond high school. The city is in the strong position of having one community college, two four-year colleges, and one state university with modest graduate research facilities. This agglomeration of higher educational facilities supplies Burlington with a workforce suitably trained for its better-paying postindustrial jobs. This concentration of institutions for higher education is conducive to business confidence, yet this again is fortuitous rather than the result of city efforts. The colleges were established because of past patterns of city demographics, which, in turn, were largely a result of the confluence of geography and private investment.

Transportation facilities represent a component of business confidence over which local governments have some influence, though with less authority than the states. Burlington is located on a harbor on Lake Champlain. Because of this harbor, a pro-growth asset that preceded human intervention, Burlington became the nexus of several major railroads. Railroad construction was encouraged by the city during the 1800s to facilitate its growth as a lumber-processing center and transshipment point for Canadian forest products that were transported down the lake.[15] Today, in postindustrial Burlington, most of the tracks of these same railroads lie underutilized and will inevitably be torn up for lucrative waterfront construction. Cheap water-based transportation and rail access are largely irrelevant to New England cities, which are neither manufacturing nor transshipping raw or semifinished materials. In fact these nineteenth-century industrial accoutrements are often impediments to postindustrial investment.

Burlington does have other transportation facilities that contribute to business confidence. An important one is the Northern Connector, Burlington's connection to a major interstate highway. This access highway and a companion one under construction from the south were the deliberate result of the Paquette administration's pro-growth efforts in conjunction with state and national programs. Here is an area in which local government's impact though not plenary is considerable. Nevertheless, the prohibitive expense of highway construction makes such projects practically impossible without state or national funding.

Although technically outside city limits, the city-owned Burlington Airport is a major transportation asset, which has enhanced accessibility to other important centers of business and facilitated the expansion of Burlington's financial community. The creation of and improvements to this crucial component of the city's business confidence is partially within the city's authority although much of the funding came from the Federal Aviation Administration.

Energy costs, unlike availability of transportation, are not usually within a city's jurisdiction. The costs of oil, gas, coal, nuclear, or hydroelectric power resources are mostly determined by private-market conditions, and often the supplier is located outside city boundaries. Notwithstanding, Burlington, in an effort to decrease escalating power costs and utilize a nearby resource, built the nation's first (and perhaps last) utility-owned wood-chip plant to produce electricity. After the price of oil collapsed in the mid-1980s and cheap Canadian hydroelectric power became available, Burlington's electricity became some of the most expensive produced in the region. Ironically, the logic of supply and demand negated a municipal strategy that would have marginally improved Burlington's business climate if oil prices had remained high. Actually, after the Progressive Coalition finally obtained control of the Burlington Electric Department, Progressive commissioners tried to make electricity rates for business proportionately higher than rates for residential customers. Vermont's Public Service Board vetoed this effort.[16] Throughout this micro–class struggle, business confidence remained high in Burlington. Even if the Coalition proposal had succeeded, business confidence would probably have been unaffected, because energy costs for most postindustrial industries, such as banking, in contrast to those for traditional industries, such as steel manufacturing, are not an important production cost.

Although Burlington's foray into cheaper energy proved to be folly (and from a business point of view unnecessary), the city's livability remained excellent by business standards.[17] Livability, an amorphous concept, cannot be reduced to a general set of variables. Burlington has special characteristics that contribute to its livability; its college-town atmosphere, sweeping view of Lake Champlain, comparatively small size, sound schools, lack of racial hostility (achieved by default since only one race is there in any numbers), and low (by big city standards) crime rate make the city an attractive point of relocation. A large proportion of Burlington's residents have moved from other places. Although the housing market is tight (vacancy rates are less than 1 percent; by national standards, a vacancy rate of 2 percent is considered full occupancy), compared with adjoining regional metropolitan markets such as Montreal, Boston, and New York, Burlington's average house price of seventy thousand to eighty thousand dollars is extraordinarily low.[18] Burlington's livability is good enough to keep many of its colleges' graduates there permanently.

But such accolades beg the question of whether the city government created and sustained these conditions. Because the basis of livability is so diverse and ultimately subjective, any answer must be qualified.[19] The presence of the colleges and the amenities of culture that they bring are mostly irrelevant to city planning efforts, as are the proximity of Lake Champlain and the lack of racial hostility. However, the existence of sound schools and relatively low crime rates are influenced in a modest way by city policy.

Burlington, like the rest of Vermont, lacks a first-rate high technology educational and research center. The city's only university, the University of Vermont, is not a first-class state institution like the University of Michigan or the University of California at Berkeley or Los Angeles. Burlington has benefitted, however, from the establishment in its suburbs of two separate private facilities financed primarily by DEC and IBM, the foremost high technology firms in the world. Again, the cause is an accident of geography. Increased prosperity in the Route 128 area, built around Harvard University and the Massachusetts Institute of Technology, has pushed up the costs of land and labor and sent expanding firms into neighboring New Hampshire, Maine, and Vermont. Burlington (and the rest of Vermont) with its modest resources could not afford to subsidize multi-million-dollar research facilities, nor is there any reason to believe Burlington could attract them. By the luck of being in the right place, Burlington has benefitted from the positive spillover effects of two institutions of higher learning over one hundred miles away.

Like most older cities, Burlington lacks open space for efficient manufacturing facilities or campus-style corporate headquarters. Some space was made available in the 1970s, however, when Burlington (like most other older northern cities) took advantage of the national government's lavishly funded urban redevelopment program to level part of the downtown. Hotels and offices sprouted on cleared land that had contained moderately priced residences. The five-term Democratic mayor Gordon Paquette made land clearance a priority. City input into such a program was indispensible since applications for the national grant funds that made it possible had to include extensive city planning. However, if the city used large amounts of national government funding to provide modest amounts of land for postindustrial retail, office, hotel, and garage construction, it was because it could not attract industrial capital. The local private (but publicly subsidized) Greater Burlington Industrial Corporation developed suburban industrial parks, and, with the aid of Vermont-backed guaranteed loans, it offered a better deal on land.[20] Burlington, even with lavish national government subsidies, could not compete with its neighboring municipalities for industrial capital. Rolling pastures, complete with subsidies, were more attractive to manufacturing investment than the confinement of city blocks.

The city land made available for new construction with help from massive national government grants contributed to local prosperity in Burlington. Prosperity is a result of accumulated business confidence and helps to sustain it. Burlington's record is impressive. By 1985, unemployment was down to 3.5 percent (half the national average); employment was up 4.7 percent from the previous year. Workers' incomes were up 6 percent, and new construction was up 7.5 percent.[21] Such prosperity attracts investment. Retail chains, for example, were drawn to Burlington for the increasing dollars in consumer hands, though suburban malls received the greater share of investment. All the city boosterism that can be marshalled cannot provide such prosperity; there must be other, independent conditions to stimulate business confidence, few of which are controlled by local government policy.

Local government has the greatest input in the areas of taxes, availability of financing, especially through loan guarantees, and direct government aid, for example, through outright grants for the purchase of equipment and construction.[22] Cities, especially those as small as Burlington, are limited, however, in their ability to subsidize new business or finance the expansion of existing businesses without extensive state or national government assistance. Notwithstanding extremely tight budgets, the Sanders administration established the Community Economic Development Office to stimulate business and targeted small business for subsidies. One of its first tangible efforts was a $12,500 loan guarantee in 1984 to an organic food store.[23] Statistics bear out the claim that small business is the engine of new job growth;[24] for small cities it is the investment area where limited amounts of funds can go farthest.

Tax reduction through local rebates or exemptions of property taxes is the most common form of subsidy to business from local government. Its use is limited, however, because most city revenues are dependent on property taxes. Furthermore, cities can do little to build business confidence through tax reductions since, for most firms, property taxes are a very small part of the cost of doing business and therefore have little influence on most business expansion or relocation decisions. In one survey of why industrial firms relocated to Florida, which has a notoriously low tax rate, less than 2 percent of the respondents cited low taxes as a factor.[25] Under the Sanders administration few property tax breaks were offered to business; other factors kept Burlington's economy healthy.

If property tax reductions contribute so little to business confidence, why are they so commonly used? Elected or appointed political leaders have within their control so few means of attracting private investment to their communities that those that are left (such as tax breaks) take on an importance out of proportion to their effectiveness.[26] Only cities like Burlington that already have a good business climate can afford to fend off business demands for tax cuts or other publicly financed subsidies.

Strong business confidence is difficult to destroy. Policies such as significantly raising taxes on business, placing a temporary moratorium on new construction, or other capitalist destabilizing measures could, but not necessarily would, destroy business confidence. Only so drastic a measure as calling for and leading a general strike for higher wages or more control over production—such as the opponents of Bernard Sanders feared would happen if he were elected—could negate business confidence.

Merely the election of a socialist mayor and radical aldermen is not enough to cause a decline in business confidence. Just as the election of Communist mayors in Italy (where sometimes even businessmen run on the Communist party ticket) has not resulted in massive capital flight, so too the election of radicals to Burlington's government has not destroyed business confidence. Unless the mayor and his allies deliberately enact policies that are inimical to capital accumulation, this healthy business environment will be unaffected by who sits in office. Since both capitalism and Sanders' type of socialism favor economic development, there were some convergences on policy during his administration, though Sanders' record on issues affecting business confidence was mixed: aid to small business but obstruction of a new highway. The effectiveness of factors outside Sanders' grasp has helped to keep the confidence of business in Burlington strong, and this confidence has strengthened the hand of the Sanders administration with business.

Many factors go into creating business confidence, and business confidence, once established, is difficult to destroy. It provides some restraint on city policy and can survive despite measures taken by the city regime. Any program the radicals in Burlington want to implement, for example, must be measured not only by Republican and Democratic partisan hostility and the restraints imposed by the state of Vermont but also by the possibility of economic stagnation.

The policies of city governments have little positive or negative effect on business confidence: local governments have only limited resources for attracting and keeping capital, but a city regime that is unreceptive to business demands, especially in a city whose populace is socialized to desire ever-increasing economic growth and its perceived rewards, cannot weaken business confidence. After five years under a socialist regime that attempted socialization of the local television franchise, refused repeal of an inventory tax on business without a replacement levy, extracted concessions from a major developer, and for those five years obstructed the construction of a major highway to the city's downtown that was avidly sought by the business community, the business climate in Burlington did not noticeably suffer.

Communities that, like Burlington, are blessed with the prerequisites of business confidence have the luxury of increased leverage (and thus autonomy) in dealing with the demands of capital. Local governments and communities that cannot provide the requirements of capital will suffer the negative effects of capital flight.[27]

THE POSTINDUSTRIAL RESTRUCTURING OF CAPITAL

The restructuring from industrial to postindustrial capital gave the Sanders administration increased leverage to bargain with the business community. Because of the efforts of the previous administration, the national government (through the Urban Renewal Program), and the local financial community, Burlington had laid the foundation for a postindustrial boom. With business confidence high, city political elites were able to make demands on real estate developers. Ironically, it was the health and vibrancy of capital that allowed the Sanders administration to challenge business hegemony.

The postindustrial restructuring of capital has drastically changed Burlington as the city's economy has experienced the withering of manufacturing and the blossoming of finance and other industries that produce intangible services. A postindustrial economy is characterized by an emphasis on the production of specialized knowledge and its ever-quickening transmission.[28]

It follows that such a society is increasingly preoccupied with the computer and other forms of efficient communication. As previously mentioned, the greater Burlington area is dependent on computer production to sustain its economy. It produces hardware for the computer industry and uses those machines in its financial industry, colleges, and the large hospital complex affiliated with the University of Vermont. Terminals are everywhere. The sales of information and systems that collect information are the preoccupation of the most expansive sector of the business community.

The resulting shift in investment from the older manufacturing sector to the newer high technology industries and the service industries that utilize high technology equipment has transformed the city's very being and its possibilities. The relocation of manufacturing facilities out of Burlington has accelerated. Improved, capital-intensive manufacturing techniques have led to drastic workforce reductions in those industries that have not already fled to havens of cheap labor overseas or in the American South. Older core cities, such as Burlington, which anchor Standard Metropolitan Statistical Areas in the Northeast and the Midwest, do little large-scale manufacturing, even though their explosive growth in the last century was based on their utility for manufacturing. Exemplifying this trend, Burlington has lost its textile industry, which dominated the city's commercial activity from the turn of the century to the 1950s.

Since 1970, this process of deindustrialization has accelerated nationally. The architectural litter of abandoned high-ceiling, high-rise manufacturing facilities, some of Victorian vintage, is striking. Burlington has its share of these obsolete factory buildings, which have found new life as retail and office space. One converted textile mill houses Burlington's largest industrial employer, General Electric. However, this is an exception. Being a monopoly defense supplier of Gatling guns, GE Burlington has little incentive to modernize, an undertaking that would probably entail relocation. Nevertheless, Burlington demonstrates that the predictions of the 1970s that Northern cities were facing certain demise or would become the arid playground of the unemployable and suburban thrill-seekers have proved to be inaccurate generalizations.[29]

Many Northern cities have experienced a postindustrial restructuring from a manufacturing base to an expansive service sector. This new economic vitality marks what we might call a winner city.

This service sector of the economy, which has provided the bulk of new jobs in the past two decades, has been underwritten to a large extent by national, state, and local government. Cities such as Burlington, Boston, New Haven, Stamford, and San Francisco have been the beneficiaries of large amounts of funding by all levels of government (in particular the national) from such programs as Urban Renewal and Model Cities. Government funding has also increased exponentially the growth of the private, nonprofit sector (a euphemistic term that often hides the interests of various producer groups).[30] The proliferation of programs enacted during the 1960s and 1970s (especially Medicare, Medicaid, and the expansion of student aid and research grants to universities) has provided an immense margin of growth for cities fortunate enough to have large research hospitals, universities, and institutes. With three colleges, one university, and Vermont's largest medical complex, Burlington has benefitted enormously from the expansion of social funding.

The contribution of the private sector to the ballooning service sector in these winner cities has been the construction of corporate headquarters and of regional offices throughout the United States and the rest of the world.[31] Burlington is not home to any *Fortune* 500 headquarters, but it is home to local bank headquarters and regional corporate offices. Burlington (like other winner cities) has seen its financial services and related employment grow at an impressive rate despite the labor-saving functions performed by computers and other automated equipment, such as satellites and fiber optic cables that provide immediate transmission of electronic data.

An increase of government, nonprofit, and corporate services causes an expansion of a subsidiary service sector that caters to the institutional/functional needs of larger, specialized service areas and to the personal needs of the employees. The more prestigious and highly paid side of the service sector is comprised of lawyers, accountants, and other professionals. The number of BMWs and Mercedes in Burlington's downtown attest to their presence there. The more menially reimbursed side of the service sector is comprised of Burlington's far more numerous cashiers, janitors, waitresses, and office temporaries who serve both managers and the professional classes. As much as even a socialist mayor might dislike this inequitable bifurcation of wage earners, the creation of jobs is a political priority. Sanders and his team worked to attract a large department store to the downtown shopping area knowing that it would provide only a handful of well-paying managerial positions and a much larger number of retail and clerical jobs that would pay only what is necessary to retain help. Being a winner city does not necessarily mean that all or even most local inhabitants will have improved standards of living. In sum, winner cities are those that have been rewarded with large increases in employment in the service sector which to some extent compensate for an abrupt decrease in jobs in the manufacturing industries.

Cities are changing entities that are neither always favored by new investment nor consigned forever to economic decay. As economist Bennett Harrison has theorized, cities and regions go into periodic economic declines that last until new conditions develop that create an environment conducive to profitability. Harrison cites the conditions necessary to create this new profitable environment: a pliant labor force that will take almost any job offered regardless of pay or conditions, a supply of readily accessible investment capital, funds available from the national government to create the type of infrastructure needed by the new industries, and the provision of services and subsidies instrumental to pro-growth strategies by state and local government.[32]

Specific to this study, New England as a region and Burlington as a city have followed this pattern. As the textile mills left the city in the 1950s, employment stagnated. Burlington, being the preeminent regional banking center in Vermont, had capital available for promising business investment. The last criterion (government subsidies from all levels of State) was provided when urban renewal was implemented in the city in the 1970s. The central city, in part, was leveled and then sold to private investors at a fraction of the cost. If the logic of capitalism and metropolitan growth is examined, economic decline may well be a necessary precursor to economic growth and restructuring. This theory may help to explain why the formerly economically depressed region of New England is now comparatively healthy; industrial capitalism went into decline there first. In the 1980s, because of growth and employment in the service sector, New England's economy has been successfully restructured to postindustrial uses. Postindustrial economic investment patterns now favor Burlington, but this will not last indefinitely.

RESISTANCE IN POSTINDUSTRIAL BURLINGTON

With the postindustrial restructuring of Burlington there has been a marked drop in the numbers of the city's traditional working class (in Marxian terminology the proletariat), that is, blue-collar workers with no supervisory responsibilities who are directly involved in the production of goods.

Jobs in the service sector have replaced the blue-collar jobs. Subsequently, the workers in the new jobs have been removed from the daily friction and devastatingly stark alienation that is the most oppressive aspect of the production process and therefore are much more likely to be nonunionized than are industrial workers. Union organizing in the United States in the postindustrial 1980s results in one hundred thousand to two hundred thousand new union members in the private sector every year; only 7 percent of the service sector is unionized.[33] Burlington reflects this national pattern. Residual manufacturing firms such as GE Burlington and utilities such as New England Telephone remain unionized. Also, increasing numbers of municipal workers are unionized, including Burlington's teachers, police, fire fighters, and many of its rank and file municipal workers.

The increasing numbers of nonunionized postindustrial workers and the decreasing numbers of unionized factory and municipal workers creates divisions in the wage-earning class that are visible in Burlington as in other cities and other nations. The large cohort of lower-paid service workers who are not affiliated with a union show no overt expressions of class solidarity with the well-paid workers at GE Burlington.

In local politics a more important division exists between the traditional working class and the so-called new middle class of professionals. The latter are by and large not part of the manufacturing process. A true postindustrial creation, the new middle class is directly tied to the production of information. New middle class members produce, disseminate, or apply information. Most are wage earners, although some are petit bourgeoisie, who have advanced degrees. Many work for the State or the nonprofit sector. Because of their class contradictory positions, the new middle class can identify as wage earners with the proletariat, and they resemble the bourgeoisie by seeking to control the work process.[34] But as workers who seldom own their own workplaces and do not work by the hour, they really identify with neither class.

In Burlington, members of the new middle class tend to be the organizers and a good portion of the membership of the new social movements. These movements represent the postmaterialist left, which opposes various forms of domination and oppression in society that are not directly class-based. The new middle class can be found in Burlington's very vocal peace, ecology, and feminist movements, all of which clashed with the Sanders administration over economistic priorities.

The membership of the new social movements also includes many countercultural followers. In Burlington the counterculture is composed of people who are either out of the class system, such as the unemployed and students, or people who are mostly casual workers. The people in this last category work (so they are within the class system), but they work only to achieve subsistence and eschew any careerist goals. Also, the relationship between the nonclass and the administration and its working-class supporters was marked by uneasy collaboration for mutual goals and bitter recriminations over conflicting values.

In the forthcoming chapters the reader will discover that in Burlington the demands by women for comparable worth were resisted by blue-collar municipal workers, the mayor's waterfront development plan was opposed by environmentalists, and the civil disobedience actions by the Burlington Peace Coalition were opposed by the administration. The postmaterialist concerns of the new social movements clashed with the class concerns of the traditional left.

Before ending this section on postindustrial urban resistance, it must be emphasized that a minority of the electoral supporters of the Progressive Coalition in Burlington would identify themselves as socialists, feminists, ecologists, or peace activists. Most Progressive Coalition adherents, like most Americans, did not oppose capitalism and had only a superficial knowledge of socialist, feminist, ecological, or anti-militarist theories. Instead of acting from the dictates of detailed theory, most of the Sanders administration supporters were reacting to tangible effects upon their lives. Usually it is only when a green space is threatened with high-rise apartments or when a proposed highway will sever a neighborhood from the rest of the city that larger groups of people beyond political activists become involved. Although their actions are guided by the resistance to some type of systemic logic, they usually remain committed to some variation of the status quo. In Burlington the core of activists raised the public's consciousness, but it would be a gross overstatement to say that most of the Sanders administration supporters were radicals.

CONCLUSION

Capitalism, with its near monopoly of profitable productive resources, has changing needs that must be met by cities to attract investment. Although a community's ability to fulfill such needs produces business confidence, city governments have limited resources and authority to fulfill them.

Despite limitations, most city governments try to attract investment. This policy reflects both the desire of elected leaders to remain in office and the well-socialized progrowth values of the citizenry. The less a community has that will foster business confidence the more city government will try to offer as compensation for such deficiencies.

Although enticement is the general rule, there are local government challenges to the business community, especially to specific projects that disrupt neighborhoods. As Burlington demonstrates, however, local government challenge does not mean the automatic collapse of business confidence. Burlington's radicals used local state autonomy to effectively blunt challenges from business. Yet this local autonomy, as will be discussed in the next chapter, was restricted by the federalist system. In the end even a socialist mayor must respect the immense authority that the capitalist system has over productive investment in the United States.

4
Burlington Within the Federalist System

Many of the restraints on and directives to Burlington's policy originate from parts of the federal system. For this study the federal system is the totality of what is commonly called government (in the United States) and the relationships between its constituent parts. Since local government has the least amount of autonomy within the federalist structure, it is crucial to this study to know what limits are placed on local authority by other levels of government. As this chapter will reveal, many of the Sanders administration confrontations were with Vermont state officials and many were shaped by Vermont laws. Because of this conflict, an analysis of the limits to local reform that treats the relationship of the local government to the state and national levels as a neutral background (merely the terrain for conflict between larger historical forces) would be deficient. In reality the federal system prescribes and proscribes local policy options in a most arbitrary fashion. A structure with that much authority must be studied both independently and in conjunction with other structures.

Despite the dramatic impact that federalism has on the autonomy of local government, the demands it makes on the citizenry, and its appropriation of immense resources (over one-quarter of the Gross National Product), the State in its totality is less than a complete structure.[1] Unlike capitalism, which is organized around the core characteristic of financial accumulation (both the goal and unifying factor of its existence), federalism has no single, overriding purpose. Instead, it has a multiplicity of purposes (some shaped from outside structures, some from within), which are often contradictory. The purpose of federalism is to reproduce the existing structural relations in society with minimal but necessary change, and thus there is no single logic to federalism; there are logics. Some are self-generated, such as bureaucratic logic; others reflect the needs of various societal systems and the resistances to them. Government under federalism is a fractured structure with limited autonomy.

Only by analyzing the distribution of authority between the levels of government, compounded by the fragmentation within each level of government, can we see that federalism is not a coherent structure. Specializations of authority are alternately delegated and usurped by higher levels of authority. The sharing of authority is common, but it alternates between cooperation and conflict. To understand local government's place in this system, we must examine its relationship to each other level.

THE RELATIONSHIP OF LOCAL TO NATIONAL GOVERNMENT

The national government uses two different power strategies to get local government to implement national policy priorities. These power strategies are mandate and enticement. Mandated policies are crude power relationships: the national government either demands that a policy be implemented or it forbids a local practice.[2] In Burlington national government mandates were not a major factor in city policy making.

The two most prominent policy areas for national mandates are ensuring civil rights and protecting the environment. The first area is of little concern in Burlington, because the city has no significant racial problem, blacks being less than 1 percent of the population, and was not in violation of the Reagan administration's conservative policies on women's civil rights. In the area of preserving a clean environment, Burlington was a willing partner in the Superfund program since it had a prominent toxic waste dump in an abandoned barge canal. On the canal cleanup, the city and national administrations both worked toward the ideal of environmental safety though Vermont's state environmental regulations proved much more stringent than those of the national government. In the larger picture, the Reagan administration's environmental enforcement policy was in a state of retrenchment; there was little possibility of a national mandate being imposed on Burlington.

The relationships that did exist between Burlington and the national government were typical of such intergovernmental associations. Local government was enticed by the national government's largesse to change policies to meet national priorities. The national government has increasingly used its superior financial resources, the greatest share of income taxes and the control of the money supply, to coax local government to establish services and projects it would not undertake alone. Unlike mandates, enticements do not provide for overt coercion; local governments do not have to accept the enticement. However, if a community wants United States funding it must make an effort to comply with national government guidelines, which vary widely with the type of grant involved.

The national enticement strategy has three different legislative forms: the categorical grant, the block grant, and general revenue sharing, each of which has differing effects on local autonomy.[3] Categorical grants offer local governments the least amount of discretion over spending national dollars. These grants when targeted at local government usually include a major contribution from the national government, a smaller state grant, and the final dollars (usually 25 percent or less) from the local municipality. Most of the national funds disbursed to cities come from these grants. Low local funding makes these programs very attractive to local political elites. States and localities must carefully apply for these grants because there is competition for the limited funds that are budgeted. To receive the funds, localities must meet all or most national prerequisites and make their case appear more persuasive than those of other localities. Once a grant is awarded, localities, in order to keep the funding, which is often under state supervision, must follow the national government's detailed guidelines or risk the loss of future appropriations. On occasion, they must repay misspent funds to the national treasury if they fail to meet the guidelines. The strings attached to such funds set up rigid limitations. Crosscutting clauses in more than fifty major programs also make categorical grant recipients meet other objectives, such as affirmative action, relocation aid, fair labor standards, and public information access.[4] In Burlington the environmental standards from a crosscutting clause as applied to highway construction gave opponents a legal tactic to obstruct completion and force government elites to bargain with them.

The question of whether local autonomy is increased or decreased by the rule-encumbered categorical grants can only be answered by analyzing specific situations. In one case in this study, Burlington increased its bargaining power with a corporate waterfront developer by offering to apply for a multimillion-dollar Urban Development Action Grant that would allow for a mix of public amenities with private condominiums and offices. When this categorical grant could not be secured, the amenities promised by the developer were cut back; both the Alden Corporation and city officials knew the city's financial autonomy was undermined.

The dual effects of categorical aid were demonstrated in the case of the airport. Burlington's Airport Commission had obtained categorical grants for expensive additions to its facilities. However, when the city tried to tap funds from excess airport revenues for other purposes (in return for guaranteeing loans in previous years), national authorities ruled that this would be in violation of the conditions attached to categorical grants the airport had received. In fact, the Federal Aviation Administration blocked a $1.7 million grant until the Board of Aldermen reversed their position on using airport revenues.[5] Without funds for expansion from the national government, Burlington's airport would have remained underdeveloped and would likely have stunted the city's economic growth. With national funding, the airport's subsequent material success could not be redistributed to other city programs. Do categorical grants increase local autonomy? The answer is yes only if local and national goals are synonymous. If they differ, local autonomy is not increased (or can actually decrease) unless the national guidelines are not enforced.

While categorical grants have unpredictable effects on local autonomy, block grants are more likely to increase local autonomy. Block grants, first enacted in the 1960s, were attempts by the national government to pass money to states and localities targeted to general goals, such as law enforcement or local employment, and with fewer restrictions than categorical grants. States and localities would have leeway within the general categories to fund their own priorities.

Although by 1983 only 14 percent of the total grants-in-aid funds that came from the national government were in block grants,[6] the money provided by one, the Community Block Development Grant (CBDG), funded many different neighborhood programs. Especially innovative, Burlington had a neighborhood planning assembly in each ward that made recommendations on the use of CBDG money to the Board of Aldermen.[7] Other programs, such as Burlington's shelter for battered women and the land trust program (designed to buy land and preserve it for affordable housing), received partial funding from block grants. With fewer specific restrictions than categorical grants, block grants increased the Sanders administration's ability to provide services to its citizens, and though a prominent national study concluded that when aid formulas were shifted from categorical to block grants, low-income groups received fewer benefits,[8] the Sanders administration specifically targeted many of its programs to such populations.

The quantity of local state autonomy produced fell dramatically because the Reagan administration continually pared away block grant and other funding.[9] Largely because of such cuts, by the end of 1985, Burlington's treasurer, Jonathan Leopold, predicted a city deficit because of a shortfall of $630,000 in national aid during fiscal year 1987, a considerable sum for a community of thirty-eight thousand.[10]

The Reagan cutbacks in funding markedly reduced general revenue sharing (GRS), the form of grant-in-aid most preferred by local officials. Having the fewest restrictions, GRS money can be used to fund a host of programs that can range from reactionary to very progressive, mostly at the discretion of local leaders. In 1983, GRS money was only 7 percent of the national government's aid budget, however, and with block grants only 14 percent,[11] the amount of financial autonomy established for localities by these funds was severely limited. The cutbacks in national spending by the Reagan administration that included cutbacks in both block and categorical grants and the termination of GRS in 1986, further aggravated the revenue shortfall in Burlington. National enticement strategies are dwindling; if the 1980s rate of national government contraction persists, local autonomy within the federal system will be almost entirely a state matter.

THE RELATIONSHIP OF LOCAL TO STATE GOVERNMENT

In the hierarchic federal system, local government is subordinate to the state. In fact, the very existence of local government is a state prerogative. Juridically, this has long been so. In the 1860s, an Iowa judge proclaimed the still binding dictum known as Dillon's Rule that details the precarious legal existence of municipalities:

1. There is no common-law right of local self-government.
2. Local entities are creatures of the state subject to creation and abolition at

the unfettered discretion of the state (barring [state] constitutional limitations).
3. Localities may exercise only those powers expressly granted.
4. Localities are "mere tenants at the will of the legislature."[12]

An analysis of state/local relations merely from a legal view would lead to the conclusion that there is total state suzerainty over local government. All power relationships between these two levels would be postulated as crude, with the state mandating its will.

This is an overstatement; there are mitigating factors that limit the arbitrary state/local relationship articulated by Judge Dillon. Since states devolve some of their authority to local governments, it can be inferred that there are actors, groups, and institutions that demand some measure of local control.[13] These actors, sometimes in the form of locally elected state legislators, can act as a brake on the state's propensity to invoke Dillon's Rule. When the state administrators of Vermont asked the legislature to revoke a previous right given to Burlington to tax rooms and meals, the rural-dominated body went along with Burlington's elected representatives and refused to pass the legislation.

The functional specialization of policy making also acts to increase community authority. Zoning, for example, is almost universally a matter of local discretion. The functional distribution of authority to govern land use is local government's most important power. The Sanders administration repeatedly attempted to use this power to guide waterfront development. Although states limit such authority and frequently supercede it through environmental or other ordinances, the need for local expertise acts as a buffer to state intrusion.

States often delegate authority to local communities through home rule legislation, or in state constitutions. In such legislation, consistent with Dillon's Rule, the state defines the powers of localities and allows localities to fill in the details within the boundaries set. Unfortunately for Burlington, the state of Vermont did not have home rule provisions until 1988. The state legislature repeatedly rejected Burlington's progressive policy changes. In lieu of home rule, states have different legislative strategies for providing authority to local government.

Before the 1988 statewide referendum on home rule, the relationship of Burlington to Vermont, from a simple legal view, was one of clear subordination of the former to the latter. Vermont did not offer any choices for the form of local government, nor did it specify a particular form. Instead, Vermont enacted all local government by special acts of the state legislature, with each enactment deliberated on separately. On the face of it, this procedure is very restrictive to local autonomy since the state can prescribe a governmental framework without local approval. In practice, however, Vermont historically placed fewer impediments to authority than might be supposed. Consistent with New England's historical and cultural emphasis on local government, until 1984 Vermont allowed municipalities to enact changes to their charters, and (unless the legislature vetoed such changes or they ran counter to existing Vermont statutes) the changes were accepted automatically. The restrictive nature of special act provisions was ameliorated by allowing localities to alter and thus expand local authority. In 1984, in keeping with the bias of Dillon's Rule against local government, the Vermont legislature reversed the law. All changes in municipal charters were denied without the specific approval of the legislature. Some argued that this new policy was so encompassing that even if Burlington legislated any new tax for longer than one year, it would have to be submitted for Vermont's approval. Burlington's autonomy suffered a severe blow when Vermont, arbitrarily applying its juridical authority, made local government explicitly subordinate to the state.

Like the national government, states can either mandate or entice local governments to implement policies consistent with state desires. States can and do pass legislation that forbids local government from enacting certain laws.[14] However, in Vermont, the charter change procedure made this type of negative power strategy superfluous in most cases. Mandatory state legislative directives on local government, unlike the small number of national mandates, are common. Such mandates can cause resentment by local leaders, especially when an additional expenditure is demanded from the local budget without state compensation. In Burlington, many negative state mandates were accepted as constants and not challenged even by the city's radical leadership. For example, much of the telephone company's property holdings remained tax exempt by a nineteenth-century state legislative provision, despite the city's primary reliance on property taxes for revenue. The Progressive Coalition expressed no outrage over this blatant business subsidy; it was just another example of what they would correctly perceive as a pro-business bias.

States use enticement strategies in addition to mandates to persuade localities to establish and fund programs. Since the revenue-gathering capacity of localities is limited by federalist and other structural constraints, optional state dollars can persuade a city like

Burlington to implement policies it would not normally consider. To keep state educational grant dollars, the city reassessed its Grand List of taxable properties, despite the local unpopularity of this policy; Burlington's homeowners and renters had previously voted down tax appropriations to pay for the program.

Like direct state aid for various projects and programs, most aid from the national government in the form of categorical grants must pass through state administrative offices to localities. States usually contribute a portion of such funding from their own revenues.[15] Such pass-through funding ($12.3 billion nationwide in 1972) allows state officials an effective veto over much national/local funding.[16] Implicitly, state highway officials made a veiled threat to eliminate pass-through funding for highway construction in Burlington when city officials obstructed progress of the Southern Connector. Explicitly, the state highway commissioner threatened that the city would have to repay national funds already expended (as will be discussed in Chapter 5) if the state-approved highway was not completed.

Thus, the question of whether state aid to local government increases or decreases the amount of local autonomy depends on the constraints and benefits of the particular case. As in the national/local relationship, the criterion for evaluating whether local autonomy has been expanded seems to be the amount of congruence that exists between local and state officials or, if not that, then the extent to which the state has abdicated its responsibility to enforce the conditions of aid. Under the Paquette regime, the state-planned highway was solicited by city elites, so one could say autonomy increased. In the early Sanders regime, when the same plan was opposed and the state threatened retaliation, autonomy shrank.

What remained without question was that the state of Vermont had, until 1988, the juridical authority to terminate the very existence of Burlington or any other locality in the state; a latent threat to restrict local autonomy was ever present. When the state offered a positive strategy of enticement, a locality's decision to spurn such a program was an invitation to a possibly more onerous state mandate at the locality's expense.

LOCAL GOVERNMENT'S RELATIONSHIP TO OTHER LOCAL GOVERNMENTS

The local state's unequal relationships to the state and national levels are not exhaustive of the possibilities of government-to-government relationships within the federalist system. Local government is also in a competitive relationship with each neighboring municipality (and potentially the universe of other municipalities). A crucial problem for local governments is that people who have moderate to extensive wealth and valuable skills can relocate across city boundaries at will, and local governments have no authority to coerce them to stay. Most businesses can and do also pass through the permeable boundaries between cities.[17]

Since incorporated communities are equals before the law in most states (those allowing big city annexation policies being the exception), cities cannot impose restrictions on the surrounding suburbs and exurbs even if they have deliberate policies to entice businesses and the more affluent populations away from the urban core. When Vermont Telephone moved from Burlington to South Burlington, the city administration tried, unsuccessfully, to retaliate by asking the state Public Service Board to deny all rate increases based on the cost of the new building. To control intercity capital flight, Burlington sought to tap state authority. Legally, Burlington could not directly challenge South Burlington's authority to raid its resources since both communities were legal equals in the competition for capital investment.[18] Without the authority to prevent labor and capital flight or the jurisdiction to prevent other cities from accepting such valuable resources, cities compete by trying to establish a high level of business confidence. The relationship of local government to local government is one of legal equality and unequal resources.

Although the complexity of national to local, state to local, and local to local governments seems to be enough to demonstrate that federalism is a structure of confused organization, this picture remains incomplete. Within local government, just as within the national and state governments, there is a fragmented organization that disaggregates authority even further. Burlington's government is a confused combination of two ideal models of city government: the mayor-council and the commission.

The city of Burlington received its first charter in 1865 from the state of Vermont. By the end of that century it had three boards of departmental commissioners, a mayor, and a Board of Aldermen, a structure that has changed only incrementally ever since.[19] In 1981, Burlington had twenty-three different commissions ranging from one with elected representatives that governed the important School Department to one with appointed delegates that governed the politically inconsequential Department of Cemeteries.[20]

The appointed commissioners receive their offices in several ways that accurately reflect the internally fragmented nature of Burlington's government. Excluding the popularly elected School Board commissioners, eight are picked by the mayor, twenty-one by the aldermen, and more than ninety are appointed by the City Council, which is comprised of the mayor and the Board of Aldermen.[21] Most commissioners have three-year terms (one year longer than the mayor or any alderman); some have four, and a few five. Once appointed, these commissioners, who exercise executive authority, are autonomous of both the mayor and the Board of Aldermen. Because the commissioners hold longer terms of office, a mayor and the majority of the Board of Aldermen must form a single, cohesive, partisan majority for at least four years to ensure control of most of the commissions. Unless such successive majorities occur, it is impossible to have even indirect electoral accountability for the commissions. And even if a partisan majority is sustained and a commissioner is appointed by this majority, a commissioner after taking office is not subject to recall during his or her term in office except for dereliction of duty or malfeasance (both difficult to prove). The end result is that accountability is insulated from the ballot box.

The pattern of representation of Burlington's commissioners further demonstrates a lack of political accountability. Since one must volunteer for the unpaid position of commissioner to be even considered for appointment, it is not surprising that these commissions have often had memberships unrepresentative of the city's diversity. The commissioners who were appointed under the combined Democratic and Republican majority during the period under study, for example, have proven to represent disproportionately the wealthier areas of Burlington. Of 104 commissioners serving in 1982, only 4 came from the poorest wards in the Old North End. By comparison, one affluent New North End ward had 33 commissioners, and the wealthiest ward, situated in "The Hill" (a neighborhood of stately houses surrounding the University of Vermont campus), had 31 commissioners.[22] These two wealthy wards alone controlled most of the city's executive offices, all with no direct electoral accountability. This example of self-selection by elites verifies the conclusion of almost every basic American political science textbook that those with higher levels of socioeconomic status dominate the more difficult and influential types of political participation.[23] The Sanders administration's persistent victories helped to favorably alter these proportions, without actually reversing them to lower-class advantage.

Representation within the commissions was undemocratic not only by class but also by sex. The excessively high proportion of male officeholders was incongruous with the city's population profile, in which women are in the majority. Despite a vibrant women's community that supported the Progressive Coalition and the presence of women from all three partisan factions on the Board of Aldermen, the token number of women commissioners on hand in 1981 was increased incrementally. In one instance, when twenty positions for commissioner were filled at one sitting by the Board of Aldermen, only three women were confirmed. Interestingly, that evening the Design Review Board, one of only a few boards with significant female representation, received its fourth female member (out of a total of five members).[24] The stereotype of women as holders of aesthetic roles was perpetuated by the aldermanic board's action. Since none of the three contesting partisan organizations was overly concerned about an equitable balance by gender, the portion of the executive branch represented by the commissions remained under the domination of a majority of unelected males. Their affluent neighborhood origins only compounded the undemocratic tendencies of the commission form of government.

Under Burlington's charter, the commissions serve as a fragmented executive authority, often at odds with the mayor, who remains the chief executive more in name than substance. The mayor's authority under the city charter makes the position alternately weak and strong. Concerning appropriations, the mayor is a member of the Finance Board, along with the president of the Board of Aldermen, the city treasurer (a mayoral appointee subject to aldermanic approval), and two other aldermen elected by the board. This means that if the mayor's party fails to control the Board of Aldermen, the Finance Board will not be under his partisan control. Euphemistically, the charter says the Finance Board will "assist" the mayor, who submits the budget each year. Since shaping the annual budget is an important tool for setting the political agenda, if the mayor and his party can control the Finance Board, some of the planned fragmentation of city government can be overcome. Unfortunately, the Progressive Coalition controlled the Finance Board (and the presidency of the Board of Aldermen) for only one year.

After completing the proposed budget, the Finance Board sends it for approval to the Board of Aldermen, where the mayor has no vote. The board can cut any proposed appropriation by a simple majority vote; it can increase funding by a more difficult to achieve two-thirds vote. That it was the intention of the authors of the Burlington Charter to design a fiscally conservative framework of government is made evident by this fragmented distribution of authority biased toward those who want to limit government size, spending, and authority.

Despite the mayor's diluted budgetary authority, he retains one important strong-mayor feature: veto power over the Board of Aldermen's resolutions and proposed laws (requiring two-thirds vote by the board to override). Once the Progressive Coalition elected aldermen to more than one-third of the seats, Mayor Sanders' negative powers as designated by the conservatively biased charter were put to use to block conservative proposals. Thus the mayor is a strong mayor only in the sense that he has a formidable authority to say no. In terms of positive power, the mayor's ability to initiate new policy is shared with and dominated by the Board of Aldermen, which must originate such policies.

Like the mayor, the thirteen members of the Board of Aldermen are elected for two-year terms, six one year and seven the next. The election of all thirteen at once would have tended to cement alliances between mayoral supporters on the board and the mayor himself. Instead, the charter effectively separates the parliamentary contests from the chief executive's election, and this separation further fragments an already complex scheme of government.

The key to a conservative government framework is not merely divisions; overlapping delegations of authority that protect the status quo are also necessary. The Board of Aldermen is not identified in the charter as a legislative body; it is considered an "administrative" body in combination with the mayor and his appointed officers, who must be confirmed by the board.[25] With the members of the Board of Aldermen sitting on the City Council and the Board of Finance and controlling the Board for Abatement of Taxes, the aldermanic council overlaps both legislative and executive functions. If we look at Burlington's city government in its entirety, executive authority is everywhere. In fact, without the unity of a sustained majority controlling the Board of Aldermen, the mayor's office, and the commissions, there is almost no point in referring to Burlington's "executive authority," since as a collective institutional entity it can only exist through the cement of cohesive political parties or factions.

Before our analysis of Burlington's contribution to the convoluted structure of the federalist system is complete, it must be noted that in addition to the commissions, the mayor, and the Board of Aldermen, there is another source of competing government authority. When 5 percent of the voters of Burlington sign a petition calling for a referendum on a particular issue, an election is held, and the voters become their own unmediated legislative body. This elegant exercise of relatively undiluted authority surrounded by what is otherwise a morass of conflicting institutions squandering local sovereignty allows Burlington's citizens to supersede a local government framework designed not to work effectively. Direct democracy, though labeled a part of the federalist system by scholars, is really the antithesis of the disaggregation of authority under federalism. Since referenda by the unorganized public is the exception rather than the norm for public-policy making, Burlington's government in its entirety remains an example of an institution designed to be confused, cautious, conservative, and of extremely limited scope.

To recapitulate, the whole of federalism is not more than the sum of its parts, because its parts do not truly integrate into a whole structure. Authority is in some places specialized; in others it is diffuse and overlapping. The federalist system is not immune to change, but unless other societal structures and their resistances that reflect more coherent power relations forcefully alter the status-quo bias of the State, change remains incremental at best or moribund. A panoply of institutional veto opportunities allows privileged populations to maintain an intolerable, narrow range for reform that vacillates between liberal and reactionary change.

THE RELATIVE AUTONOMY OF THE LOCAL STATE

The internally fragmented and permeable quality of the federalist system as a whole, specifically when compared with local government's tertiary position of authority within the federal system, makes the question of local state autonomy seem moot. But local government does have authority. If it were only a local committee for the ruling bourgeoisie, there would be no Sanders administration; if it were only an appendage of state government, there would be no state/local government policy clashes.

In the federalist system, no common value unites each agency and policy; instead, the system reflects a diversity of values. Thus, at a glance, the State appears to have a conglomeration of interests. On a more subsidiary level, however, the State does act to perpetuate itself as a bureaucratic organization.

A logic that is a lesser rationale for the perpetuation of the State is contained within the common systemic needs of bureaucratic agencies. Bureaucratic logic when applicable to the State is subordinate to the functional purpose provided by the legislature that created the bureaucracy in the first place. Burlington's Library Commission, for example, is concerned about the number of books circulated, and the Streets Commission is concerned about the flow of traffic. Nevertheless, these two agencies with very different purposes could be united against a city proposal for a general reduction in service.

Public bureaucracy is a part of the State that is subordinate to but not wholly under the control of elected officials. Burlington's Electric Department, which alternately encouraged and then sabotaged the Sanders administration's efforts to municipalize the local cable television franchise, represents a bureaucratic niche of authority that provides a limited measure of autonomy to the State. Public bureaucracy can deflect or champion democratic demands from outside the State, muffle conflict through the myth of the State as an apolitical organization, and defend the authority that is inherent in specialized knowledge. Each of these functions provides public bureaucracy with relative autonomy and with a logic of its own. When elected leaders and bureaucratic heads agree, the logic of bureaucracy can be used to defend or expand local state autonomy; when they disagree, they squander the modicum of authority the local state has.

The local state also derives autonomy from its functional and dynamic role as the reproducer of the existing structures in society. Both materially (i.e., through business subsidies) and ideologically (i.e., by reciting the Pledge of Allegiance in the schools), the local state sustains a variety of institutions. In addition, the local state is both the site of conflict between supporters of unequal relations and the site of resistance to unequal relations. Structuralist Marxist theorists have developed an entire literature around the need for the State in advanced capitalist nations to help reproduce capitalism.[26]

The late Nicos Poulantzas, the most advanced thinker on the structuralist theory of the State, argues that the State is the materialization and the concentration of society's class relations. The State's institutional form and policy biases are congruent with the relative strengths of class relations in society as a whole. Thus the State, instead of being merely the site of power struggles, is also a power relationship itself.[27] Poulantzas argues that the State reflects class relations, particularly between the capitalist class and the working class, and these class relations are the real source of unequal power relations. Poulantzas stresses that because the State is a materialization of class relations, it has a responsibility to reproduce the existing unequal relations. To accomplish this contradictory task it must have some autonomy.

Burlington, a local state, has a small measure of State autonomy.

Yet even under a socialist mayor, the city acted to fulfill its historical task of reproducing capitalism while trying to improve the conditions of the working class. City policies under the auspices of Burlington's elected radicals demonstrated the dual and contradictory role of the local capitalist state: allowing the private development of the water-front while demanding public amenities, delaying but finally accept-ing a highway designed for the needs of downtown business, and abandoning the municipalization of local cable television for a cash payment and vastly increased service delivery. Capital in its hege-monic position retains the upper hand, but the general public re-ceives concessions that it would not have without the vigorous strug-gle carried on by the Progressive Coalition and its supporters on local state terrain. Unequal relations were reproduced but not without tan-gible benefits for the working class.

Since the State, and to a lesser degree even the local state, has a measure of autonomy, a theorist is tempted to specify exactly where such autonomy is located. Poulantzas has studied this question of what happens to the locus of authority of the State when opponents of capitalism capture the electoral apparatus of the State. His observa-tions are relevant to the Progressive Coalition's capture of Bur-lington's City Hall. According to Poulantzas, when the left captures part of the apparatus of the state, it does "not necessarily control the one or ones which play the dominant role in the state and which therefore constitute the central pivot or real power."[28] Instead, the locus of authority that promotes the interests of capital will move to another part of the State, one not controlled by the left. Our study of Burlington will demonstrate this point repeatedly. This point is partic-ularly germane to the United States since the structure of federalism allows the lateral movement of authority within a level of government (Board of Aldermen to the commissions), and, if that is not sufficient protection, provides avenues of appeal to the higher levels of state or national government. Vermont's Public Service Board repeatedly acted on behalf of corporate capitalist interests and against Prog-ressive Coalition municipal tax reforms and a proposed municipaliza-tion of cable television.

CONCLUSION

The autonomy of the local state described in this analysis is modest but not negligible. Despite the hierarchy of authority that makes the local state subordinate to both the national and state governments,

particularly the latter, cities do have resources and a sphere of jurisdiction. The common and particular needs of bureaucracy give the
unelected portion of the local state some autonomy, even from the
elected officials, and though this bureaucratic autonomy has no es-
sentialist purpose, it has roles determined by society's unequal power
relations. The local state embodies such values and changes policy,
within limits, to reflect the changing strengths and weaknesses between structures and resistances. The role of reproducing society's
unequal structures provides the State with necessary autonomy to
prevent destructive conflict and also makes city government a major
site of class and other kinds of conflict. The local state, despite having
a small allotment of authority, has nevertheless been the target of the
agents of resistance in Burlington.

The next four chapters will describe the interplay between capitalism and federalism and the struggle by Burlington's Progressives
to create a more equal society. In addition, the struggle within Burlington's left will have its effect on the Progressive Coalition agenda.

A FRAMEWORK FOR ANALYSIS

Before these cases are presented, however, it is necessary to intro-
duce the framework of analysis. Because so few left theorists have
published analyses of reform, one serious problem for left urban
theorists has been the lack of a framework within which to evaluate
reforms on the local level. Since the proletarian revolution in the advanced capitalist nations has not arrived and will likely never do so, it
is imperative that a theoretical mechanism be established to evaluate
the reform of existing and future left governments. One prominent
left theorist, André Gorz, has created a framework to judge whether a
reform is democratic socialist or merely reformist.[29] I have taken his
categories and altered them away from their economistic bias to reflect the pluralistic demands of the new social movements. Also, I
have added another category of reform to identify policies that are
actually a step backward.

Democratic Structural Reform
A democratic structural reform is a change in a structure that benefits
those who are dominated by challenging the essential logic of that
structure. Such a reform puts human needs and demands (which ide-
ally should be defined by the citizenry itself) ahead of the needs of a

dominating structure. The most extreme type of democratic structural reform is revolutionary. An example of a revolutionary reform is a city government's making all citizens' incomes approximately equal through a steeply progressive income tax.

Nevertheless, the breadth of democratic structural reform allows for reforms that are less than revolutionary and thus more feasible for adoption. It has been argued that Burlington's land trust program is such a reform.[30] The land trust buys land to keep it off the market, where its price has been bid up by developers. Moderately priced housing is built on the land; the homeowners rent the land at fixed, under-the-market rates. If the program continues, eventually most residential real estate in Burlington will sit on city-owned land, which will help to ensure affordable housing for moderate-income people. Since the land is originally purchased at market rates rather than confiscated without payment, this reform is not revolutionary. However, it acts against the long-term interests of capital by serving a human need (affordable shelter) and removing something valuable from the marketplace (real estate). When land ceases to be a commodity and instead becomes a social right, democratic structural reform has been achieved.

Liberal Reform

Liberal reforms provide benefits to those who are dominated; unlike democratic structural reforms, however, liberal reforms accept the logic of the particular structure under challenge. By accepting and accommodating structural logic, liberal reformers frame their proposals more modestly. This is not to say that such reform is inconsequential. Most of the reforms enacted by the Progressive Coalition in Burlington fall into the category. Some argue that the combined effects of many pieces of such legislation could push a system to socialism.[31] This study will dispel any illusions that liberal reform centered purely within the local state as it is now constituted could push a system to socialism.

Reactionary Reform

Reactionary reforms are really not reforms at all; they are changes that actually increase the authority and command of resources to structures that dominate, and thus they benefit those who have historically been dominators. The word "reform" has been chosen in this definition because this is the terminology used by proponents of such changes when presenting them to the public. In Burlington, the reassessment of property at a uniform market rate for both business and homeowners was a reactionary reform that cut taxes for business and redistributed the burden to homeowners and through increased rent to apartment dwellers. In effect, there was a redistribution of income upward, the opposite of democratic structural reform.

The spectrum created runs from democratic socialist reform on the left to reactionary reform on the right. Most reforms do not fit precisely into one category. Any given program may have more than one aspect. In Burlington, the Progressive Coalition's tax proposals had both liberal and reactionary aspects. Only when the content and probable effects of proposed and enacted reforms are dissected can they be placed within the spectrum. The analyses in the next four chapters will use this spectrum.

5
Economic Development

The major thrust of the Progressive Coalition's program was economic. Three issues loomed large: development of the waterfront, construction of the Southern Connector highway, and the development of a municipal cable television system.

WATERFRONT DEVELOPMENT

Burlington has always utilized its lakefront. In fact, its first real growth was due to its location on Lake Champlain. During the 1840s railroads were first constructed to serve the sawmills and other wood-derivative industries on the waterfront. With state encouragement, twelve acres of the lake were filled in for railroad construction, and by 1869, twelve wharves had been built. After a growth period of half a century (with periodic business downturns), Burlington's waterfront declined precipitously. In 1897, western United States lumber interests convinced Congress to pass a tariff on Canadian lumber, effectively ending its entry into the United States.[1]

During the 1970s a portion of the city center adjacent to the waterfront was redeveloped with extensive funding from the national government. Urban planners rediscovered the waterfront and sought to transform it from an underutilized industrial zone into a mixed-use area for recreation, commerce, and residences.

By the time Mayor Sanders and his two supporters took office in March 1981, a local developer, Antonio Pomerleau, reputed to be Burlington's richest citizen, purchased an option to buy eleven acres of unused Central Vermont Railway land on the waterfront for $120,000. Pomerleau initially planned two eighteen-story skyscrapers and two twelve-story structures, which would have dwarfed all other buildings along the waterfront. Burlington's Planning Commission rejected the proposal to build these cement and steel edifices, which would block the magnificent lake view from portions of the city. Two days after Sanders won his first term as mayor, Pomerleau resubmitted a scaled-down design on March 5, 1981, for two nine-story buildings and a seven-story structure that would house a hotel, condominiums, and retail space.[2]

Interestingly, Pomerleau, whom traditional Marxists would categorize as part of the local ruling class, struck up an unpredicted and much gossiped about friendship with the newly elected socialist mayor.[3] Notwithstanding their friendship, the mayor resolutely opposed the Pomerleau plan. In fact, in May 1981, Sanders, using a mayoral prerogative that needed no approval from the hostile Democratic/Republican-controlled Board of Aldermen, set up a Waterfront Task Force to propose development guidelines and thus avoid entrusting the waterfront development to the vision of any individual entrepreneur.[4] From the beginning, Sanders and the Progressive Coalition aldermen demanded of any developer public access to the lake. The Coalition's demand was not novel. Sanders' predecessor, Gordon Paquette, had made the same demand, and when Sanders took office there already existed a Citizens' Waterfront Group organized and led by Rick Sharp, a lawyer and an environmentalist. The citizens' group had its own plan for ensuring public access, expanding the amount of city-owned property adjacent to the railway acreage, and building a public marina.[5] A loyal Democrat, Sharp would prove to be a consistent critic of both Pomerleau's plans and Sanders' initiatives.

Later in 1981, Pomerleau again changed his waterfront development plans to a towering twenty-two-story building housing $200,000 condominiums surrounded by smaller buildings housing a hotel, retail space, and more condominiums. This $30 million plan sailed through the Planning Commission, chaired by Republican William Aswad, a local engineering executive and a proponent of growth. The key to approval was the solution provided by David Sellers, the Yale University architect hired by Pomerleau, who added height in order to expand public access down below.[6] The logic at work here was that of capitalism: since there was a minimum threshhold for profitability after all costs were incurred, a specific number of units would have to be offered at a certain price for it to be attractive to investors. Following this logic, public access at the pedestrian level could be saved only by depriving the greater Burlington public of visual access to the lake. Notwithstanding the friendship between Sanders and Pomerleau, the radical mayor remained opposed to a huge building that would be restricted to the wealthy. Although the mayor could not, under the city charter, overrule the Planning Commission's approval, he could tie up the development in the state courts for an extended time. For a businessman, money invested without an increment over time is money lost. The mayor's use of negative power relations proved to be a decisive stumbling block for Pomerleau's plans.

Fortified by Progressive Coalition aldermanic victories in the March 1982 elections, Sanders, skeptical of the commitment of the Waterfront Board (a subcommittee of the pro-business Planning Commission) to the public interest, tried to create a new, larger commission that would have greater input. This new commission would include the existing Waterfront Board, aldermen, and the watchdog Citizens' Waterfront Group.[7] Most important, this new commission would be answerable to the Board of Aldermen, whose resolutions are subject to a mayoral veto. This proposal was an obvious end run around the Planning Commission, which was dominated by pro-business ideologues.

The Waterfront Board, as a subcommittee of the Planning Commission, sought to preserve its autonomy under William Aswad's leadership by refusing to incorporate into this larger entity. Aswad was leery of Sanders' motives and expressed fear that Sanders would buy the land and make it a city park.[8] Sanders had considered the possibility.[9] However, estimates of the market value of the land ranged up to $500,000 an acre; this cost plus the permanent removal of this land from the city's Grand List of taxable properties would make voter approval of such a purchase unlikely. Indeed, Sanders must have been wary of such a proposal. When he was first elected in 1981, a sizeable property tax increase was decisively defeated on the same ballot; the tax revolt was a factor in Sanders' initial victory and in his subsequent victories. Planning Commissioner Aswad's fears would be difficult for the Progressive Coalition to realize as long as they had to play by the capitalist rules of "just" compensation that are enforced at all levels of the federalist system.

In November 1982 while the mayor was trying to redirect the authority to plan from the appointed officials of the Planning Commission to elected officials, Antonio Pomerleau dropped his option to purchase the railway land. It would cost Pomerleau $100,000 a year to keep the option, with no promise of imminent development.[10]

Subsequently, the property was up for sale by the Central Vermont's parent company, Grand Trunk of Detroit. The land was already zoned for moderate-density development, forty residential units an acre. Although with little city input the land could be sold and developed with limited numbers of houses or condominiums, there were clauses in the zoning ordinances and a city master plan allowing for some city review. Nevertheless, at this juncture Sanders saw a political opportunity to remove waterfront development from Aswad's bailiwick.

In December 1983, Sanders asked the Board of Aldermen to approve interim zoning for two years; under this proposal, no development could proceed without the assent of the aldermen and Sanders. This would effectively displace the Planning Commission's rule over waterfront development.[11] Predictably, Aswad opposed the diminution of his commission's authority.[12] Also predictably, the hostile Board of Aldermen in an almost totally partisan vote defeated interim zoning seven to six, with one Democrat defecting to the Progressive Coalition position. The primary argument against interim zoning was that the time for talking was over. Opponents of interim zoning argued that it was time for building.[13]

After the aldermanic rebuke, the mayoral race began heating up, and Sanders' opponents tried to exploit the waterfront issue. Judith Stephany, the Democratic nominee, advocated a community "development corporation" for the waterfront; this was another end run around the Planning Commission, but one that would likely insulate development proposals from citizen input.[14] This proposal was so poorly thought out that when queried by reporters Stephany could not say what it would cost or how quickly it could be put into effect.[15] Since Stephany was trounced at the polls by Sanders in March 1983, any objections to the plan became moot. Waterfront development remained in suspended animation.

Despite editorials being regularly published in the *Burlington Free Press* that the Sanders' anti-business stance would stifle investment,[16] that June a group of out-of-town Vermont investors, in partnership with the famous architect Benjamin Thompson, purchased the railway property, with a project in mind that would dwarf Pomerleau's $30 million plan. Thompson had achieved national fame for his urban designs: Boston's Faneuil Hall, Baltimore's Harbor Place, and Manhattan's South Street Seaport.[17] This was a link between Vermont's wealthy elite and a prominent national corporate firm. Sanders praised Thompson's work both publicly and privately,[18] even though Thompson's previous projects were clearly urban preserves created for those well-heeled elites who could afford conspicuous consumption.

With waterfront development now seemingly imminent, the mayor's office, the aldermen, the planning commissioners, and the Waterfront Board tried to compromise on new zoning rules that would reduce residential density to twenty houses, guarantee that a scenic vista of the lake would not be obscured, and increase open-space requirements.[19] The compromise failed to receive the approval of each fraction of government. Soon after, the Planning Commission attempted through its own offices to implement interim zoning that would effectively keep waterfront development under its control. However, the Vermont legislature had passed a law the previous year requiring that notification by any town considering interim zoning must be made to neighboring municipalities before such interim zoning can be implemented. Therefore the commission's hasty zoning plans were nullified on procedural grounds. Because of state limits on Burlington's actions on land use, one of the few prerogatives cities have with which to shape their destiny, Burlington lost all the gains it had made on controlling waterfront development.[20]

In a decision reflecting both partisan and bureaucratic differences, in August 1985, a joint committee of city aldermen and planning commissioners rejected interim zoning for the lakefront. Sanders was pushing for a new ordinance that would guarantee eight acres of open space out of a thirty-six-acre development plan. A prominent local architect, Colin Lindberg, claimed this would effectively preclude development of the land.[21]

While the mayor's office, the opposition-dominated council, and the Planning Commission were locked in a jurisdictional battle, the Alden Waterfront Corporation (Ben Thompson and the Vermont investors) bought a crucial piece of property on the waterfront, the vacant and historically designated Green Mountain Power Building. Although the power company had rejected all initial bids, including a hasty one offered by the city and one by Alden, the development corporation eventually triumphed when the Board of Aldermen, by a partisan Democratic/Republican vote, refused to outbid Alden.[22] Since the aldermen balked, the city's right of eminent domain remained unexercised. While the Green Mountain Power negotiations continued, Alden bought one other waterfront parcel and options on five more.[23] In this instance, the dispersion of authority throughout

Burlington's city government paralyzed it. By contrast, the Alden corporate leaders had a clear goal and pursued it without any internal impediments.

The Alden Corporation astutely chose to take a conciliatory strategy with the mayor by publicly pledging cooperation and continuously meeting with him and his aides in private meetings.[24] These meetings were much criticized by the opposition aldermen, the Waterfront Board spokesman, the reliably hostile *Burlington Free Press*, and even the generally pro-Coalition *Vermont Vanguard Press*. What really irked all of the above parties was that Alden refused to reveal the names of its investors until forced by mounting public pressure to do so in February 1984. Interestingly, one of the original ten investors, a native of Vermont, is also an heiress to the Dow Jones and Company fortune. She is reputed to be the daughter of one of the richest four hundred individuals in the nation.[25] With this kind of backing, it was not surprising that Alden's ten investors could quickly outbid the city of Burlington's thirty-eight thousand residents for the Green Mountain Power Building.

While Sanders was negotiating with Alden for public access, height limitations, moderately priced housing, and open space, various ad hoc citizens' groups were independently organizing to modify or oppose Alden's waterfront development plans. The Citizens' Waterfront Group pushed for open negotiations and a public bike path that would run the length of the shore. Sanders publicly blasted that group, accusing it of becoming an arm of the Democratic party; both leaders of the Citizens' Waterfront Group, Rick Sharp and Howard Dean, were registered and politically active Democrats.[26] The Waterfront Group's consistent goal of an unimpeded bike path running the length of Burlington's shoreline was sidetracked by the mayor several times, including when he disapproved of a $2 million bond referendum in 1983 to finance the proposal. The referendum failed by a narrow margin at the polls. When the mayor's waterfront plan was finally adopted by the Board of Aldermen in 1984, Sanders then supported a $750,000 bond for a shore-length bike path.

Wisely anticipating the high level of public interest and potential opposition in Burlington, the Alden Corporation agreed to public hearings on the project that would go to all six of the affected neighborhood planning assemblies. The Alden Corporation saw these hearings as an opportunity to build grass-roots support, even though these public assemblies had advisory input only. Ben Thompson, himself, became the lead public relations man, personally selling the proposed $100 million project. Thompson, using a sophisticated slide presentation at City Hall, laid out a proposal that included a community marina, a public park, an inn, expensive condominiums, and subsidized housing—700,000 feet of construction in all, with eight stories being the maximum height of any building.[27] Sanders had also tentatively won the right to buy back the waterfront property if Alden's plans were ultimately rejected.[28] Also tentatively, the city would get a cut of the profits. The Alden public relations work paid off in late February 1984 when a predevelopment understanding passed through the Council unanimously.

In return for Alden's concessions, the Progressive Coalition offered more than their goodwill. Burlington promised to apply for a federally funded Urban Development Action Grant (UDAG) to cover $17.5 million of the cost of the project.[29] The Coalition was attempting to take a categorical grant and redirect it from its intended purpose of subsidizing the redevelopment of a depressed area that would not otherwise be invested in. The Coalition hoped to use UDAG money as a bargaining enticement to extract concessions from Alden for moderate-income housing and public recreation, and the Sanders Administration promised to support a change in the city's low-density zoning regulations to accommodate the nonconforming Thompson plan.[30] If the purpose of the Coalition was to extract concessions from wealthy investors and to prevent the waterfront from becoming an exclusive playground of the rich, the deal that was struck at least appeared to accomplish these objectives.

These concessions did not stop environmental critics. The Waterfront Coalition, an ad hoc citizens' committee, demanded more parkland (and a greater setback from the lake) and opposed a proposal to fill in several acres of the lake to enlarge the project.[31] An underlying problem the Waterfront Coalition was reacting to was that the more open space Sanders bargained for, the more land Alden wanted to create out of the lake. Every public concession was countered by a corporate demand. The most serious criticism of the project came from the Citizens' Waterfront Group, which argued that under the public trust doctrine, any land created by filling in the lake reverts to city ownership after the original occupant vacates it. Thus, according to this argument, a good portion of the land to be developed by Alden was in fact already owned by Burlington and could only be leased from the city or used for public purposes.[32] Although Peter Clavelle, director of the city's Community and Economic Development Office and Sanders' ally and appointee, acknowledged the public trust doctrine, the legal interpretation remained unclear. Did the public trust doctrine mean that the property must be used in part for public purposes, which the Alden plan did accommodate, or did it mean that the city is the ultimate holder of title? A win in court would have meant that the city received up to twelve acres of waterfront property at the price of court costs; a loss would have delayed development. Any city litigation ran the risk of undermining investor confidence in other shorefront projects.[33] Throughout the negotiations with Alden, the city used the public trust doctrine to extract concessions.

While environmentalists argued for strategies that the development-minded Sanders administration chose not to take, the Vermont Transportation Agency was trying to win approval over opposition from the Progressive Coalition for a highway through to downtown. Acting in tandem with the Transportation Agency, Vermont's Environmental Protection Agency threatened to refuse a permit for parking for the waterfront project unless the Southern Connector highway was completed. The dubious logic involved here was that the Alden project would clog city streets and raise air pollution levels, but the new highway would speed cars along and relieve this congestion and thus disperse pollutants. Critics of the state plan persuasively argued that the highway would actually increase traffic and pollution.[34]

Despite the opposition's protests and the state environmental agency's threat, Burlington's aldermen approved the Sanders waterfront plan, known as the Alden Plan, with only one dissenting vote on June 11, 1984.[35] With city approval finally in its pocket, Alden had no problem raising its 80 percent of the waterfront financing; Burlington was not so fortunate. The UDAG grant was not approved in 1985. Since federal appropriations for categorical grants by 1985 were dwindling because of the Reagan administration's cutbacks, the applications from competing cities, which were not "winner" cities like Burlington in the national/international war of competition for new investment, took precedence over Burlington's request for such aid.[36] With UDAG money a foreclosed option, city officials pondered other ways of financing the city's part of the deal. Meanwhile, Alden dropped any promises to build moderately priced apartments or to scale back the project from $100 million to $42 million.[37]

The favored proposal called for setting up a tax incremental financing district. This variation of the basic property tax dictates that tax revenue collected on the improved waterfront property would be pledged exclusively to finance a bond issue that was floated to pay

Burlington's share of the project. Any shortfall would be the city's responsibility. This proposal would require approval by the Vermont state legislature.[38]

Despite the funding obstacles, the Sanders administration vociferously defended the waterfront plan against any alteration that was not part of the Alden Corporation's new scaled-down plan. The ever-persistent Citizens' Waterfront Group managed to get enough signatures on petitions to force a June 1985 referendum on pushing the setback of buildings from thirty feet, as specified in the Alden proposal, to eighty feet. A spirited campaign by Rick Sharp for the proposal was countered by a formidable opposition composed of the Progressive Coalition's elected officials and a Republican alderman, William Skelton. The proposal was defeated by a vote of 2,710 to 2,104.[39] Environmental concerns did not redirect development imperatives that both the Progressive Coalition's elected officials and the Alden Waterfront Corporation had agreed on.

One referendum victory was not enough to save the Alden Plan; the funding problem still loomed. A referendum on a $6 million bond, which needed a two-thirds vote of approval (a city charter provision), was set for December 10, 1985. If approved the bond was to be paid off at $500,000 a year through the tax incremental financing plan. Although the Alden Corporation signed an agreement to be liable for the $6 million bond, if the developer were to go bankrupt, any shortfall would have to be made up by the city treasury.[40]

Sanders lobbied the School Board Commission, which is dependent for funds on property taxes, to support the plan. Such backing was crucial to generate public support, since the opposition Democrats broke with their Republican allies and opposed the bond measure on fiscal grounds.[41] Specifically, Sanders wanted the School Board to give up its portion of the property tax levy on the waterfront development property; the Sanders administration proposed that these funds be used to pay off the bonds. Since the School Board levy was set at 57 percent to the city's 43 percent of the property taxes collected, the Board's approval was crucial to the plan's success; 43 percent of the taxes collected on the waterfront project could not meet the bond payments. To improve the likelihood of a favorable vote by the School Board, Peter Clavelle, director of community and economic development, offered a plan to have the city guarantee the 57 percent to 43 percent ratio of any tax revenues received from this project over the amount needed to meet the bond installment payments.[42] Despite this offer, the School Board refused to back the plan, fearing the consequences if revenues fell short of expectations. In addition, School Board members noted that the designation of a tax incremental financing zone would have to be approved by the state of Vermont, an unlikely proposition.[43]

As the date of the referendum approached, the School Board's rejection of the plan could only have encouraged the diverse coalition that was forming to campaign for a public rejection of the proposal. Two groups of political opposites united to oppose the plan: the Vermont Greens, an environmental group, united with the Citizens for America, a right-wing organization.[44] Many of the Greens were former supporters of Sanders who had broken with him because of his pro-development policies. Smitten by charges of selling out, Sanders countered the opposition Greens: "There's an illusion that all we have to do is keep pushing a developer and keep pushing a developer. We feel we pushed him as far as we can go and we feel we got significant concessions."[45] Despite Sanders' claims, the opponents of the waterfront development plan ran a spirited campaign with almost no funding but good coverage by the local press.

The waterfront development plan was supported by an unlikely coalition of elected and appointed Coalition members, the *Burlington Free Press*, the *Vermont Vanguard Press*, the five Republican aldermen, and most of the business community, including the Lake Champlain Regional Chamber of Commerce and the Downtown Burlington Development Association.[46]

On December 10 (with one quarter of the voters turning out), the plan managed to garner a 53.4 percent majority vote, less than the 66.6 percent required by the city charter to approve the bond. The working-class wards, Sanders' most loyal supporters in past elections, either voted against the plan or approved it narrowly. Judging by letters to the editor of the *Burlington Free Press*, the projected cost of the condominiums starting at $175,000 and reaching up to $300,000 fostered a division within such neighborhoods about whether the public benefits of such a plan outweighed the enmity engendered by the establishment of an enclave for the rich. In fact, only one ward, the wealthy Hill section, approved the plan by the necessary majority.[47] Upon the defeat of the bond referendum, the Alden Corporation immediately claimed it was abandoning the project.[48]

After the Alden Plan failed at the polls, the Sanders administration went into litigation with owners of waterfront property. Teaming up with the state administration of Vermont, the Sanders administration sued under the public trust doctrine to take title of the filled land along the shoreline. In a parallel development, the Vermont legislature rejected a proposal put forth by Rick Sharp and Howard Dean to create a Burlington port authority that would build a park on the waterfront land, in effect rejecting the public trust doctrine.[49] Meanwhile, litigation took its plodding course.

During the summer of 1986, the Sanders administration began out-of-court negotiations with the Central Vermont Railway and other affected landowners. Using the public trust doctrine as justification, the city of Burlington demanded a fifty-foot walkway, a one-hundred-foot setback, one-quarter of the land for public parks, a bike path, a boathouse, a public marina, and various other public amenities. The railway's lawyers found the demands outrageous and broke off negotiations.[50] Peter Clavelle publicly admitted that private investment would "be chilled" along the waterfront until the public trust litigation was completed.[51] Developers knew the legal question was complex. Just what did "the public trust doctrine" mean? The court could rule a narrow interpretation that suited the Central Vermont Railway or it could agree with the Sanders administration's expansive interpretation, which at its most extreme would result in title reverting to the state of Vermont.

With negotiations stalled at the end of 1986, the Board of Aldermen set up a negotiating team with representatives from all three parties. This team too failed to reach a compromise with the railway, and the Alden Corporation, exasperated, sued the city. They claimed that they were losing money because they could not sell the property they owned while the city was needlessly harassing them in court. That fall the Sanders administration's position was fortified by public opinion; three nonbinding and loosely worded referenda that backed urban waterfront development, the public trust doctrine, and waterfront rezoning were passed by overwhelming margins. The Board of Aldermen took the cue and voted to rezone the waterfront by a nine-to-one vote. New regulations enforced a one-hundred-foot public access space along the water and commercial development in a separate zone with strict height limitations. The railway threatened suit against the regulations. With the support of all three political parties and the environmentalists, a $2.8 million waterfront bond issue was passed by a better than two-to-one margin in March 1987. City-owned lakefront property would be upgraded, with the most expensive improvement a community boathouse. While the Sanders administration planned to buy additional key acres of waterfront land with future bonding proposals, the Vermont courts made a preliminary finding on the public trust doctrine.[52]

The decision of Justice Stephen Martin satisfied none of the parties, nor did it produce any clear losers. The railway did have legal title to thirty-one acres of land, but that land was "impressed with the public trust doctrine" and had to be "used for a public purpose," such as "restaurants, hotels, shopping centers, or a sports stadium." Assistant City Attorney John Franco appealed because the decision alluded to "the public trust in name only and completely gut[ted] its substance." Using lawyerly logic, Liam Murphy, an attorney for the Central Vermont Railway, claimed that condominiums and offices would be acceptable under the criteria offered since they were not listed as unacceptable. Nevertheless, he would also appeal. Justice Martin left open the possibility for further litigation by refusing to specify an exact definition of the public trust doctrine; he claimed that this was impossible because what is in the public's best interest changes over time.[53] Thus, all proposed development projects on the filled land would be subject to his approval.

In November 1988, the Sanders administration with the support of the other two parties decisively moved to prevent developer encroachment along most of the railway property that immediately abutted Lake Champlain. A $6.4 million bond issue to buy and upgrade waterline property (thereby isolating the property behind it) was sent to the voters. The bond issue passed by the necessary two-thirds margin.

In the end, most of the waterfront land remained in private hands. No doubt, the nature of what will be built on the land will be decided in the Vermont courts, and the public trust will, for the most part, remain subordinate to private gain.

PROPOSED REFORM AND ALTERNATIVE REFORMS

The Alden Plan, the major waterfront development reform proposed by the Progressive Coalition's elected and appointed representatives, was a liberal reform. Sanders and his cohorts negotiated with Alden for a public marina, a public right of way, public parkland, and in the plan's initial stages a promise but not a binding commitment to build moderately priced housing. By negotiating these concessions the Progressive Coalition sidetracked the likely result of unimpeded development, a waterfront preserved exclusively for the wealthy that excluded both moderate- and low-income citizens not only from residency but even from trespass. Although there were benefits included for the dominated in the Sanders/Alden proposal, the logic of capitalism was clearly accommodated.

Both the proposed bond package (originally a hoped-for UDAG) and the preservation of the existing thirty-foot setback requirement were needed to maintain profitability, that is, to satisfy the investors. A radical mayor and radical aldermen acted in unison to protect a plan that was the result of extended negotiations in a hostile environment. The Planning Commission, opposition aldermen, the local business community, and the almost always reactionary *Burlington Free Press* would have compromised much sooner to the Alden Corporation's benefit. Sanders and the other Progressive Coalition representatives in city government probably worked out the best development plan they could, especially after the enticement of the UDAG money was no longer possible.

The waterfront plan accommodated the Alden Corporation's need for profit, and, as the Progressive Coalition's lower-class supporters noted, included amenities that, ironically, hastened the entire city's transition to an enclave for the wealthy. The immediate goal of public access and more public parkland was a strike against self-segregation by the wealthy. Nevertheless, the project would have increased the pace of gentrification in the city. By the time of the bond proposal defeat, the Old North End neighborhood where the overwhelming majority of the city's poor reside was experiencing exploding real estate values. In this neighborhood where the median household income in 1979 was $10,103 compared to $25,893 in the nearby New North End, gentrification was not creeping; it was racing.[54] Realtors were in such a frenzy for Old North End properties that one dilapidated house selling for $25,000 never made it onto the market. It was purchased by an absentee landlord and divided into smaller, more profitable units.[55] By 1984, in the Old North End, multifamily dwellings that previously had sold for under $40,000 could not be found in livable condition at that price.[56] In Burlington as a whole, rents jumped from an average of $270 a month in 1980 to $360 in 1981; this 30 percent increase occurred in the depths of the worst national recession since the 1930s.[57]

Also, real estate speculation in the Lakeside neighborhood at the opposite end of the waterfront development project was enriching for those who owned property. For example, even before the first shovel of dirt for the Alden Plan would have been turned, a twenty-eight-unit condominium development in Lakeside was sold (with 113 people on a waiting list) in one day.[58] Although the Sanders administration, to its credit, has expanded federal rent subsidies, set up a land trust, and attempted to build moderate-income housing, most of Burlington's residents, who are renters, will inevitably be paying skyrocketing rents. Sanders, a critic of gentrification, argued: "The principal victims will be tenants. If a house doubles in value, everything else being equal, rents will go up substantially."[59] This multimillion-dollar project would have accelerated an involuntary migration of Burlington's poor. Ironically, since low-income residents are strong Progressive Coalition supporters, the radicals risked losing a crucial component of their precarious electoral plurality.

Nevertheless, the economic benefits of waterfront development have been well touted by Democrats, Republicans, and Progressive Coalition members alike. Fifteen hundred permanent jobs were projected to be created by the project; unfortunately, these new opportunities would overwhelmingly be clustered in the lower-paying end of the service sector. The likely beneficiaries of these opportunities will be Burlington's ubiquitous student population. Still, as Mayor Sanders has said, fifteen hundred jobs are "not to be sneezed at,"[60] particularly in a community with only thirty-eight thousand citizens.

Besides jobs, the other economic benefit widely praised was increased tax revenue that easily could have been over $1 million a year to a city government that is heavily financed by property taxes. Unfortunately, this increased revenue would be diverted for many years to pay off the $6 million bond that the city proposed to float to pay its part in the project. Until the bond is paid, the city would collect a flat $100,000 a year.[61]

Economic development under the Alden Plan would have put strains on the public infrastructure and the immediate ecological system. While the Progressive Coalition's elected and appointed representatives were negotiating with Alden, the city's sewers were reaching their capacity for waste treatment. Already, during storms fecal matter would back up and flood into the basements of the wealthy New North End neighborhood. Fearing a complete breakdown of the treatment system, Vermont environmental officials at one point suggested building a bypass for untreated wastes that would take them directly into Lake Champlain, surely an ecological tragedy.[62] The state also pressured the city into a temporary moratorium on new sewer hook-ups; this effectively prevented all new development except in low-density areas where septic tanks are allowed. The Sanders administration, not wanting to jeopardize economic development, quickly encouraged a public yes vote for a $22 million bond issue to expand the capacity of the sewer system.

This, however, would not take care of Burlington's fundamental sewage problem. Like many other older municipalities, Burlington had a combined storm and sewage drain system; excess rainwater meant human excrement in Lake Champlain, an estimated 825,000 pounds in 1986.[63] Although the proposed bond did not raise enough to fully segregate the two systems, it did allow for an increase in treatment capacity enough to allow economic development to proceed.[64] To totally separate the systems, stop any leaks, and provide adequate capacity for treatment might cost up to $130 million.[65] The cost for increased economic development that would not destroy local ecology was staggering. Nevertheless, with tripartisan support, the $22 million bond passed easily, despite the populist, anti-tax public that had swept Sanders into office. Burlingtonians, like most Americans, cling to a fundamental faith in economic development as an almost unquestioned good. The thorny issue of the costs of development compared with the benefits of such development was lost in a chorus of boosterism. And those costs were not small; charges to city users will increase at least 10 percent a year from 1987 through 1990 on a base of about $260 a year.[66]

The equation more development equals more trash was a minor feature in the public debate, though the problem of where and how to dispose of bulk waste was frequently at the top of the local political agenda. Burlington, like many other communities, disposes of its garbage in a landfill. This landfill did not meet the state of Vermont's comparatively strict environmental standards. The city was under a seemingly perpetual order to close the dump and eventually did convert it into a park.

The trash disposal problem preceded the Sanders administration; as far back as 1978 the voters of Burlington approved a $10 million bond issue to build a trash burner. The burner would sell steam through a pipeline to the University of Vermont Medical Center Hospital at market rates. After numerous feasibility studies, Sanders set up a committee of three businessmen headed by his confidant Antonio Pomerleau to study whether or not the plant would be financially sound as proposed.[67] In the Resource Recovery Facility Study, the business committee predicted the plan as proposed would have been financially burdensome to Burlington. With the unofficial imprimatur of the business community, the Progressive Coalition's elected representatives and the opposition aldermen unanimously killed the plan. Interestingly, the plant was killed almost strictly for economic reasons, despite the persistent but ignored effort of the Burlington Environmental Alliance to kill it for ecological reasons.[68] Costs and the state of the current technology were the issues that were dealt with in the bulk of the report completed by the mayor's committee.

The Resource Recovery Facility Study revealed the economic orientation of the committee and of the major sponsor of the study, Mayor Sanders. Despite complaints by the adjacent town of Winooski against the air pollution that would emanate from the proposed plant and complaints from Burlington's Environmental Alliance, the mayor's committee all but ignored ecological concerns. Out of a seventeen-page report, one sentence spoke of air pollution. Even the concern of that one sentence was monetary, a fear that "substantial additional capital expenditures for 'scrubbers' and the like would be necessary."[69] Nevertheless, the killing of the trash plant was an ecological victory.

The mayor and the Coalition examined only one option for the immediate future: keep the dump open. After the December 1983 rejection of the trash plant, the city faced a state-imposed deadline of July 1, 1984, for closing the dump. Instead of closing it, the Sanders administration proposed a plan to prolong its life by building trenches to prevent an ongoing pollution of the surrounding ground water.[70] In marked contrast to the sewer referendum, voters decisively turned down the Progressive Coalition's bond issue to pay for these improvements. If Burlington could not resolve its current ecological problem of disposing of bulk wastes, how would it cope with the inevitable increased bulk wastes resulting from economic development?

The overwhelming majority of the members of the Burlington community and the elected officials of the Progressive Coalition (with Alderwoman Zoe Briener the only exception) placed ecological issues at a much lower priority than economic issues.[71] The logic of economic development and the logic of ecology are not compatible; ecological concerns do not bring increased tax revenue and more jobs, goals that both procapitalist and prosocialist elected officials have in common.

An ecological logic would demand that this mostly sylvan acreage owned by the railroads should have been either preserved or returned to its original wetland status. The ecological priority is that man must not dominate nature. The Sanders administration had an unprecedented opportunity to preserve natural ecology and at the same time retard the process of gentrification. To follow such logic, the Sanders administration would have had to oppose development and in doing so would have protected the natural world against a world constructed by man for profit.

If the Sanders administration and the citizenry had been anti-growth rather than pro-growth, there would have been a ready impediment to derail economic development. When the $22 million bond issue for sewers was placed on the ballot, a decisive rejection would have maintained a moratorium on new sewer hook-ups. In its place, a more modest sewage system designed for existing capacity could have dealt with the existing pollution problems. This would have effectively stopped new economic development. The problems of unequal income distribution, gentrification of existing housing, and possible capital flight would not have disappeared, but the preservation of open space and the maintenance of a community of accessible size would have been possible. A moratorium on new development would have been a democratic structural reform because it would have totally ignored the needs of capitalist expansion. A moratorium would have been an ecological reform, concerned equally with the preservation of the nonhuman world and the indivisible human world. Unfortunately, this is a goal that will seldom be sought by most opponents of capitalism since capitalists and socialists both favor economic growth. The values and logic of ecology as a resistance strategy were antithetical to the Alden/Sanders waterfront development plan with its proposal to fill in several acres of the lake and to build a seven-story waterfront hotel, 150 luxury condominiums, a parking garage, retail stores, restaurants, a boathouse, a marina, and offices.[72]

What would a democratic structural reform utilizing waterfront development look like? A democratic structural reform that would benefit the dominated, irrespective of capital structure's logic, could, though unattentive to ecological concerns, address the needs of workers. Subsidized housing for the working class fits this criterion in Burlington, which has a desperate housing shortage. From this perspective, the waterfront could best be used to build subsidized housing exclusively for low- and moderate-income people, while maintaining access to the lake for all of Burlington's citizens.

This approach, however, is untenable. With waterfront land costing up to $500,000 an acre, the cost of the thirty-one-acre railway property alone would be $15 million. Any revolutionary action such as expropriation without compensation would be promptly struck down by any court in the land; public use litigation has proved that point. Purchasing the property with the hope of national government funding (a liberal approach) would be ill advised; the Reagan and Bush administrations stopped almost all financing for new public housing construction. Thus, the city would have had to obtain a two-thirds vote of approval to float a bond in order to build the project at an expense much greater than that of merely acquiring the land. Passage of such a bond would have been unlikely: the portion of the population of Burlington that is comprised of homeowners has in the past expressed disapproval of the small number of public housing projects that do exist, and they have successfully stopped virtually all new efforts to build new public housing in recent years. In this scenario, the democratic majority would likely reject either a democratic structural or liberal public housing reform.

If by some unlikely chance a referendum failed to stop such a project, the resulting division of the dominated classes into homeowners and renters would likely motivate the homeowners to move their resistance efforts to new terrain, the state courts. As we shall see in the Southern Connector issue, this time-consuming strategy can result in an effective veto or at least a prolonged delay for almost any proposed reform.

This hypothetical scenario of democratic structural reform making has been extended to this pessimistic conclusion to suggest why some items never even reach the political agenda, despite the preponderance of human need. (And if affordable shelter in frigid Vermont is not conceded as a human need, then any human demand cannot be considered legitimate.) Thus, for housing, national sources of income are drying up, state funds are almost nonexistent, and a local citizenry burdened by a regressive property tax is predisposed to forego such expenditures. Furthermore, a municipality's ability to raise funds for human needs is severely limited, and fractionalized local government only complicates the problem.

The closest that the Sanders administration could come to a lakefront development plan that would have been a democratic structural reform answering the dire need for housing was a proposal for inclusionary zoning. This was a liberal reform demanding set asides for moderate-cost residences within a larger project. With a hostile political environment of business-minded Democrats and Republicans dominating the Board of Aldermen and the commissions, a mere

promise to try to build moderate housing was all that could be extracted from the Alden Corporation, and even this was allowed to lapse.

If the Sanders administration had been attacking waterfront development from an ecological perspective, its goals would have been
attainable. The federal system, inclined toward the status quo, could
have been used to prevent any new development merely by the refusal to expand the capacity of the sewer system. This logic was not
compatible, however, with the economistic orientation of the leaders
of the Progressive Coalition, who were more concerned with who
owned and who had access to the waterfront than with the ecological
consequences of the built environment.

THE SOUTHERN CONNECTOR

Coexistent with the waterfront development project, the Southern
Connector controversy preceded the March 1981 election of Sanders
and his supporters. The Southern Connector was a proposed four-
lane highway that would link the downtown area with the nearby
interstate highway, Route 189. The plan for the two-and-one-half-mile
highway was originally conceived in 1965 and took detailed form in
the 1970s, when a portion of the downtown was razed and part of the
central city was rebuilt. At the time, a large, upscale pedestrian mall
was planned. It was later completed by the refurbishment of Vic-
torian-era buildings and the construction of new retail outlets. The
resulting complex offered space to a profusion of small businesses.
Like all major malls, the Church Street Marketplace and the adjoining
Burlington Square Mall needed an anchor, a large department store to
draw crowds of shoppers to frequent the surrounding smaller stores.
A recommended and perhaps necessary condition to attract and keep
a large store in the mall was easy access for suburban shoppers by a
modern highway.[73] Since a large mall of forty-two stores was already
serving South Burlington and an extended bout of litigation was
needed to prevent another even larger proposed suburban mall in the
nearby town of Williston, the majority of Burlington's retail business
community favored the speedy construction of the Southern Connector.

The financial-business community also supported the construction of the Connector. Since urban renewal, Burlington's razed downtown areas had sprouted office towers. Today's Burlington skyline is

composed of glass and concrete buildings identifying the municipality's transition from a manufacturing center to a postindustrial city.

The traffic situation resulting from the commute to the downtown offices and retail stores is further compounded by the flow of
traffic to and from the four institutions of higher learning (including a
medical complex) that are adjacent to the downtown area. The conglomeration of all these commuting destinations and a mediocre bus
transit system results in traffic congestion. For example, a study prepared in 1984 for the city of Burlington found that 11,384 residents
from sixteen surrounding towns commuted to Burlington as their
place of work. While this number seems insignificant to any resident
of a large metropolitan area, it is formidable for Burlington, a city of
thirty-eight thousand.[74] Most of these suburbanites are traveling
downtown through a series of clogged city streets at the usual morn-
ing and evening rush hours. This situation preceded the Sanders administration. During the Paquette administration, urban renewal
funding from the national government combined with lesser state
and city contributions were used to raze a working-class neighborhood. The uses of the resulting subsidized open space was shaped
by a master plan that emphasized commercial development. The subsequent transformation to a densely concentrated business district in
Burlington's city center created the need for what was originally estimated as a $16 million highway.

The city residents who must brave Burlington's overloaded
streets voted by a two-thirds majority to build the Southern and
Northern connectors in 1979 to funnel traffic to and from the interstate highway. Putting both of the connectors together on the same
ballot was a wise political calculation by Mayor Paquette. Since the
Northern Connector was not a contentious issue among the city's residents, it helped smooth the vote for the more disputed southern
counterpart. Subsequently, by a two-thirds vote, city voters passed
the bond issue of $2.7 million, about 10 percent of the total cost; the
proposed state and national government funding of the other 90 percent of the cost was crucial to the success of this pro-development
referendum vote. In the original Southern Connector plan, two
dozen houses, twelve garages, eight industrial buildings, and a large
warehouse/bottling plant would be razed.[75] With Burlington's voter
approval in 1979, the support of most of the business community, and
the funding promised by the state and national governments, construction of the Southern Connector, like that of its northern counter-

part, appeared, to the relief of the investment community, to be ensured.

Besides the investment community there were other interested parties: the neighborhood associations. The South End Community Organization, the Lakeside Organization, and the South Cove Neighborhood Organization united to oppose the Southern Connector because it would effectively slice off their communities from the rest of Burlington.[76] These groups refused to passively accept the traffic solution that would benefit downtown business interests, suburban commuters, and other neighborhoods of the city that were helplessly mired in pass-through traffic. Under the unofficial but tenacious leadership of Joan Beauchemin, a community activist, these neighborhood associations managed to delay construction of the connector until it was redesigned from a four-lane to a two-lane road.

Because of the traffic jams in the South End, Lakeside, and South Cove neighborhoods, especially during the change of shift at the massive General Electric plant, some of the residents of these communities supported the connector even though they would be isolated by it.[77] Apparently, the consequences of a business-built environment shaped the consciousness of some to believe that the only solution was one compatible with the needs of business. In fact, throughout the period under study, the most vociferous opponents of the Southern Connector who ran for the Board of Aldermen from the ward encompassing the South End, South Cove, and Lakeside have lost. Neither Joan Beauchemin, who ran a very close race, nor Samuel Sampson, who was easily beaten, could put together an electoral majority in their wards. Both ran as Progressive Coalition candidates opposed to the connector. It remains unclear whether there was actually a majority opposed to the highway, as proposed, in these three southern Burlington neighborhoods. Since voters cast their ballots for a variety of reasons, it is difficult to specify exactly why Beauchemin and Sampson were defeated.

Nonetheless, the neighborhood opponents of the connector found an ally in Bernard Sanders, who campaigned against the highway in his 1981 uphill mayoral campaign. His position was that no road should be built. Sanders' victory, along with that of his two supporters, gave the coalition of neighborhood groups a narrow base of elected officials who opposed the highway. Unfortunately, with the bond money already appropriated and a hostile Board of Aldermen, the mayor and his allies could, at best, run a delaying action. Without an aldermanic majority, the Progressive Coalition could not reverse the plan and legislate an acceptable alternative. Even with a majority, it is questionable whether an alternative plan could have been implemented. Terrill Bouricius, Coalition member of the Board of Aldermen, preferred the construction of light rail transportation for city residents and commuters, but this option was never placed on the public agenda as an alternative for serious consideration.[78]

The opponents of the Southern Connector, at a disadvantage electorally, sought to exploit all the ready-made veto opportunities provided by the fragmented federal system of government. They used the state court system to stalemate progress on the connector. For example, in October 1981, highway opponents working with Mayor Sanders claimed that the city's 1979 referendum appropriating money for the connector was actually illegal and thus not binding. Sanders and other highway opponents argued that Paquette's city clerk, Frank Wagner, wrote a letter to the state applying for highway funds, declaring that "The voters of the City of Burlington approved the local portion of the cost for the project at the annual city meeting held March 1, 1977."[79] The vote actually took place two years later. Since state law mandated that the vote for highway money must come within eighteen months of the city's application, this procedural flaw seemed to be a promising way to void the entire appropriation process completed so far. This strategy ultimately failed on legal grounds, but it illustrates one of the numerous entry points within the federal system that can be used by opponents to delay or veto public projects.

A more important and successful approach to delaying the connector was provided by the existence of a polluted barge canal. The proposed route of the connector crossed an old, abandoned barge canal, a legacy of the 1800s, when Burlington was a mill town for Canadian lumber. After the canal was closed, an early gas works, the Burlington Gas Light Company, was established that extracted gas from coal. The coal tar byproducts resulting from coal gasification were toxic and identified generations later by the national Environmental Protection Agency (EPA) as possible cancer-causing chemicals. However, at the time the gas works was functioning, the byproducts were dumped in the canal without penalty. In the late 1970s, the national government, through Congress, created a Superfund of $1.6 billion to clean up the most egregious toxic waste dumps. Although the EPA had the authority to sue for compensation of the clean-up work, the Burlington Gas Light Company was defunct;

therefore, an attempt was made to sue its successor. After a prolonged investigation, other dumpers were cited, including Burlington General Electric and the city of Burlington. When the first 115 sites were listed by the EPA in October 1981, Burlington's barge canal was ranked among them.[80]

Problems with removing the toxic wastes from the canal were formidable. The amount of accumulated, contaminated muck in the barge canal was initially reported to be enough to fill ten thousand large dump trucks. There was a fear that removal might pollute Burlington's lake-fed water supply in the process. Another problem with removal was what to do with the polluted muck: Should it be safely stored for centuries while it decomposes, or can it be detoxified?[81] Although various solutions were proposed (from building an overpass and thus ignoring the pollution to sophisticated pumping and on-site treatment projects), state and national environmental regulations remained an obstacle to construction of the connector.

In 1982 while environmental concerns were preventing the beginning of construction of the highway, William Aswad, chairman of the Planning Commission, asked the Vermont Transportation Agency to continue engineering studies, despite an aldermanic directive to do otherwise. Aswad maintained he was acting within the commission's authority.[82] William Aswad's role as a promoter of business interests was enhanced by the fragmented commission system: both the waterfront development project and the Southern Connector project were originally more under his commission's authority than that of the elected officials.

Concerning the highway, Aswad was far from disinterested. As an engineer at General Electric, Aswad had planned the route of the connector despite potential conflicts of interest. He situated the road to end in a large, looping curve that would result in the demolition of a warehouse next to his employer's property. If the road took a direct route, as Vermont Transportation Agency officials had recommended, General Electric would have lost a good portion of its parking lot, a choice that was between $0.5 million and $1.2 million less expensive than the warehouse route. When the Rosetti Brothers, owners of the warehouse sued rather than lose their place of business, the *Burlington Free Press* reported: "Aswad has maintained a file for nearly two decades, since at least 1967, at his place of employment at General Electric Company, concerning the Southern Connector which shows that he has been regularly consulted over the years by General Electric management concerning their wishes to this project."[83] In

1984, Samuel Sampson, a Coalition member of the Planning Commission and longtime foe of the connector, released the damning Rosetti lawsuit information to the public. Sampson accused Aswad of having a conflict of interest; Aswad in turn argued that he had abstained from all decisions affecting General Electric. Aswad's use of the Planning Commission's power for his employer's interests is an example of how organized interests can permeate government for their own purposes; Sampson's role on the commission demonstrates that resistance groups can penetrate the federalist system. Also, the Rosetti challenge illustrates that the business community is not a solid phalanx; business will fight business through the offices of government for narrow, selfish gain.

Although it was a difficult battle, Sanders and his cohorts proved to be formidable foes of Aswad and his Planning Commission, which was dominated by business interests. In May 1985, after thirteen years as chairman of the Planning Commission, Aswad resigned, complaining loudly of his frustration with the Sanders administration. At the time, Aswad correctly noted: "The past two planning directors have been largely ignored by the city. The City Planning Commission has been decimated."[84] During his three terms in office, Sanders had submitted budgets that gradually reduced the Planning Commission to a skeletal operation. More important, the money was redirected to the Community and Economic Development Office, a department created under the Sanders administration and headed by the mayor's appointee, Peter Clavelle. This office effectively usurped most of the functions of the Planning Commission and centralized authority for economic planning in a City Hall office. Sanders redirected and centralized authority in his office despite a city charter that specifically places planning responsibilities under an autonomous commission.

It took the Coalition four years to dislodge from city government one outspoken foe on the Planning Commission, but throughout the period under study, the connector had plenty of other advocates in and out of government. In the 1983 mayoral campaign, James Gilson, the Republican nominee, claimed: "People voted yes, and no individual, not even the mayor, had the right to subvert the will of the people."[85] The Democratic nominee, Judith Stephany, echoed her support for the speedy construction of the Southern Connector.

Since Burlington owned a half-acre of land in the path of the connector, if Sanders had so wished, he could have refused to turn over the title to the state and thus further delayed the road's progress. But

Sanders had changed his mind about the road by the time of the 1983 election. After commissioning a private poll that found that most of Burlington's residents preferred a highway to be built,[86] Sanders shifted his position from outright opposition to a four-lane highway to support of a scaled-down, two-lane road, the so-called Pine Parkway. He allowed the crucial land transfer to occur in February 1983.[87] The pro-growth attitudes of the community at large were in contradiction to the neighborhood activists' opposition to the road. Since the latter were strong supporters of the Coalition, Sanders was searching for a compromise that would not divide the ranks of his electoral majority.

In 1973 the City Planning Commission and the Street Commission favored a local road expansion similar to Sanders' two-lane Pine Parkway proposal. However, after state engineers planned a four-lane route, both commissions came to accept the state plan in 1977, and thereafter almost monolithically supported it.[88] Predictably, Republican Governor Richard Snelling and Transportation Secretary Patrick Garahan categorically rejected the Sanders compromise in February 1983, saying that a two-lane proposal would result in the forfeit of $14.25 million in federal subsidies.[89] In effect, the state was saying that their preferred construction of this project was the same as the national government's. If Burlington wanted the money, it would have to accept the plan already provided for in a specific categorical grant proposal. Despite the implied threat from the state, Sanders did not give in and accept the state plan.

While the state of Vermont was claiming that the four-lane highway was a take-it-or-leave-it proposition, the cost of the project, including a projected $3 million for the barge canal cleanup, was escalating. Originally both connectors were slated to cost $27 million; by 1983 the projected cost was $43.5 million. Despite this jump in needed expenditures, the cost of both highways declined for the city when the national government changed the formula for cost to be borne from federal government 75 percent, state 15 percent, city 10 percent, to 95 percent, 3 percent, 2 percent, respectively.[90] National government enticement encouraged highway supporters.

While state officials, with the national government's financial muscle, were pushing for immediate construction, Sanders appointed in July 1983 a six-member panel (half representing business and half opposing the connector) to study the proposed highway, a classic delaying action. The mayor's panel later disbanded after stalemate precluded any majority conclusions from being forwarded to the mayor.[91] At the same time, the state proceeded with studies about the most efficient way to extract the barge canal's wastes, but construction remained stalled.

Action on the connector seemed inevitable; the directives and logic of economic development were shaped like a puzzle, each piece dependent on the rest of the pieces' being put into place to complete the picture. National officials tabled a city-sponsored economic development grant for $6 million designated to help build a 474-car parking garage that would service an expanded hotel (eventually a $4 million one was approved) and a proposed 70,000 square foot department store. But the Porteous, Mitchell, and Brown Company, a regional department store chain, demanded commitment on construction of a parking garage before they would commit themselves to the Burlington Square Mall;[92] this was the crucial anchor store that the downtown merchants coveted. Also, the state's approval of the waterfront project was made contingent on construction of the highway.

Progressive Coalition supporters and other highway opponents challenged every argument for building the connector. Samuel Sampson claimed air pollution would be increased, not decreased, with the highway's completion. Armand Beliveau, a retired engineer, claimed traffic congestion would get worse, not better.[93] On July 19, 1984, Sanders asked for yet another study on the connector, arguing that the state design would impede rather than promote access to the city. The same day, state Transportation Secretary Patrick Garahan crudely counterattacked, threatening that Burlington would have to reimburse the state for the six million dollars already spent on the project. Later, a top federal highway official confirmed that Burlington would have to pay five million dollars for any design changes.[94] Despite Garahan's threat, in July 1984 the Progressive Coalition with one Republican alderman voted to study modifications to the Pine Parkway proposal.[95]

While the elected representatives studied and fought, the state pursued its case for the connector in court against both neighborhood activists and angry businessmen facing relocation. In late August 1984 a court-appointed official declared the highway a necessity. On the face of it, this decision allowed the state to exercise its power of eminent domain in order to purchase property in the proposed route of the highway.[96] This development elated highway proponents only until the presiding justice ruled he had no authority to enforce the official's findings. Shortly afterward, Rosetti Brothers, the main business opposition to the Southern Connector, dropped its opposition after its warehouse was spared by rerouting the highway through the General Electric parking lot. (No reason was given why design changes for business were possible.) Neighborhood activists could not be so easily placated. The environmental debacle remained; it fortified the neighborhood activists' hopes for continued delay of highway construction. To cross the barge canal, four state permits and one from the national government would be needed.[97] This process, typical of the labyrinthine federal system, promised numerous opportunities for opponents to forestall and perhaps kill the project unless a compromise to their liking was offered.

By the 1985 mayoral election, Sanders, maneuvering for a scaled-down road, now argued that he wanted an ecologically safe proposal. Steven Goodkind, the city's director of public health and safety (a Sanders appointee) was arguing that the best solution would be to leave the barge canal wastes alone rather than risk the effects of a cleanup.[98] This suggestion, if adopted, would effectively preclude the building of the highway along the state-planned route. While the Sanders administration was putting forth its best environmental argument to oppose the Southern Connector, it was also negotiating a land swap that would trade one acre of city-owned waterfront for ninety-five undeveloped acres in the Intervale. The Intervale was an expansive green belt that was being nibbled away by developers, the Burlington Electric Department, and the illegal city dump. The city's plan for these ninety-five acres was not to preserve them; instead, most of the land would be used to bury city sewer sludge.[99] Despite policies to the contrary, the Sanders administration's declarations that an ecologically safe solution to barge canal pollution must precede highway construction were given some credence when a new city-sponsored alternative to the state's proposed route was announced.

In April 1985, the Sanders administration commissioned yet another examination of the connector problem, the Burlington Urban Design Study under the leadership of Peter Owens, landscape architect. Owens produced a plan that would follow most of the previously planned route as a two-lane road but would curve around the barge canal without crossing it. The canal would be covered, in part, by a greenhouse, where water hyacinths, which naturally filter out pollutants, would be planted. Also, a new bike path paralleling the road would be built.[100] The plan seemed to answer all the opponents' questions. For the Sierra Club and the Burlington Environmental Alliance, who joined the neighborhood opposition when the pollution of the barge canal became public knowledge, Owens proposed an ecologically safe, low-technology solution to the waste problem. And for the neighborhood activists, he designed a two-lane highway that had no chain link fence, that melded into the streets of the cityscape, and that preserved the access of their community to the rest of Burlington.

In July 1985, Sanders presented the new plan to highway officials in Washington, D.C. The alternative plan left room for the addition of two more lanes in the future if needed. The national officials said the plan was acceptable to them and that it was up to state officials to make a final decision.[101] This revelation undermined the state contention that the federal highway officials were totally committed to a four-lane highway. Sanders was now also optimistic about state officials. In November 1984, Madeleine Kunin, a quasi-liberal Democrat, was elected governor. Transportation Secretary Patrick Garahan, a hard-line Republican, was replaced by Susan C. Crampton, a Democrat. Sanders' initial optimism proved to be unwarranted, however. In an August 1985 meeting, Sanders and Crampton failed to agree on the new proposal. Crampton argued that safety demanded a four-lane highway; she cited three studies that had reached this conclusion. After the unsuccessful meeting, Sanders merely expressed the obvious: the Southern Connector would be further delayed.[102]

Despite Sanders' predictions of delay, the $900,000 cleanup of the canal financed by the Superfund was begun in early October 1985. The accumulated wastes, dumped for fifty-two years by the Burlington Gas Light Company, were not totally cleaned up. The EPA project was designed to remove only the surface materials, 1,444 tons in all. The waste was to be solidified by mixing it with other materials, and then it was to be trucked to an out-of-state hazardous waste dump.[103] More cleanup than this would be needed before the connector could be built.

During October 1985, State Transportation Secretary Susan Crampton met for four hours with Mayor Sanders over the state/city differences on the connector. Sanders and Crampton agreed that a new study should be undertaken to determine whether a four-lane (the state's position) or a two-lane highway was needed; the recommendation of the study would be binding on both governments. They could not agree on who would do the study, who would pay for it, and how long it would take. Also, they could not agree on whether the highway section traveling through the barge canal should be on pilings (the city's position) or traditional landfill (the state's position). The city hoped that pilings would reduce the chance of pollutant escape to

Lake Champlain. It was imperative that decisions be made because, Crampton warned, the state of Vermont was considering transferring the funding to another highway project. If an agreement could not be made soon, such funds might be cut out of the budget by a future United States Congress.[104]

Local businessmen, who were vociferously defending the waterfront proposal, added further pressure for an agreement. Shouting back and forth with the mayor during a November meeting of the Downtown Burlington Development Association, they accused Sanders of obstructionism. The business consensus was clearly to let the road proceed on the state's terms.[105] The pressure was finally relieved on November 15 when the city of Burlington and the state of Vermont signed an agreement on the Southern Connector. The agreement provided that the EPA would make the final decision about the route of the connector and that the earlier urban design study completed by Peter Owens would be used "to the fullest extent possible."[106] Although the agreement was hailed as a victory by Sanders, such ambiguous phrasing seemed to leave the door open to further conflict. As part of the agreement, A. Harry Atkinson, a local businessman and opponent of the connector, dropped his lawsuit against the project, which had effectively stalled it for months.

Joan Beauchemin, a Sanders supporter, neighborhood activist, and opponent of the Southern Connector, wholeheartedly endorsed the state/city agreement. Claiming that Owens' urban design recommendations were "enforceable by law" if not followed to "the fullest extent possible," Beauchemin announced that the new agreement met the complaint of the South End. She also defended the mayor, who had consistently been accused by the *Burlington Free Press* Editorial Board of delaying construction of the connector: "For someone who is characterized as unable to work with state officials, Sanders certainly seems to have done extremely well in hammering out a compromise against some pretty tough odds on a volatile issue."[107]

While the neighborhood activists were mollified by a new road design, the EPA was not. The pumps at the clean-up site became clogged and unuseable, and the EPA ordered another study of the barge canal before any new clean-up operations could begin. While work was halted, inflation continued; by 1986 the cost was projected at $50 million. Because of environmental constraints, by the end of 1987 the original barge canal route was jettisoned, and the planning began for an alternate route through a residential/business district. The slow process of obtaining rights-of-way for a new route further delayed the Southern Connector.[108] Vermont's Transportation Agency still preferred the original route over the canal. The new route would mean new displacements of community residents and businesses. The fragile compromise established between community activists and highway proponents would likely be torn apart.

PROPOSED REFORM AND ALTERNATIVE REFORMS

In fighting to prevent construction of a four-lane Southern Connector, the Progressive Coalition and its neighborhood activist and environmental allies did not implement any reform. Instead, their limited success was to block a reactionary project and leave open the possibility that further delay could be obtained through the courts by activists opposed to the compromise agreement. The Southern Connector was conceived as a pro-business development project. The real impetus for a no-compromise, four-lane highway project was not the much-argued safety issue.[109] The most interested proponents were the business class who would materially benefit from construction of a highway; specifically, the downtown business community was interested in gaining profit, not preventing automobile accidents.

In Burlington, the actions of William Aswad and the Planning Commission produced a multilayered pro-business economic development package. Burlington's wealthy suburbanites would travel the Southern Connector to retail buying locations or commercial offices. Wealthy condominium owners on the redeveloped lakefront could make the reverse commute to the IBM or DEC complexes in the adjoining suburbs.

The likely scenario would be a beautiful script written for realtors, landlords, developers, and retail business owners who cater to the upscale crowd. As land prices increased, manufacturing would hasten its migration to the nearby suburbs, the South, or the Third World. In its place would come expensive, luxury residences, more and higher office towers, and a few large department stores with their satellites of expensive shops. Perhaps even a city-subsidized convention center would be built to help attract tourists and businessmen to fill the various high-rise hotels either proposed or now under construction.

The construction of a four-lane highway through downtown Burlington would accelerate the city's evolution to a dual economy. The supposed payoff to the dominated classes for all this construction is more jobs. However, the type of jobs produced by such development is just as important as the creation of these jobs. As Michael Harrington and Mark Levinson have empirically demonstrated, the United States is evolving into a dual economy. As relatively well-paying, unionized manufacturing jobs disappear, the resulting occupational structure is topped by a thin layer of well-paying jobs; underneath is a thick layer of poor-paying jobs.[110] The 25 percent of Burlington's residents who fall under the poverty line would likely not choose to become minimum-wage workers at part-time jobs. Vermont's relatively high welfare payment schedule offers little incentive to single parents with children to take such low-paying work. Instead, many of them would be displaced by higher rents and forced to migrate. Burlington's students would take the minimum-wage jobs, their temporary residency assuring them of low pay. The end result would be not so much a new highway as an artery in a larger map of postindustrial capitalism.

If neighborhood fears of the imperatives of economic development in the automobile age are well founded, the proposed highway could well be an ecological nightmare. Although the Sanders administration had a record of compromising ecological needs for economic development to benefit the dominated classes, the final two-lane, alternative design proposal offered by Peter Owens would at least have prevented a potential ecological disaster. The ambiguous qualifying phrase in the state's acceptance, "to the fullest extent possible," is potentially dangerous to the ecology of the community.

Although well-crafted, Owens' proposal, were it to have been adopted, would have been another example of a liberal, compromised reform. Although the Owens road would perhaps have satisfied most of the neighborhood activist opposition, the resulting scaled-down construction would have left open the option for expanding the road later. As in the Sanders administration's waterfront projects, there were some public benefits provided by the Owens proposal. The road built under this proposed reform would not have been, at least in its initial stage, devastating to residential homeowners in the three affected neighborhoods. Also the health and the drinking water of the entire community would not have been threatened by an ill-conceived proposal to pump out and treat the nearly ten thousand dumptruck loads of toxic waste that were never extracted under the Superfund program. Nevertheless, despite these benefits, the underlying logic of capitalism would have been accommodated. The inner city would have been constructed in such a way that business-controlled economic development could continue despite its negative effects on Burlington's residents. Neither national nor state highway planners were sympathetic to the Sanders administration's attempts to stop the highway. Officials at both levels of federalism considered the needs of growth to be more important than any of Sanders' arguments.

Terrill Bouricius' proposal for a light rail was closer to being a democratic structural reform.[111] Construction of a mass transit facility, an inherently democratic form of transportation, in a city as small as Burlington would provide unambiguous benefits to residents, fulfillment of a human need irrespective of capital's needs. If a transit line were limited to Burlington's city limits (not one of Bouricius' suggestions), it would be a purer democratic structural reform. It would relieve many of the city's impoverished families from having to spend large portions of their incomes on automobile-based transportation. It would provide a constructive base to oppose all future highway requests. A highway would facilitate the suburban invaders' entry to and exit from the city and their daily creation and withdrawal of the city's productive resources, which promotes class segregation and shields assets from taxation by city authorities. A well-planned and well-funded, self-contained mass transit system, however, would facilitate residential access for Burlingtonians to existing productive resources, no matter how unequally distributed. It would be a transportation system created for the community itself, not one designed for suburbanites.

The balloon containing this democratic structural reform fantasy is easily popped. Mass transit systems are extremely expensive; even a city the size of Buffalo, New York (ten times the size of Burlington), strains under the financial burden of such a capital intensive undertaking. Buffalo's modest 6.5 mile project will cost an estimated $530 million; the United States and New York state governments will pay most of the cost.[112] Unfortunately, the current rail transit programs under construction are likely to be the last that are lavishly financed by national government funds for the forseeable future. The national government formerly paid for the greatest part of mass transit development, in proportions similar to the proposed financing of highway construction that made the Southern Connector a feasible project in the first place. Because of successive cuts in mass transit aid by the Reagan administration, few new systems will survive past the planning stage. A city the size of Burlington, restricted to revenues from property taxes, could not consider such a project without massive amounts of national government funding.

In addition, even if Burlington were to build a light rail transit system, it could not afford to run it. Burlington's population of thirty-eight thousand, most of whom have automobiles available, could not provide the number of fares needed to sustain such a system. To have enough fares, lines would have to be extended to the suburbs in a fashion similar to Boston's Metropolitan Transit Authority. Since this would facilitate the influx of the suburban commuters, the transit reform would no longer be a democratic structural reform enhancing the life-chances of Burlington's residents. In fact, it might even worsen the employment opportunities for city residents by increasing employee competition for existing jobs. Also, it would encourage Burlington's wealthier citizens to relocate to the suburbs. Unfortunately, the possibilities for a democratic structural reform to replace the Southern Connector, one that would benefit the mass of Burlington's citizens is not beyond imagination, but facing the constraints of capital and federal cutbacks in aid for mass transit, it proves to be unfeasible.

MUNICIPAL CABLE TELEVISION

The Progressive Coalition attempted and ultimately failed to procure a municipally owned cable television system in Burlington. In May 1983, two months after being reelected for the first time, Bernard Sanders put the issue on the political agenda by appointing a committee to study the shortcomings of the privately owned Green Mountain Cable Television franchise. At the time, Green Mountain Cable was hooked up to seven thousand Burlington residences and businesses, part of a larger regional system of twenty-eight thousand subscribers. The mayor's study committee was guided by an unsuccessful Progressive Coalition candidate for alderman, Huck Gutman, who claimed: "My only presupposition is that cable TV is presently unsatisfactory. . . . What is essential is that we get better service for no or a moderate increase in rates." The formal charge of the committee was to compare Green Mountain Cable's service to cable service in other communities, especially in the number and variety of channels available. Almost as if it were an afterthought, it was announced that the city panel would look at municipal cable ownership.[113]

Mayor Sanders, Alderman Peter Lackowski, and Alderman Bouricius, all socialists, preferred the option of municipal ownership.[114] But with two years of red-baiting hostility framing the Coalition's actions, they were careful to couch this proposal in neutral language. The Republican-dominated *Burlington Free Press* Editorial Board saw through the subtlety, however, and correctly surmised that a municipal socialist proposal was in progress. The day after Sanders made the cable television committee announcement an editorial warily entitled "Committee Should Stick to Issue of Cable TV Quality" argued:

> The idea of municipal socialism of a cable television service is flawed for several reasons. It represents an unnecessary intrusion of government into the arena of private business. It violates the unwritten principle that government should not interfere with the communications media. And it is economically unfeasible for the city to take on such a commitment when so many other important problems remain unsolved.
>
> The city's takeover of the system would send a negative signal to other firms that might be considering Burlington for their operations. . . .
>
> With the city in control of the cable system, channels doubtlessly would be pre-empted for the type of programming that could be classified as propaganda.[115]

The entire business-based counterargument to a municipally owned cable television station was articulated even before the idea was formally proposed.

To try to municipalize the ownership of Green Mountain Cable, a subsidiary of Cox Communications, a *Fortune* 500 company, would be a considerable undertaking, even without the enmity of the local daily newspaper. In 1982, Cox Cable, the fourth largest cable company in the United States, had 1.3 million customers; Vermont's 28,000 were a decidedly small part of their business. Also, most of the public's complaints about Cox were minor: too few channels (twelve), no local programming, and the substitution of the Cox-owned Spotlight channel for the popular all-movie channel, Home Box Office.[116] There was one serious complaint: 30 percent of Burlington, including the affluent New North End and the downtown mall, were not wired for cable. Since Cox was planning to rebuild the antiquated system, which dated to the 1950s, all of these objections could easily be accommodated. As an existing enterprise, Cox was dealing from a position of strength. No doubt anticipating a municipalization recommendation, Cox purposely decided not to cooperate with the Gutman committee.

Nevertheless, Huck Gutman and the committee commenced their attack by challenging Green Mountain Cable's right to choose programming, something Cox controlled from company headquarters in Atlanta. Huck Gutman argued that "the decision should not be by what is in the interests of the best profits but in what is the best interest of the community."[117] Green Mountain countered that they hired a local firm to poll the public for their choices. According to Robert Hart, the local manager of Green Mountain Cable, programming should be the viewers' choice, not the municipality's. Gutman also demanded more local access, including coverage of aldermanic meetings, disputing Green Mountain Cable's previous assertion that there was no demand for such programming.

While the mayor's committee was peppering Green Mountain Cable with various demands, the autonomous city-owned Burlington Electric Department (BED) began its own study of a takeover of the local cable television service under BED's authority. With neither aldermanic nor mayoral approval, the BED's five-person civilian commission ordered a fifty-thousand-dollar study on the economic and technological possibilities of a municipal takeover. Robert Hart, faced with two city-government challenges, from the mayor's committee and the BED, asserted that Cox would "fight it all the way."[118] Meanwhile, Burlington city government's right hand (the BED) and left hand (Gutman Task Force) appeared to be tentatively and independently grabbing for the same object; unfortunately this organism had no central nervous system to coordinate the body as a whole. In June 1983, realizing that the city's two independent efforts could leave it open to a divide-and-conquer strategy by Green Mountain Cable, Mayor Sanders publicly endorsed the BED's efforts. Also, by this time, Sanders had stripped away the patina of impartiality about cable ownership and declared: "In terms of a monopoly, if somebody has to make money on [cable], I would rather see it be the city . . . than a corporation from Atlanta."[119]

Although Sanders was committed to the municipalization of local cable television, in retrospect, it seems that the BED had more limited bureaucratic objectives. Under the title, "Utility Not Interested in Cable Takeover," Timothy S. Cronin, the director of public information for the BED, published a revealing editorial in the *Burlington Free Press*. He explained what the BED did not want: "Our intentions do not center around municipal ownership of the cable TV system or entertainment programming decisions"; and he explained what the BED did want:

Fire and security alarms could be offered at a reasonable price in all residential and commercial buildings; medical alert systems can be installed linking chronically ill outpatients and others with hospital emergency services; remote reading of utility meters; traffic light synchronization; energy management systems which would reduce energy waste; expansion of library services; data transmission among all city departments to reduce costs.[120]

If we look at the content of the majority of Cronin's demands, we find a bureaucratic shopping list. The goals of energy management and remote readings of meters are specific to the BED's needs as a municipal electric utility. Most of the remainder of the list would please many of the other autonomous city departments from the library to the streets. This list of bureaucratic priorities presented Green Mountain Cable with a negotiating agenda that would ultimately lead to BED's support of Cox in the ownership fight.

Two days after Cronin's July 27, 1983, article, Sanders' cable television panel publicly recommended that the BED apply to the Vermont Public Service Board for permission to build and run a fifty-five-channel system. This proposed system would wire all buildings in the city free of charge, charge monthly fees of three dollars or less for basic service, provide an electrical load management system (a BED goal), provide fire and police alarms, and set up a seventeen-member programming board, nine of whom would be elected. Cox countered that their cable franchise was exclusive and that the city had no legal right to infringe on it.[121] The cable company's position had legal authority: in 1979 the Vermont legislature had given plenary authority to the state Public Service Board (PSB) to regulate cable television systems, thus undermining city claims of jurisdiction.

In contrast to the fifty-five channels and minimal monthly rate the mayor's committee promised, in September 1983, Cox Cable Communications requested from the PSB a 100 percent rate hike (to a basic service charge of twelve dollars a month) to finance an expansion of the Green Mountain system to thirty-five channels. Cox would also install a two-way system for the transmission of information and electricity management and bring back Home Box Office. Most important, the company would expand the cable system into parts of Burlington that were not already served. The proposed rate of return for upgrading the system would be a hefty 19 percent.[122] Cox was trying to co-opt the BED by acquiescing to its bureaucratic goals and to placate the existing public complaints about Green Mountain Cable's service. Cox claimed that all these concessions had been years in the making, but their appearance was much too close in both timing and content with the municipal threat to Green Mountain Cable's monopoly position to make it believeable that this was all mere coincidence. Nevertheless, there were two crucial differences between the public and private proposals: the basic rate to be paid and the recipient of the profits reaped.

The Gutman panel's optimistic assertions of a monthly rate of only $3.00 appeared to be slightly low. In January 1984, the BED published its commissioned study by Rice Associates. The study, reflecting the goal of the party paying for the study, favored a municipally owned system. Although the average rate was projected at $13.50 a month for forty-two channels ($1.50 higher than Cox's request), a three-tiered system would be established with the lowest basic monthly service starting at $4.00 a month for ten channels. Also, the report went on to say that if a municipal system were built, remote meter reading and various energy management systems would save the city $2.5 million to $7 million in fifteen years.[123] Robert Hart, the spokesman for Cox, had maintained all along that Rice Associates had a reputation in the cable business for favoring municipal systems.

When the Rice report was revealed to the public, a portion that contained legal advice on how to proceed against Cox was kept secret. Green Mountain Cable sued the BED under Vermont's right-to-know law for public disclosure of their opponent's legal strategy. Hart claimed: "It's our position that that's public information."[124] This is a perfect illustration of government's permeable quality. Because government is a structure that has a certain degree of democratic process, it remains more open to scrutiny of its operations than does business. When the BED pondered an attack on Cox's monopoly, Cox demanded access to its foe's game plan. The BED had no such authority to make Cox's strategy public. The prerogative of capital to keep its operations secret was virtually unchallenged.

After the Rice study was completed, the cable television dispute was removed from the municipal level to the state level. The Vermont Public Service Board became the forum, and Cox's bid for a rate increase became the immediate issue. The BED requested and received permission from the PSB to have an intervenor status, which gave the BED the right to cross-examine witnesses and to present evidence.[125] If Cox were allowed to proceed unchallenged, the PSB's approval of a Cox rate increase and plan for rebuilding would be a virtual fait accompli. To replace the Cox system, Burlington needed to prevent Cox from expanding its cable service. Cox, well prepared with a small battalion of lawyers, engineers, and consultants, took the offensive with a proposal before the PSB that would give Burlington, Rutland, and Montpelier each their own television studio with their own public access channel. Since Rutland, Vermont's second largest city, and Montpelier, the state capital, were not considering municipally owned cable television franchises, Cox was craftily playing a divide-and-conquer strategy. Now two Vermont communities, historical rivals of Burlington, stood to lose concrete public benefits if Burlington succeeded in preventing the Cox rate increase. Also in the Cox proposal were an education channel and a leased-access channel (crucial to remote meter reading). Finally, fifty-four channels were offered instead of twenty-eight, a major concession. James W. Brown, BED director of rate research, was already displaying signs of capitulation: "If it really is a plan to implement the things you're listing, it sounds encouraging. Perhaps Cox is really beginning to live up to its responsibilities."[126] The Sanders administration tried to reverse the Cox momentum; the Coalition testified before the PSB advocating a municipal takeover based on the conclusions of the Rice report.

In April 1984, the Board of Aldermen unanimously endorsed a resolution directing the city attorney's office to draw up the necessary legal documents to apply to the PSB for a municipal cable television franchise.[127] Tentatively, Democrats, Republicans, and Progressives united behind the Progressive Coalition and the existing BED proposal. Without doubt, it was the BED's authorship of a municipal plan that persuaded aldermanic Republicans and Democrats to vote for a city-owned franchise. Despite the aldermen's unusual resolve, during June the BED succumbed to Cox and unofficially supported the firm's expanded plan as presented to the PSB. One obstacle to the Cox bandwagon was that Green Mountain Cable was challenging a new increased street excavation fee Burlington had levied in state court.[128] Cox refused to compromise on this issue. Since this issue was outstanding, Sanders had a publicly defensible reason not to accept the BED/Cox agreement, which needed approval by the aldermen. The Sanders administration continued to press for a municipally owned franchise; in fact, Sanders chose to turn up the heat on Cox. The mayor demanded a $1.25 million payment and a percentage of Green Mountain's gross receipts in return for a city agreement not to compete with Cox for Burlington's cable franchise.[129] Despite Sanders' efforts, by September the Burlington Electric Department's capitulation was complete; it formally severed itself from Sanders' position. BED's commission voted four to one to accept the Cox plan and asked the aldermanic committee to likewise accept it.[130]

On September 17, 1984, the BED/Cox compromise was debated by the Board of Aldermen. Republicans and Democrats, reverting to their usual pro-business attitudes, dropped their previous support for a municipal cable system and now supported the BED position. Chance intervened on the side of the Progressives: three Republicans, who certainly would have supported the plan, were absent. The resulting Progressive Coalition majority voted down the compromise.[131] One week later, when the missing Republicans had returned to their seats, they teamed up with Democrats to vote seven to five to reject a municipal cable system; the mayor vetoed their resolution, and the five Progressive Coalition aldermen sustained the veto.[132] The Sanders administration was in an isolated position: a majority of the aldermen opposed the Coalition proposal, and the key BED commission also rejected it.

Sanders and his supporters pursued the Progressive Coalition program in front of PSB hearing commissioners. Using capitalist values to fight capitalism, Sanders argued that the Burlington franchise should be open to all competitors: "You have a major corporation with high-priced lawyers saying it does not want any market competition for 12 years and that consumers should have no say in the matter."[133] The Progressive Coalition's arguments were to no avail. Although the PSB never formally rejected the city's application for municipally owned service, the board tentatively accepted the Cox rebuild proposal in October 1984 and issued the final go-ahead in February 1985. The PSB pared Cox's rate request down to $10.50 a month but allowed Cox to add a surcharge to Burlington cable users to cover the cost of the city's street excavation fee.[134] With Cox and the PSB in virtually complete agreement, Sanders' anger knew no bounds.

Although the PSB's ruling was an unambiguous Cox victory, the city could and eventually did appeal the board's findings to the Vermont Supreme Court. As with the Southern Connector resistance strategy, the Sanders administration now resorted to using the federal system's numerous veto possibilities to frustrate Cox's building plans. In early February 1985, before a long, drawn-out battle could occur, Cox announced its intention of selling off all its Vermont franchises, pending PSB approval, to a group of Vermont and New Hampshire investors. Cox's official explanation was that it was acting to restructure its cable business and thus was sloughing off its smaller franchises. Two of the prospective owners met with Sanders to discuss the differences between the city administration and the cable franchise.[135] Cox's promised battle-to-the-end was now close to ending. It is difficult for the public to know whether Cox placed the Burlington franchise on the block only for reasons of corporate efficiency or whether the threat of continued litigation from City Hall influenced its decision. Unlike the federal system, the business realm has no Freedom of Information Act that Cox must obey; business does not have to divulge its decision-making process unless it is accused of breaking the law.

By now Burlington's position was strictly one of obstruction. In mid-February, city officials refused to sign an agreement with Cox that would allow the company to lease BED poles to string new cable wires to serve Burlington's elite New North End neighborhood. Burlington officials were delaying any decisions while negotiations with the prospective owners of Green Mountain Cable were taking place. Also, the Sanders administration requested the PSB to block the sale of the franchise because the city's application to the board as a competitor had not been acted upon.[136] On a partisan vote, the Democratic/Republican aldermanic majority passed a bill that would allow Cox to use the poles and thus proceed with the rebuilding and expansion of the system; Sanders vetoed the measure.[137] The Sanders administration as usual had no powerful allies. According to the Rice study, the majority of Burlington's residents endorsed municipal ownership. Nevertheless, their collective assent could not overcome the opposition of both Cox Communications and the state of Vermont.

Even if Cox had acquiesced in its battle with Burlington's Progressive Coalition, there were legal questions that might preclude city ownership. One formidable barrier was the lack of a provision for a municipal cable television franchise in Burlington's charter. Although it contained provisions for a municipal water utility, an electric utility, and even a gas utility, on other ventures in municipal socialism it was silent.[138] To complicate matters, the Vermont legislature had recently changed its procedure for accepting municipal charter revisions. From 1963 to 1984, the state-mandated procedure to amend municipal charters was minimal; a public warning, a public hearing, and then a copy of the amended charter filed with the Vermont secretary of state were the only requirements placed upon a city. If the state legislature did not expressly forbid the charter change and if the change did not contravene existing state laws, the new language was accepted by the state as legally binding without state legislative action. In 1984, the Vermont legislature altered the procedure; now all charter changes had to be specifically approved by the legislature to be legally binding.[139] The veto power of the state expanded dramatically. Either the

Vermont Assembly or the Vermont Senate could merely fail to act, as legislatures are wont to do on most proposed legislation, and a municipal charter change would be denied. An earlier effort by Burlington to diversify its revenue base by adopting a gross receipts tax on meals was soundly rejected by the 1984 state legislature; there was little reason to believe the state would act in the city's favor on a more ambitious project. State infringement on local autonomy provided a tall hurdle for Burlington to jump.

Charter authority was not the only legal question confronting the Progressive Coalition's efforts to socialize Burlington's cable television network; there was the question of the franchise. Burlington's cable franchise was originally affirmed by a thirty-year contract between Green Mountain Cable and the city in 1952. John Franco, a Progressive Coalition member and lawyer for the city, claimed that with the expiration of the contract, the city owned the franchise.[140]

Complicating this reasoning was the fact that in 1979 Vermont had created the Public Service Board, an autonomous state agency, and had given it plenary control over cable television regulation within the state. With the PSB's consistent pro-utility bias, the city's chances of winning this legal battle were not auspicious. Furthermore, Burlington was fighting a losing battle with the PSB over electric rates. With the combined strength of Cox's financial clout and the state of Vermont's pro-capitalist bias in its agencies (PSB) and laws, the Sanders administration's plans for a municipally owned cable system were increasingly less feasible.

Thus it was not surprising that on March 29, 1985, the Sanders administration accepted an offer of $1 million cash from the prospective owners of Green Mountain Cable, the Mountain Cable Company, to settle all city claims. This $1 million would be paid to the city to drop its bid to become a municipal franchise and also to cover street excavation fees while the system was being rebuilt. Mountain Cable also agreed to pay a 5 percent gross receipts tax, which might pull in $150,000 a year, and to rent space in City Hall for an additional $35,000 a year. With the advent of federally imposed rate deregulation, Mountain Cable agreed to limit rate increases to 5 percent or less. In addition to dropping its municipal franchise bid, Burlington would support the sale of Green Mountain Cable from Cox to Mountain Cable, support Mountain's rebuilding program, and agree to street pole attachment of Mountain's cables.[141] Cox's approved rate of $10.50 would not be challenged when the company was assumed by the new owners. Soon after the deal was announced, the Board of

Aldermen unanimously approved it, a financial coup for Burlington's cash-starved treasury.[142] Even the hostile *Burlington Free Press* Editorial Board about-faced and congratulated Sanders.[143] In return for this cash bonus, Burlington, for the indefinite future, would not have another opportunity to control a key communication technology, cable television, within its borders.

In the end, the Sanders/Mountain Cable deal was modified against the city's wishes and negated by U.S. Congressional action. Effective January 1, 1987, cable television rates were deregulated by the Federal Communications Act of 1984. Mountain Cable filed for a 19 percent rate increase, far above the level allowable as specified in their contract with the city. The Sanders administration took them to court to extract a compromise on the rates. No compromise was offered by Mountain Cable, and it prevailed in Vermont Superior Court, which found that national law overruled the city contract's provisions over rate regulation.[144] Shortly after, Mountain Cable sold its franchise to Adelphia Corporation for a substantial profit. Mountain Cable had paid $45 million for the franchise; it sold it for a whopping $117 million. Robert McGill, one of the owners of Mountain, predicted another rate increase.[145] This increase was assured despite the failure of Mountain Cable to ever wire downtown Burlington. Burlington's deal looked much better on paper.

PROPOSED REFORM AND ALTERNATIVE REFORMS

The municipal socialization of Burlington's cable television would have been a democratic structural reform. In fact, it was the conservative opposition, the *Burlington Free Press* Editorial Board, that assessed the potential outcome if the Progressive Coalition were to establish a municipal cable service:

With the city in control of the cable system, channels doubtlessly would be pre-empted for the type of programming that could be classified as propaganda. Just as government should not be operating newspapers or television stations, it should not be allowed to take over cable television. There are adequate forums for Sanders and his allies to express their opinions without putting a communications system in their hands. Such a step would be dangerous and could expose viewers to the worst sort of demagoguery. Local commercial and educational television channels offer ample amounts of local programming.[146]

The business community's fears of and arguments against a municipal cable television system that would have Progressive Coalition input illustrates the rich potential of municipal television as a democratic structural reform.

By utilizing local access and possibly by pooling resources with a state-supported institution, such as the University of Vermont, the Progressive Coalition could produce programming to counter the existing monotony of commercial propaganda. Undoubtedly, the city would own its own access channel, which could provide alternative views to the public. While it is true that private cable systems offer many communities a local access channel (as in Cox's proposal), it should be kept in mind that the station's program manager usually has final say on who and what will be broadcast. A Progressive Coalition cable television service would have no such private enterprise master. The Progressive Coalition's proposed seventeen-member board in charge of programming would likely provide access to a plurality of ideological viewpoints, something contemporary programming fails to do. Since the majority of the programming board would be elected, voters could remove incumbents if their choices of programs seemed arbitrary.

The *Burlington Free Press* editorial claims that Sanders and his allies have adequate coverage of their views in the community. In Burlington this is true. However, there is no reason why the Progressive Coalition's countercultural message should be limited to Burlington. After all, most of the nation has no access to the radical point of view in its most utilized mass media, television. However, as the nation becomes increasingly wired with cable, any local station will have the capability of being broadcast by satellite to the rest of the United States. Although there is little reason to believe a radical station (were it to come to the air in Burlington) would be carried by many privately owned cable systems, there are at least several other progressive cities on the opposite coast that probably would. Very likely, all of Vermont that was wired with cable would receive Burlington's own channel and programming.

Cable control by the Coalition could have provided a forum for the socialization of values that contradict those of capitalism. At times the Progressive Coalition has deliberately and actively battled the effects and needs of capitalism. A locally controlled television station would provide at least a statewide medium to mobilize popular resistance to capitalist ideology. It is this possibility of establishing a socialist alternative, a dialectical response to capitalist ideology, that makes municipal ownership of a local television station controlled by elected radicals a possible democratic socialist reform. Such a service would fulfill a human need not simply irrespective of the needs of capitalism but actually combatting capitalism.

To many, calling cable television a "human need" might seem preposterous. The *Burlington Free Press* Editorial Board would agree:

Even though it has been said before, the fact that cable television is a luxury bears repeating. That any government should consider it as an essential says much about the scale of official priorities. People who are dissatisfied with the service provided by private systems have ways and means of making their displeasure known to the firms' management. They can complain about the service and ask for improvements. If there is no response to their requests, they can cancel the service.[147]

Despite the fact that only four channels are clearly available in the mountainous Burlington area to those who are without cable, there remains the fundamental question of whether or not television fulfills a human need at all.

To label television as an unneeded luxury is to ignore that most human needs are constructed; they are not constant throughout history. Except for such items as medicine, shelter, clothing, and food, there are few irreducible human needs actually indispensable for existence itself, and even these vary widely in different societies. As civilizations advance in material wealth, the threshhold of human need rises. Refrigeration, telephone service, electricity, and running hot water were not recognized in the United States as basic human needs in the 1800s, but today they are. The Progressive Coalition has recognized that cable television is on the threshhold of the rising expectation level of human needs.

If it had been possible, a majority vote by Burlington's residents for a municipal cable system could have resulted in the wiring of all residents' homes and places of work free of charge; after installation, the Gutman panel proposal would have allowed basic service at a token cost. This action would have ratified the Coalition's perspective that cable television answers a human need as defined by the community itself. In fact, it would have established cable television as an entitlement. Such a vote would be an example of a community defining its own human needs instead of allowing capitalist entrepreneurs or corporations to create new needs for the purpose of profit. Unfortunately, a majority referendum vote for municipal cable television would have been merely a symbolic exercise since institutional actors of both the federal (Vermont PSB and the BED itself) and capitalist (Cox) structures denied the local majority's attempt at democratic structural reform.

Some might argue that a city ownership of its own cable system would be a democratic structural reform simply because the community, rather than private investors, would own a profitable portion of the local means of production. On the contrary, municipal ownership in itself and without democratic control is not a democratic socialist reform. For example, Burlington already owned the electricity franchise and the water works in the community. While this base for municipal socialism is not negligible, it cannot be characterized as democratic socialist reform.

In fact, these bureaucracies bear an uncanny resemblance in structure, operation, and service delivery to their equivalents in the private sector. Without democratic control, through, for example, the elected board that was proposed for Burlington's cable television system, municipal cable television would probably act in a bureaucratic and hierarchical fashion similar to that of the Burlington Electric Department. When considering a municipal cable system, BED looked to its own needs; remote meter reading and energy load management reflect those needs. The content of programming and customer rates, those issues that concerned the viewers, were expressly not BED's concern.

Public ownership without democratization, which the commission system of government almost guarantees, merely substitutes bureaucratic logic, in this case the BED's expressed functional goals and needs, for capitalist logic and needs. Benefits for the majority are low on the bureaucratic agenda. Municipal ownership in itself is usually a liberal reform; sometimes it can even be a reactionary reform. Only if the enterprise being socialized is also democratized by allowing maximum feasible participation by all sectors of the population can municipal socialization become a democratic socialist reform. The proposed seventeen-member board of programming overseers under the municipally owned cable system proposal was a step in this direction.

Although the Sanders administration spent considerable time and effort trying to socialize Green Mountain Cable, the combined strength of the state of Vermont and the business community vetoed the effort. Not only did the state Public Service Board successfully pigeonhole the Coalition's proposal for a municipal system, but also Cox, with the PSB's approval, created a plan for an alternative to a municipal cable television service. This one-two punch strategy ensured that Burlington's cable television system would remain in the capitalist domain for years to come. The Sanders administration proposal was reduced to a form of economic plea bargaining.

The grudging acceptance of capitalist ownership by the Sanders administration characterizes the final adopted reform as a liberal reform. The needs of capitalist corporations to make a profit were preserved by Vermont's Public Service Board, and there were also benefits to Burlington's dominated majority. First, a local access channel (which Cox originally denied the demand for) was finally conceded. Second, a local educational channel that would assist Burlington's teachers was to be built. Third, the new system was to have a considerably greater number of channels, fifty-five, than the thirty-four that were originally planned. Fourth, eventually all of Burlington would have the option, if one could afford it, to hook up to cable. Finally, the city treasury was enriched by over one million dollars. Few of these reforms would have occurred (or at the very least their scope would have been reduced) had the Progressive Coalition never attempted a municipal takeover of local cable television.

In addition to meeting these reformist demands, Cox promised to build a two-way cable system that would provide for remote meter reading and other data transmission. Although this reform was to indirectly help the majority of Burlington's citizens by providing more efficient service and coordinating autonomous city departments, the primary recipient of benefits would be the BED and other autonomous city bureaucracies. It was these goals, laid out in Thomas Cronin's *Burlington Free Press* article, that were first met by Green Mountain Cable. Cox's successful co-opting of the BED by meeting most of the Electric Department's espoused goals was not even a liberal reform. Instead, it represented, as a single instance, how the flexibility of the capitalist structure allows it to meet the internally generated bureaucratic demands of the federalist structure. Structures of power relations can sometimes accommodate each other to provide a united front against resistance groups or classes. Even if the Sanders administration had controlled the BED commission from the beginning of the two-year struggle to municipalize cable, the possibility that the municipal cable television fight would turn in the Coalition's favor was unlikely. The Public Service Board's failure to even hold hearings on the city's application demonstrated its distaste for municipal cable franchises. Also, the expense of buying out and then rebuilding Cox's existing facilities would have required a referendum approval from the public to borrow millions of dollars in a city already overburdened by property taxes. Because the city and ultimately its taxpayers would have to pay a fair market compensation (a legally enshrined capitalist rule), municipal socialization advocates would bear the burden of convincing Burlington's citizenry that they could not afford such a "luxury."

CONCLUSION

If we evaluate all three economic development issues covered in this chapter, we can conclude that democratic structural reform at the municipal level is very difficult but not impossible. Each issue under consideration in this chapter—waterfront development, the Southern Connector, and municipal cable television—resulted in either a liberal reform or the prevention of a reactionary reform.

Specific to waterfront development there was a simple solution to preserving a wooded lakefront tract: do nothing! Without the public subsidy of an enlarged municipal sewer system, development could not proceed. However, the price would likely be paid later. Business confidence would have subsided, and new investment would have migrated over the suburban border. The high price of ecological democratic structural reforms would have been economic stagnation. And any other public use of the entire property would be contingent on the largesse of the national or state governments; this simply was not forthcoming.

The Southern Connector highway compromise (if ever implemented) was another liberal reform. Here too, a mass transit alternative as a democratic structural reform was virtually impossible without extensive federal subsidies. In this case as in the previous one, a reactionary reform, enhancing capitalist development at the expense of working class citizens, was decisively modified to provide public benefits.

Finally, municipal cable was a democratic structural reform on the Progressive agenda. Although initially it appeared feasible, the state Public Service Board, in effect, vetoed the Burlington proposal with the complicity of the Burlington Electric Department and Cox Communications. In this case the benefits extracted for compromising to a liberal reform were impressive. Despite the incurred costs, capital left the battlefield bloodied but victorious.

In two of the three cases, waterfront development and the Southern Connector, the outcomes were not final. The federalist system gave the Sanders administration leeway to maneuver, but that leeway was mostly limited to creating obstacles to development. When the administration took a positive tack, through the municipal cable television and the Sanders/Alden development plan, federal vetoes were used against the Progressives. Institutional stalemates left only one proposal, cable television, actually resolved; the other two were either postponed (waterfront development) or tentative (Southern Connector).

The next chapter analyzes progressive tax initiatives. The reader should expect to find similar levels of accomplishment despite formidable efforts on the part of the Progressive Coalition.

6

The Search for a Progressive Tax

The Progressive Coalition struggled for a tax proposal that would effectively place the burden of municipal costs more on the wealthy and the business community. The Coalition proposed the following major tax initiatives at the local level: shifting the property tax burden from homeowners and renters to business, levying a gross receipts tax on meals and rooms, levying a street excavation fee on utilities, and taxing business and not-for-profit corporations for childcare services.

The battle by the Sanders administration to maintain the inventory tax (a property tax on business) and to legislate the other taxes was the culmination of efforts to move away from a tax base almost wholly dependent on real estate. It should be kept in mind that Bernard Sanders was elected in 1981 in part because of a proposed sixty-five cents per hundred dollars of assessed property increase in the real estate property tax by the then Mayor Gordon Paquette. The Paquette-sponsored sixty-five-cent tax hike came after ten years of gradually increasing property taxes along with deteriorating basic services and infrastructure. From the public's point of view, Paquette's devotion to urban renewal and increased private investment in the redeveloped downtown came at the expense of citywide services. Even a longtime Democrat and Paquette supporter, Stratty Lines, who owned a local downtown diner, claimed the mayor "seems to be building a monument to himself."[1]

The proposed 1981 tax increase, a 31 percent increase in the general city property tax, was designed to reverse years of neglect. Paquette's proposed budget included funds for eight new police officers, eight new firefighters, dumptrucks, police cars, a street sweeper, salary increases, books for the library, and other regular city services. Paquette asserted that the dramatic 31 percent increase was merely "this year's inflationary costs, not last year's or the year before. We're not playing catch-up."[2] Paquette was exaggerating: although 1981 was a double-digit inflationary year, the cost of living index was never even close to his proposed increase. Such sharp increases are common in newly developing cities, but Burlington was a mature community with virtually no population growth. Despite Paquette's denials, Burlington was trying to remedy past neglect.

Mayoral challenger Sanders agreed with many in the community that services were deficient and more revenue was needed; he did not propose fiscal retrenchment to counter the proposed tax increase. Instead, Sanders proposed "new sources of tax revenue for the city rather than the same old tax on property which comes down heaviest on homeowners."[3] Sanders wanted downtown merchants to repay the city-guaranteed $1.5 million bond that financed part of the Church Street Marketplace, a downtown pedestrian mall. He would solicit a substantial fee from the tax-exempt University of Vermont and its adjoining Medical Center and fight for property tax reclassification that would result in higher taxes on business property and lower taxes on residential. Sanders even envisioned a city income tax to eventually replace the property tax: "Just as the state places a piggy-back tax on federal taxes, we could place a piggy-back on state taxes. . . . The advantage of this approach is that it will affect only about 12 percent of our households—the most affluent 12 percent, rather than all homeowners."[4] Paquette's consistent property tax increases and Sanders' counterproposals provided the context of the 1981 mayoral contest, which also asked voters in a separate question to approve the 31 percent tax increase.

At the time Sanders was first elected mayor, voters were decisively repudiating the proposed tax measure. Upon taking office, Sanders proposed and the public accepted a scaled-back twenty-five-cent tax increase. Through his next two reelection campaigns, Sanders held the line on the general property tax. Despite this restraint, Sanders endorsed various temporary splinter property taxes to fund specific projects such as resurfacing the streets and sidewalks or upgrading the police department. Sanders did not want to suffer Paquette's electoral fate by ignoring basic services.

Accurately judging the temper of the times, the Sanders administration wisely co-opted the property tax revolt. In the late 1970s,

Massachusetts and California voters passed referenda enacting drastic property tax cuts. Homeowners of all income brackets were allying with commercial and industrial property owners to combat the spiraling cost of property taxes. When Burlington's voters rejected the Paquette tax increase, they were the tail end of a nationwide revolt at the state and local levels. By 1977 every state had in some way acted to blunt the ire of property taxpayers. In Vermont, as in twenty-five other states, property tax circuit-breakers were passed.[5] In Vermont, the circuit-breaker program was a very modest state-financed rebate to those who paid high property taxes. Subsequent events proved that rebates were insufficient to blunt the anger of Burlington's property owners when they voted.

Tax policy has conflated the interests of those who own residences with those who own profit-making property in keeping property taxes low. Because all of Burlington's taxable property was assessed at 100 percent of fair market value, a de facto low-tax coalition was created between middle-class homeowners and the business community. This policy dates to 1977, when Vermont enacted, at the behest of the business community, a law mandating this assessment procedure. This reactionary reform favored profit-making property owners at the expense of homeowners and renters. Previously, commercial and industrial properties were classified at different rates, which allowed them to be taxed at higher levels than residential properties. The rationale behind tax classification is that a business, whether manufacturing or commercial, is actually creating profits on the premises. By contrast, people who own their own homes do not realize any increment, in what is usually their largest lifetime investment, until they sell.

The business community profited by pushing for the enactment of tax laws that demanded property-value reassessment periodically and tax levies based on fair market value of real property only. This business windfall occurred when property tax burdens were proportionately shifted from factories and offices to houses and apartments. It follows that in a tight rental market like Burlington, tax increases on rental properties are soon passed on to the tenants, so landlords are only temporarily at a disadvantage. With the weight of taxation shifted, most homeowners and renters (most of whom are modest wage earners) found themselves in an unspoken alliance with the business community. A common demand was made: hold the line on property taxes.

The Sanders administration was presented with a dilemma.

Property taxes had to be kept down for Progressive Coalition candidates to be reelected, but at the same time, the ambitious projects of the Progressive Coalition were very expensive. Thus, throughout the tenure of the Sanders administration, there was a search for new revenue sources.

PROPERTY AND RELATED TAXES

Before Mayor Sanders' victory, Burlington had for many years collected a tax on business inventories. Inventory taxes are paid once a year on machinery, fixtures, and stock. For some businesses, there are ways of evading such taxes. One oil storage company on Burlington's lakefront pumped out its oil and sent it to tanks across Lake Champlain in Plattsburgh, New York, to avoid paying the inventory tax when it came due.[6] For many businesses, however, such tactics are impossible because their inventory or other taxable assets are fixed. Although the inventory tax was a tax on business, it arbitrarily fell heavily on some businesses but barely touched others.

While Burlington kept its inventory tax, surrounding Vermont communities began abandoning inventory taxes after the state of Vermont legislated such a local option in 1975. The effect was intensified competition between localities for new business investment. In fact, when Sanders was elected in March 1981, the nearby town of Shelburne and twenty-one other Vermont communities repealed the inventory tax. The problem with such a tax is not that it spurs a great wave of capital flight but that it is a deterrent to new investment. Christopher Barbieri, spokesman of the Vermont Chamber of Commerce, commented: "Repeal could provide the item that tips the balance favorably" when it comes to new investment.[7] An inventory tax was one good reason for businesses that were capital intensive or that had to maintain high inventories of goods to invest in communities other than Burlington.

Business people continually complained about the burden of the inventory tax. In fact, they complained about all property taxes levied on them. In August 1981, the Fidelity Mutual Life Insurance Company of Philadelphia won a $220,000 cut in their tax bill—over one-third of the total. Such a drastic cut was approved by the aldermen in a closed-door session. Sanders, failing to use his veto, acquiesced. Since F.M. Burlington, Fidelity Mutual Life's local subsidiary, was the largest property owner in Burlington, a tax cut of such magnitude could only come at the expense of other taxpayers. F.M. Burlington owned the Burlington Square Mall and the nearby Radisson Hotel, Burlington's largest commercial complex. The company was a direct recipient of money from the national government to help build a parking garage that aided the hotel's expansion, and F.M. Burlington's complex was built on land cleared under the Department of Housing and Urban Development's Urban Renewal Program, an indirect but costly subsidy. Apparently, Fidelity Mutual, F.M. Burlington's parent corporation, was not satisfied with such huge national government subsidies alone. After the city's approval of the tax cut, Fidelity Mutual labeled it "a gesture of good faith, a step in the right direction."[8] Since Fidelity Mutual had been preparing a court challenge to the city's assessment, more than "good faith" was at stake.

Many of the complaints from Burlington's business community about the property tax stemmed from the fact that the city had not conducted a property reappraisal for almost thirty years. While any new building, improvements to property, or property that changed hands were appraised at contemporary fair market values, older residences that were not sold in recent years remained appraised at values that predated the inflationary 1970s.

Actually this failure to reappraise had the effect of making a notoriously regressive tax, the property tax, somewhat progressive, particularly for older and poorer residents. The Old North End, where most of the city's poor lived, had little new construction and, among single-family homeowners, few property transfers; thus many of its buildings remained undervalued by 50 percent or more. In fact, the average house in Burlington was assessed at about 20 percent of its actual sale value. This undervaluing helped to slow an upward pressure on rents that all of Burlington was experiencing. However, in the affluent New North End and the redeveloped downtown, new construction was occurring and being appraised at current market value; thus, the wealthier classes were haphazardly paying proportionately more of the share of the city's tax bill than were the moderate- and low-income earners. It was a case of mildly progressive taxation by default. Such progressiveness depended on the community's willingness to forego the reappraisal of property values.

Burlington's tardiness in reevaluating property was not unique. Subsequently, the state of Vermont acted to spur property reappraisal throughout the state by manipulating school funding to local districts. State school aid to communities was progressively based on a ratio of the number of school children to the Grand List. Without reappraisal, a real-estate rich (but not income-rich) city such as Burlington overstated its need for state funding by understating its wealth using this formula. By comparison, most of Vermont, a rural state, is real-estate poor, and distribution of state education dollars was a contentious issue, since state education assistance was widely needed. According to the U.S. Census, in terms of personal income, Vermont is one of the poorest states in the region and ranks number thirty-six in the nation in per capita income using 1980 statistics.[9] It was in this context that the Vermont legislature passed a law with positive and negative sanctions to both cajole and coerce reappraisal. Under this act, funds to Burlington schools would be cut by an estimated $137,000 if reappraisal were not implemented; however, $65,000 additional would be given to Burlington's educational department if it cooperated. In March 1982, the Board of Aldermen unanimously voted for reappraisal after the schools (which have their own budget, property tax line, and elected commission) promised to loan the city $500,000 interest free to completely reappraise all of Burlington's property. At the time of passage, Sanders commented, "It's a good deal."[10] For many homeowners and renters, property tax reappraisal proved otherwise.

The city's dependence on property tax revenue convinced the Progressive Coalition of the need to attempt taxing traditionally tax-exempt property. Burlington's colleges all are tax exempt, from their fraternity houses to their profitable bookstores. In fact, in Burlington, an incredible 45 percent of all property is tax exempt, granted that status by the state of Vermont. The large not-for-profit sector, typical of postindustrial cities, was crippling the city's ability to raise needed revenue. A few of the smaller colleges paid nominal sums to the city; however, the immense University of Vermont (UVM), with ninety buildings on four hundred acres, paid nothing and intended to keep it that way. Granted, UVM provided certain services to the city (known as payments in lieu of taxes), but these services were clearly insufficient to meet Burlington's need for cash. In the 1981 election, Sanders publicly proposed that a fee of $500,000 a year be placed on UVM, less than 0.5 percent of the university's $112 million budget. UVM resolutely refused.[11] In March 1982, the Sanders administration tried another approach, requesting that UVM pay taxes on the president's residence, fraternity houses, and the bookstore, which were not used exclusively for educational purposes.

Although this initiative never passed the Republican/Democrat-dominated Board of Aldermen, UVM did not remain a passive spectator. A UVM-sponsored study released in October 1982 claimed that the university provided $1.8 million in services to the city, ranging from allowing city residents to use the library to providing the city's fire department with a UVM Rescue Squad ambulance.[12] A few weeks later, Mayor Sanders picked apart this self-serving UVM study. For example, Sanders pointed out that the largest item of the claimed $1.8 million in services delivered was $852,160 for bad medical debts incurred at the medical center by city residents. The mayor retorted, "Those debts are clearly built into the fee structure. . . . Those who pay UHC [University Health Center] fees are paying that debt."[13] Thus Sanders countered UVM's formal justification for tax exemption, which rationalized bureaucratic privilege at taxpayers' expense. UVM's vociferous defense of its tax-exempt status demonstrated that it was not merely capitalism that impinged on the city's autonomy. The not-for-profit bureaucracy also acted to protect its needs, which, like those of capital, were legislated and enforced by the state of Vermont.[14] Nevertheless, Sanders later tried to scale this wall of legal privilege.

In 1986, the Progressive Coalition, with some support from the Democratic and Republican aldermen, put a proposal on the March ballot to tax all nonreligious and not-for-profits at 25 percent of their assessed value. A mayoral committee stacked with business persons had proposed this tax in 1985, a period of fiscal stress for Burlington. With little opposition outside of that from UVM, the proposal swept through by a three-to-two margin. The next step was the permission from the Vermont legislature for a city charter change to allow this tax. Predictably, it was voted down.[15]

Tables were turned in 1986 when the University of Vermont needed permission from the city to construct a new business school building. President Lattie Coor sought to make peace with the Sanders administration and offered to help rebuild and widen a busy street intersection, provide more parking for students, hire a traffic officer for the busiest times of day, and develop seven acres of UVM land for student housing. In addition, the university would pay thirteen hundred dollars for every fire call made and help pay for new fire equipment.[16] A detente settled over UVM proper and the city of Burlington.

Nevertheless, what was true about relations between Burlington and UVM proper was not true about relations between the city and UVM's semi-autonomous medical center. During June 1987, the Sanders administration boldly billed the Medical Center and Hospital of Vermont (MCHV) for $2.8 million and initiated a suit challenging its tax-exempt status. Sanders claimed: "There was a time in our country, perhaps 100 years ago, when hospitals actually were for all intensive [sic] purposes really charitable institutions." Citing the small amount of free care and the bill-collecting procedures of the hospital, Sanders claimed that this historical charitable status should be revoked.[17] To no one's surprise, the MCHV challenged the assessment in the Vermont courts, and, despite devoting only 1 percent of revenues to free care, the hospital unequivocally won the suit. Not even the parking garage was taxable! Although Sanders had claimed in true socialist rhetoric that "history will be on our side," it would not be for the foreseeable future.[18]

While the not-for-profit sector was fighting any Progressive Coalition attempt to tax it, in February 1983 Judith Stephany, the Democratic nominee for mayor, was arguing for the repeal of the city's inventory tax. According to Stephany, tax repeal would cost the city about three million dollars, but keeping the tax would cost more in the long run since the inventory tax would deter new investment; upon repeal, the shortfall could be made up by tax classification.[19] Sanders, since his election, had taken a mostly different approach to tax reform than Stephany, but he was lobbying the Vermont legislature without success for tax classification, a way to redistribute the burden of the property tax onto business. While Stephany proposed a tax cut exclusively for business, Sanders was asking the Board of Aldermen to reduce the general property tax by ten cents per hundred dollars. Since repeal of the inventory tax would make such a tax reduction impossible, the mayor's proposal exposed the consequences of Stephany's pro-business position.

Sander's position on the inventory tax was not totally inflexible. He frequently challenged business groups (who, oddly enough, asked the socialist mayor to speak at their forums) to come up with an alternative tax that fell on business to make up for lost revenues if the inventory tax were to be repealed. He was adamant about there being a business tax of some sort: "There is no way in God's Heaven I will ever support doing away with the inventory tax unless there is another tax on business to replace it."[20] Until the very end of 1985, repeal was the only response from the business sector; Sanders' opposition to repeal kept the inventory tax on the books through 1985. The threat of a veto by the mayor, which would have amounted to his using the status quo bias of the federal system, prevented the pro-business reform of inventory tax repeal from appearing on the aldermanic agenda until business offered an alternative tax on itself. The inventory tax did provide 12.5 percent of the total taxes collected.

Sanders, wary of his predecessor's fall, held the line on property taxes in 1982, 1983, and 1984, except for temporary small property tax increases for specific departments. This policy could not continue indefinitely since inflation, federal aid cutbacks, and the Coalition's development plans required that there be more revenue. By January 1985, the administration projected that the new fiscal year's budget, which started in July, would have a $650,000 deficit; a $.27 tax increase would be needed to cover it if no alternative sources of funds were found.[21] In addition, Burlington's school system, a virtual parallel local government, was running a large deficit. The state-enforced dependence of municipalities on the property tax and the local property tax revolt were on a collision course.

To avoid the collision that could effectively sink the Sanders administration's economic initiatives, the mayor proposed an increase in city fees. Sanders' response dovetailed with nationwide efforts by cities to collect revenue from user fees and other fees. By 1981 such fees accounted for 23.2 percent of revenue collected by cities.[22] Although late to follow national trends, Burlington was ahead of the rest of Vermont communities, which received a whopping 99.3 percent of their local tax revenue from property taxes, the second highest dependency in the nation.[23] Sanders offered a simple fee proposal: a property transfer charge of 0.5 percent. (The state already levied a fee of 0.5 percent.) It would raise a projected $300,000 a year in real-estate-investment-rich Burlington. The property transfer fee needed aldermanic, city voter, and state approval, respectively.[24] Although such a tax would be just as regressive as the property tax when placed on moderately priced homes, moderately priced homes, for the most part, were no longer being built in Burlington. Buyers of high-priced condominiums and commercial properties would presumably be paying for most of these transfers. Predictably, local real estate interests were steadfastly opposed. Despite such opposition, the Board of Aldermen voted to put the transfer fee on the March 1985 ballot.

Sanders' 1985 mayoral challenger, Democratic nominee Brian Burns, offered to support the tax if single-family houses were exempted. Burns also advocated a modest city-funded property relief program to low-income renters.[25] Burns' sincerity was in question, since he refused to offer any proposal to pay for these progressive programs. The issue became moot when Burns was trounced by Sanders in the March 5 election.

On that same March 5, 1985, ballot, Burlington's voters approved the following charter changes sponsored by the Progressive Coalition: the property transfer tax, a 1.5 percent rooms and meals levy for the schools, and a broadly worded section that would allow the city to abate the impact of the coming property reappraisal on taxpayers through tax classification or other means. With the first and second steps of charter change completed, appointees testified at the state capitol for approval by Vermont's legislators, the final step.[26] Both the 0.5 percent land transfer tax and the 1.5 percent room and meals tax matched existing state levies. By the end of March, the influential Municipal Corporations and Elections Committee of Vermont's lower house rejected all proposed city charter changes by an overwhelming 8-to-2 vote.[27] On April 17, the full House killed all of the proposals by a 71-to-46 vote. A fear was expressed by state legislators that Burlington was encroaching on the state's taxing powers.[28] Even a proposed charter change designed to soften the impact of property tax reappraisal was killed by the legislature, although it did not directly compete with any state taxing prerogative.

With state rejection of Burlington's tax initiatives, the collision between Burlington's taxpayers and the Sanders administration seemed imminent. Shortly after the defeat at Montpelier, the aldermen approved a School Board request for a public referendum proposing a one-year emergency tax increase of twenty-four cents per hundred dollars of assessed property. Despite Sanders' endorsement, the June 1985 vote was 2,441 to 2,353. The tally failed, far short of the two-thirds approval ratio necessary for passage. The School Board chairman, Francis Palm, predicted a $550,000 slash in the budget.[29] The dependence of Burlington on property taxes combined with voter resistance to tax increases acted as a vise on the municipality's budget. Subsequently, both the city and the School Board accepted lower budgets. Sanders raised user fees in most departments while submitting a 1985–86 budget that asked for no property tax increase. The seeming result of Burlington's taxpayer revolt was austerity. So far, progressive attempts at tax diversification had failed.

Although the Sanders administration had stayed within an austere budget, the completed reappraisal of Burlington's property kept the administration under siege by irate taxpayers. General Electric (GE) claimed that the city's $6,474,800 appraisal was $2,500,000 too high and asked the aldermen for a reduction. Even with the higher reappraisal figure, GE was already receiving a windfall tax break; taxes would drop from $253,883 to $197,711 a year. Apparently for GE's executives, Burlington's fiscal crisis was irrelevant; the corporate bottom line, however, was extremely relevant. The failure of the Vermont legislature to allow tax classification protected GE from paying taxes at a rate higher than that for homeowners. In fact, forty-two commercial properties and ten industrial properties received tax cuts in 1985 because of "fair market" reappraisal.[30] Sanders now called reappraisal "the reverse Robin Hood principle. . . . You're taking from the poor and giving to the rich."[31]

For Burlington homeowners, the fair in "fair market" was less than equitable. Seventy-five percent of single-family homeowners were paying increased taxes; only 10 percent registered declines. The city treasurer, Jonathan Leopold, claimed there was "an average increase for residential taxpayers of 20 percent and a decrease for businesses of 15 percent."[32] In the impoverished Old North End, an incredible 95 percent of homeowners had tax increases; three-quarters of that number had increases of 45 percent and higher.[33] Eighty-three-year-old Sadie White, an early Sanders' supporter on the Board of Aldermen, saw her Old North End home rise in value from $8,900 to $48,200. Her tax bill went up to $250; her monthly Social Security check was less than $400.[34] The Old North End was a bastion of support for the Progressive Coalition. Now, because of a state-enforced mandate, the Sanders administration had increased the tax load of the poorest part of the city, the increment of savings being passed on to an elite minority of wealthy new homeowners and the business community. Burlington's state-imposed reliance on property taxes forced a democratic regime dedicated to the working class to redistribute the burden of municipal taxation onto those who could least afford to pay it.

Nevertheless, tax classification was not totally dead. In late 1985, with a fiscal crisis looming, Sanders appointed a panel, mostly comprised of businessmen, to come up with tax proposals. The businessmen approved a trade-off. Repeal the inventory tax, and business would give its approval to a gross receipts tax on rooms and meals and to tax reclassification. With business support, the Vermont legislature approved a six-to-five business/residential ratio for assessing taxable property. Over $1 million was raised, although $400,000 was lost from the inventory tax repeal. Later, one businessman challenged the tax rate in the Vermont courts as a violation of the Fourteenth Amendment to the United States Constitution; ultimately he lost.[35]

Another property tax initiative proposed by the Sanders administration was an innovative anti-speculation tax. The Sanders administration argued that the sky-rocketing prices of real estate and rents in Burlington were exacerbated by speculators who bought property and resold it rapidly for a quick profit. Sometimes repairs were performed; often they were not. The tax proposed in 1986 would discourage speculation by taxing resale on a progressive scale; taxes would be directly proportional to the length of time the property was owned (based on a six-year time span) and the amount of profit made.[36]

Opposition party aldermen opposed the tax, claiming that high real estate prices were simply a function of too little supply and too much demand. Subsequently, Democratic and Republican aldermen, voting as a bloc, refused to put the tax proposal on the March 1986 ballot. Vermont Tenants, Incorporated, a tenant rights group, collected sufficient signatures to put the anti-speculation tax on the ballot. Janet Dunn, a prominent realtor, organized an effective campaign against the proposal for that business sector. By the thin margin of 2 percent, the measure went down to defeat.

In the fall of 1986, the Coalition watered down the proposal, reducing the original six-year turnover provision to two years (thus narrowing the net for those who would be taxed) and allowing deductions for improvements. Now the measure passed the Board of Aldermen, with Republican votes, to be placed before the voters. (Republican aldermen likely assumed a defeat at the polls since they opposed the measure.) The measure was adopted by an uncomfortably thin six-point margin. Sanders then personally took the fight to the state legislature for a charter change approval. With anti-Sanders and anti-Burlington attitudes prevailing, the lower house turned down the proposal by a ten-vote margin. Vermont vetoed the people of Burlington once again.[37]

One last attempt by the Sanders administration to levy a disguised property tax on business and the not-for-profit sector must be mentioned. Throughout the 1980s, childcare was in a crisis situation for parents who worked in Burlington. For low-income parents, the only sliding-scale daycare was provided by a center in City Hall. Its only subsidy from the Sanders administration was a reduced rent, despite urgent pleas from the center and the Women's Council for monetary help. In 1985, a commission on daycare asked for a ten-cent property tax increase to help; Sanders refused. With no subsidies, salaries were barely over minimum wage; staffing in labor-scarce Burlington was difficult to keep. In 1987 Sanders reluctantly asked the Finance Board to give $7,500 to the facility.[38]

Pressured by supporters, in 1988, the Sanders administration finally proposed a $600,000 tax on business and nonreligious, not-for-profit corporations to make childcare available to the residents of Burlington. The Democrats and Republicans refused to put the levy on the ballot until the Progressives allowed it to be amended to provide daycare only for children whose parents worked in Burlington. Many of these parents were not even residents of Burlington. The Progressives acquiesced, but Sanders angrily remarked: "It's the only time in my life I've ever heard of a [proposed] charter change being passed that won't benefit all the people of the city."[39] With the tepid public support of the mayor, it was no surprise when in the March election, the proposal was defeated. Even had it passed, the next hurdle—the Vermont legislature—would likely have tripped the proposal.

If struggle is the measure of performance, the Progressive Coalition receives credit for its attempts to reform property taxes; however, if actual results are the measure, the Coalition receives little credit for its mildly successful attempt to redirect property taxes onto business.

PROPOSED REFORMS

For real estate taxes in Burlington there were seven major proposed reforms:

- repeal of the inventory tax
- tax reappraisal of property values
- taxing speculation
- taxing property transfers
- taxing not-for-profits
- tax reclassification
- taxing for daycare

Repeal of the inventory tax was successfully thwarted by the Progressive Coalition until alternative taxes on business were agreed on. Reappraisal of property values was implemented. The speculation tax and the property transfer fee were thwarted by the Vermont legislature. Taxing not-for-profits was turned down both by the Vermont legislature and the Vermont courts. Tax reclassification was initially turned down by the legislature and later accepted. The daycare levy never made it past Burlington's voters.

The initially unsuccessful attempt by business to repeal the inventory tax was a Progressive Coalition success. Repeal of the inventory tax with no compensating levy on business would have been a straightforward reactionary reform. This local tax was one of the few taxes that remained on Burlington's business sector after the 1981 Reagan tax cuts that almost abolished the national corporate income tax. Business opposition to the inventory tax had resulted in a bill being passed in the Vermont legislature and signed into law that allowed local communities the option of repealing such a levy. The business offensive from the mid-1970s into the 1980s produced reactionary reforms at all levels of the federal system.

Since Burlington was a winner city, attracting new investment despite its elected radical officials, the Progressive Coalition could resist scare demands for repeal. The magnitude of the city's business confidence was verified in the November 11, 1985, issue of *U.S. News and World Report* (the most conservative of the three top U.S. news magazines), which ranked the "business climate" of seventy-four metropolitan areas in the nation. Burlington placed ahead of New York, Los Angeles, and Baltimore. In fact, Burlington ranked eighth, based on three factors: rate of employment, income of workers, and amount of new construction. The official unemployment rate for Burlington was 3.5 percent, 50 percent less than the national average. And employment was on the increase; the number of jobs grew 4.7 percent over the previous year. Income for the average factory worker was $20,742, which was 6 percent higher than the previous year. Also, new construction in Burlington, a crucial barometer of investment, was up 7.5 percent over 1984, which was also a banner year.[40]

Such past growth was impressive, especially considering that all of these construction activities would appear miniscule if the proposed waterfront development plan was ever accepted. With public approval accruing to the consistently reelected Sanders administration, which presided over this economic prosperity, business had important but limited influence over the policies of local government. If the businesses that wanted the inventory tax repealed—mostly wholesalers, retailers, and manufacturers—threatened disinvestment, there would likely be office and hotel developers ready to buy and transform any vacated space. The postindustrial sector's extensive need for office space was not dampened by a tax on inventory.

Despite the limited influence of business on government, business still had its public defenders among local politicians and the press. Judith Stephany and the *Burlington Free Press* Editorial Board argued for repeal of the inventory tax on the grounds that retaining it would cause economic stagnation. At one point, the editors of the *Burlington Free Press* concluded that the relocation of the New England Telephone offices from Burlington to South Burlington represented an effort to avoid the tax. This dire scenario about capital flight was shown to be erroneous by Assistant City Attorney John Franco, who reminded the embarrassed editors that the types of telephone company equipment ostensibly subject to the inventory tax had been given special tax exemption by Vermont continuously since 1882.[41] In truth, Burlington's major problem in the period under question was not that of attracting new capital. The Progressive Coalition was actually in the fortunate position of trying to shape new investment to benefit the majority rather than tailoring every proposal to the wishes of business. Without a credible threat of disinvestment, the proponents of inventory tax repeal could not marshal support to counter Sanders' opposition. If Burlington had been in a state of economic decline, business demands would have carried more weight. Even so, as this case and that of the Southern Connector demonstrate, a well-organized, resolute opposition has the advantage of maintaining the status quo of government policy. Negative power relations, such as a sure mayoral veto, made any decisive attempts at repeal not worth starting.

In the end, the business community did manage to facilitate the repeal of the inventory tax. However, it was on Sanders' terms: a tax on business had to replace it. A 1 percent gross receipts tax and tax reclassification (which taxed business property 20 percent more) were the quid pro quo for repeal. The tax reclassification was a successful liberal reform that shifted business taxation to the rate that had existed before property reappraisal.

We can give the Progressive Coalition and Mayor Sanders credit for exacting a commensurate price for accepting the pro-business reform, repeal of the inventory tax, but their support of citywide property reappraisal does not deserve such praise. Property reappraisal was a reactionary reform. Even though the state of Vermont mandated such a reevaluating of real estate prices, the undemocratic result was a shifting of the tax burden away from industry and commerce to homeowners and renters. In fact, the Sanders administration was not surprised at this outcome. After reappraisal notices and the new tax bills were sent out, Sanders made clear the difference he perceived between reappraisal in theory and reappraisal in practice. Sanders supported reappraisal in theory "because it is appropriate if you're going to tax property, you have to know what the property is worth"; but in practice, "It's been no secret to those of us in Burlington that reappraisal would bring devastation to low-income and working class homeowners."[42] These strong words and similar allusions to the financial burdens that would result from reappraisal inspired an editorial by the *Burlington Free Press* accusing Sanders of "scare tactics."[43]

If Sanders and his supporters knew that reappraisal would mean a proportional redistribution of the tax burden from business to homeowners and renters, why did they endorse such a reactionary proposal? There were three reasons. First, as already mentioned, was the state of Vermont's mandate; Burlington could ill afford a cut in state funding to its schools. Second, and equally important, was the Progressive Coalition's optimistic hope that both the public and the state would approve of new taxes not based directly on property. The property transfer tax and the gross receipts tax on meals and rooms, if adopted, could have resulted in a lowered property tax. The Vermont legislature initially vetoed these voter-approved proposals. Third, at the same time the Vermont legislature was denying charter changes to allow new forms of city taxation, the House killed Burlington's proposed charter amendment to allow tax classification.

Tax reclassification was the Progressive Coalition's proposed liberal reform that would undo the ill effects of property reappraisal, a reactionary reform. As a reform, tax reclassification would allow the city of Burlington to tax industry and commercial properties at a higher rate. Tax reclassification is based on an assumption that property that is used to create profit is qualitatively different from property that is a person's domicile. (Apartments owned by landlords actually fall in between.) Tax reclassification would allow Burlington to shift the burden of taxation proportionately but not completely from homeowners and renters to business property owners. There could have been tangible benefits for the majority of Burlington's citizens if the rate of difference in taxation had been wide enough: either reduced taxes or more city services. Despite such benefits, tax reclassification falls short of being a democratic structural reform. The final adoption of tax reclassification in 1986 proves this. Business was soon taxed more in Burlington, but within certain narrow limits. In Burlington, the business tax assessment was based on valuing property at 120 percent; residential remained at 100 percent. The business share of the tax burden was now just about the same as it was before tax reappraisal. If business were assigned all or most of the load (which would be illegal under Vermont law), Burlington's rating of business confidence would drop precipitously. Existing businesses would make plans to relocate, the likely threat of which would be enough to reverse any tax policy that would seriously impinge on business profits. In short, tax reclassification in Burlington was moderate enough to accommodate the needs of capitalism, a liberal reform.

Likewise, the property transfer fee was a proposed liberal reform. Any attempt to raise this above a few percentage points would have the counter-intentional effect of discouraging new real estate investment or, even worse, of raising monthly rents on apartments. There were definite limits to tax reform that constrained any progressive initiative.

Taxing speculation was another proposed liberal reform, one that the Vermont legislature vetoed. The watering down of the measure after an initial defeat at the polls by the local real estate lobby suggests that even liberal reform varies within the continuum of reactionary to democratic structural reform. While both tax-speculation proposals were liberal reforms, the second measure was tepid enough that the real estate community did not bother to oppose it; and while it was passed by the voters, it did not do so by a large margin. The ethos of both capitalism and its accompanying progrowth attitudes was spread wide throughout Burlington. The speculation tax mildly contradicted that ethos. Even Rick Sharp, the most visible Burlington environmentalist, was a developer. Only the most blatant profit-takers would be regulated under the voter-approved version of the antispeculation tax. Even that incursion into the marketplace was too much for the Vermont legislature.

The attempt to tax the not-for-profit sector was another liberal reform, but one that approached radical significance. Parts of the not-for-profit sector have become places for capital accumulation that accept direct taxpayer subsidies and provide a shelter from taxes. Even the business community recognized that the UVM complex was not paying its share of taxes. Although the University of Vermont and its affiliated medical center have no stockholders, they do support a large number of well-heeled elites. For example, the Sanders administration's suit against the tax-exempt status of the Medical Center and Hospital of Vermont resulted in a public disclosure of the president's salary: $110,671 in 1985 and over $140,000 in 1986.[44] Many doctors using the same facilities made probably even more. This portion of the not-for-profit sector is really capitalism without dividends or corporate taxes, and with direct taxpayer subsidies. Sanders' failed attempt to tax these institutions at least unmasked their "charitable" facade. Nevertheless, the moderate 25 percent of assessed property proposed clearly denoted this measure as more a liberal than a democratic structural reform. Even in the unlikely event that Burlington won the right to tax on appeal, the lowered rate would not threaten these institutions. They would do what all capitalists do with taxes if the market allows: pass them on to the customer.

The Progressives' last attempted tax reform, the daycare levy, was a circuitous means of laying new taxes on business and the not-for-profit sector. It was a property tax on business and not-for-profit corporations, without using the word "property." This moderate, liberal reform was effectively gutted by Republican amendment. By changing the measure to use city taxes to facilitate suburban welfare, the Republican minority encouraged electoral defeat. If adopted, the daycare levy would redistribute tax dollars disproportionately to the middle and upper ranks of the middle class. Taking from business and the not-for-profits to give to those who can afford private daycare is insignificantly progressive at best. A well-intentioned, solid liberal reform proposed by the Progressives became a marginal liberal reform; its death at the polls was expected.

GROSS RECEIPTS TAX ON ROOMS AND MEALS

As soon as Bernard Sanders was elected mayor, he began tirelessly to find a way to expand the tax revenue of Burlington by diversifying its tax base away from property taxes. While running for election in 1981, Sanders espoused a city income tax; soon after taking office, he switched his energies to fighting for a gross receipts tax on rooms and meals.[45]

Since Burlington is host to many students and business persons and a smaller number of tourists, it has many restaurants and bars. It was therefore not surprising when a special tax committee created by Mayor Sanders in 1981 recommended a rooms and meals gross receipts tax that was intended to fall heavily on commuters and students.[46]

Here was a way of taxing the often more affluent suburbanites and their progeny, outsiders against whom there was widespread resentment for their use of Burlington's public facilities, such as crumbling roads and overfilled sewers, without charge. In December 1981, Sanders asked the opposition-dominated Board of Aldermen to consider a gross receipts tax ranging from 1 percent to 3 percent, each percentage point being worth $325,000 to the city, according to Jonathan Leopold, the city treasurer. Seeking to defray criticism that such a tax was as regressive as (if not more than) the property tax, Sanders argued that a rooms and meals tax fell on "those individuals who are best able to pay. . . . Nobody forces people to go out to a restaurant, to a bar, and spend 20 or 30 bucks."[47] Thus the Progressive Coalition argued that such spending was discretionary, since it did not tax essentials.[48] For them, it seemed a feasible substitute for the property tax.

A potential stumbling block was the state's approval. Vermont already had a rooms and meals tax of 5 percent, and, like Burlington, the state was running a deficit. In fact, in 1981 the Vermont Senate passed a 2 percent increase in the rooms and meals tax that would have made the levy a total of 7 percent if the Vermont Hospitality and Travel Association (the state's restaurant lobby) had not successfully blocked the measure in the House.[49]

Despite the state legislature's failure to increase the levy, many influential state officials were opposed to Burlington's effort to piggyback a city tax on top of a state tax. When Sanders testified before Peter Giuliani, the influential House Ways and Means Committee chairman, Giuliani was adamant in his opposition. Even though the legislature had granted Burlington the right to impose a rooms and meals tax in 1949, Giuliani promised: "If it appears they [the city leaders] are serious about it, of course we will pass a bill against it."[50] Republican Governor Richard Snelling, a Burlington resident, also publicly opposed the gross receipts tax on rooms and meals, rejecting it as a "tax on outsiders."[51] In February 1982, despite the opposition of such political notables, the Vermont House surprised most observers and decisively rejected Giuliani's proposed charter bill, which would have revoked Burlington's right to impose the tax. Arguments for local control, not progressive taxation, won the battle in the House. It was one thing to deny new powers; however, it was something else to strip existing authority. After the upset, a spokesperson for the Vermont

League of Cities and Towns claimed that over 50 percent of Vermont's cities were searching for alternatives to the property tax.[52]

After the Progressive Coalition won an upset victory at the state level, the Burlington Hotel and Restaurant Association began spending copiously to defeat any anticipated referendum. The association hired Bernard Walp, a professional media consultant who had previously executed a successful twenty-thousand-dollar campaign to protect the city's landlords. In that 1981 referendum, voters turned down a proposed fair housing commission by a four-to-one margin, despite Mayor Sanders' support.[53] To pay for Wolf, forty-nine restaurateurs were asked at an organizational meeting in March 1982 to contribute one hundred dollars or more. Their goal was to change public opinion about the gross receipts tax on rooms and meals. This was an uphill battle, since a recent poll had shown that 65 percent of Burlington's citizens supported the Coalition proposal.[54] To help sway opinion, Walp distributed misleading brochures, which made the proposed tax appear to be on groceries.[55] This business-sponsored campaign would ultimately prove successful.

While the restaurateurs mobilized, Sanders had to struggle to even get the gross receipts tax placed on the ballot. In May 1982, the aldermanic opposition (five Republicans and two of the three Democrats) voted against allowing the issue to be put before the voters. Such stonewalling was surprising, even under such hostile partisan conditions, since Sanders only wanted an advisory question placed on the ballot to register public opinion on the 3 percent gross receipts tax.[56]

The Progressive Coalition, not accepting their defeat by the Board of Aldermen, gathered more than the five hundred signatures required under the city charter to place the question on the ballot without aldermanic approval.[57]

The Progressive Coalition's decision to take their case directly to the people proved to be a serious miscalculation. The June 8, 1982, vote for the rooms and meals tax was defeated by the slim margin of forty-five votes. The class nature of the vote was telling; voters in the impoverished Old North End strongly supported the measure, while voters in the two wealthiest wards strongly opposed it.[58] Perhaps the restaurateurs had beaten Sanders by convincing the public that the gross receipts tax was really a "food and beverage" tax.[59] An alternative explanation may be inferred from the simultaneous defeat of two other taxes that same day; a slim majority of Burlington's citizens may have been voting against any tax, not just property tax. Whatever the reason for defeat of the tax, Sanders lashed out at the restaurateurs' tactics. Notwithstanding his previous commitment to abide by the voters' decision, Sanders decided to ask the Board of Aldermen to pass a lower, 1.5 percent levy. Opposition aldermen defeated the new proposal on partisan lines. The gross receipts tax lay dormant for two and one-half years, only to be revived in 1985.

In January 1985, the School Board was faced with a projected $650,000 deficit. Instead of asking for a $.28 increase in the property tax (which would likely be rejected by the voters), the board, with the Progressive Coalition backing, voted for a 1.5 percent gross receipts tax that would raise $675,000.[60] Despite spoken worries of a state veto, only two Republican aldermen voted against putting the proposed levy to a public vote.[61] The first step of the three-step process of approval was completed; the next step was voter approval. From past experience, the Coalition knew voter approval could not be taken for granted.

This time the potential opposition, the restaurant sector of the business community, was divided. Since the money was for the separately budgeted and administered School Board, the usual business hostility directed at Sanders administration initiatives was not warranted. The reactionary *Burlington Free Press* Editorial Board instinctively opposed the tax.[62] However, the city's restaurateurs, who had mobilized resources to defeat the proposed tax three years earlier, were muted in their opposition and did not mount an effective anti-tax campaign. Although the restaurant sector had previously presented monolithic resistance, it now suffered from division. One restaurateur broke ranks and even argued for the tax: "If I sell a dinner for two for $75, a 1 or 2 percent tax isn't going to scare anyone away. I approve of the concept, because it's the only tax that's fair. It's a luxury tax."[63] Also those who opposed the tax were expecting a state legislative veto if necessary. Without an expensive "vote no" campaign by the city's restaurateurs the chances for voter acceptance were greatly enhanced.

Despite opposition from Democratic mayoral nominee Brian Burns and Democratic Governor Madeleine Kunin, an impressive 60 percent of those who voted on March 5, 1985, approved the rooms and meals tax (a margin almost ten points greater than that of Sanders' own reelection totals).[64] Step two of the adoption process was a stunning success for the Progressive Coalition and the School Board.

With the strong endorsement of Burlington's voters, Sanders and his compatriots aggressively lobbied the Vermont legislature to try to complete step three of the charter change process. The mayor testified that failure to support the proposal would be "striking a dangerous blow to local democracy and citizen input." He went on to ask:

What will Town Meeting Day mean in Vermont if the democratically made decisions of people of any town can be overturned by a handful of legislators on a committee who neither live in the town affected or do not understand the local town problems? Essentially, why should people come out to vote in local elections if their vote means nothing?[65]

Despite Sanders' eloquence, in April 1985 the state legislature rejected the rooms and meals gross receipts tax, along with the transfer tax and property tax reclassification charter changes. Rejection by the House reflected a fear by rural legislators from low-income areas that relatively affluent Burlington would preempt future sources of state taxation. Also, on a personal level, state legislators despised the abrasive Sanders, who lectured them during hearings for city charter changes. After the House vote of seventy-one to forty-six, Sanders commented: "The Vermont Legislature told the people that their wishes and their views as to how they want to run their government are meaningless and that the only solution to their problems is higher property taxes."[66] The recently revived gross receipts tax on rooms and meals was temporarily killed by those who controlled a key component of Vermont's government, one of many veto points in the federal system.

After the spring 1985 defeat, the city was facing a $1 million deficit. That fall Sanders established an exploratory committee packed with businessmen to study alternatives to the property tax. In a 1986 report, the committee made a compromise with the Sanders administration. It proposed a 1 percent gross receipts tax on arcades, theaters, and eating establishments and tax reclassification, with business picking up a larger share of costs. In return for these business concessions, the inventory tax would be dropped and an automatic sunset provision would be attached to the gross receipts tax. With business support, all aldermen except one Republican voted for the proposal. The state of Vermont accepted both the tax reclassification and the gross receipts tax.[67] By compromising with business and delegating to them the legislative function of writing a tax proposal, the local state, now victorious, proved that it is possible to have liberal tax reform that is acceptable to business.

Although the gross receipts tax was implemented, it remained open to challenge. Saga Food Service, the UVM caterer, challenged the tax in the Vermont courts because the university is a tax-exempt institution.[68] The hurdles that the Progressives jumped to promote tax diversification never seemed to end.

PROPOSED REFORM

The gross receipts tax on rooms and meals proposed by the Sanders administration was a reactionary reform and thus deserved its initial defeat at the polls. Contrary to the rhetoric of Progressive Coalition members, who claimed that the proposed tax was progressive because it was levied on discretionary spending and not on necessities, it was, in fact, regressive. All sales taxes (the gross receipts tax being a sales tax by another name, merely a legal maneuver) are regressive in that flat tax percentage rates take proportionately more money from low-income than high-income earners.

The primary reason the Coalition chose this gross receipts tax was that it was a levy that could be aimed at outsiders. If the tax was in any way progressive, it was in its being targeted at suburbanites who benefit from utilizing Burlington's city services such as roads and toilets but escape paying most of the costs of these services by living in the suburbs. Another reason the Coalition chose this tax was that there were few tax choices available; the most progressive tax—a graduated income tax—was unfeasible. The contradictory voter responses of defeating and then passing the tax were congruent with the inescapable costs and benefits of a regressive tax that attempts to tax suburbanites but catches in its net every city resident who wants to have a beer. In all likelihood, a gross receipts tax on rooms and meals applied strictly to outsiders would have garnered a positive vote in the first referendum, but it would be difficult to enforce (bartenders would have to be able to distinguish between residents and suburbanites) and unconstitutional (an infringement of the Fourteenth Amendment's equal protection of the laws clause).

The tax was disingenuously sold to the voters by the Coalition as being a "discretionary spending" levy. It is true that if a tax were applied exclusively to expensive luxuries, it could be justified, since workers who receive lower incomes would not be purchasing such goods or services. The purchase of caviar should be taxed on the grounds that it is not a basic necessity; such a tax is not regressive. Similarly, upscale restaurateurs who charge seventy-five dollars for a dinner for two would find a meals tax of a few percentage points no problem (nor likely would their customers). However, the tax in question is not so exclusively targeted. Inexpensive fast-food places and moderately priced restaurants would also be charging those same regressive taxes under the Progressive Coalition proposal. In fact, any worker who chooses not to carry his lunch or dinner to work would be taxed at those same rates. Keeping food prices low fulfills an essential human need for the poorer classes; any measure that raises the price of moderately priced food is decidedly regressive.

The idea that purchasing restaurant-prepared food is "discretionary" is a flawed generalization. Working parents, either couples or those from Burlington's many single-headed households, do not have much time to spend on food preparation, and now, in most families almost all able-bodied adults under retirement age are working or looking for work. Restaurant-prepared meals have become part of the rising tide of human needs, and as such they should not be regressively taxed. Burlington's radical leaders cannot consistently argue for municipally owned cable television while taxing human needs that are obviously more basic. By doing so, they open themselves to justified ridicule from reactionary as well as progressive groups.

The rooms and meals tax is regressive, not progressive, because it taxes lower-income people proportionately more than upper-income people; taxing outsiders is equally regressive. Suburban entrepreneurs, top corporate managers, and upper echelons of the new middle class would provide some revenues to Burlington's progressive city government under such a tax. The current reliance on local property taxes combined with the typical class segregation of Burlington's suburbs insulates these favored recipients of capitalist benefits from most of the city's taxes. On the more regressive side, the unsophisticated bluntness of a flat-rate rooms and meals tax falls more heavily on suburban secretaries, divorced female heads of households, students, and other suburbanites of low or moderate income. Because the proposed tax would have no minimum threshold, it would be a tax on all outsiders, not merely the wealthy.

One group of outsiders for whom the tax would be most unfair is residential students, most of whom are from moderate-income families. Since there is not enough dormitory space for students at the institutions of higher learning in Burlington, they are forced to live off campus. Severed from school cafeterias, these students often eat at fast-food and moderately priced restaurants. It would not be progressive to tax these outsiders, who actually spend most of the year as city residents. The Progressive Coalition's crude instrument designed to tax outsiders is thus a parochial response that would tax those who can and those who cannot afford to pay, alike.

In 1985, this parochial approach angered the Vermont House, which rejected the proposed charter changes needed to enact this reactionary reform. By Vermont standards, Burlington, with all its poor, is a wealthy community. For example, outside of Burlington 20 percent of Vermont's five-year-olds have no public kindergarten available.[69] Burlington's complaints of overused sewers are more than matched by rural Vermont's numerous outhouses. Because the rest of Vermont is significantly poorer, it should have been no surprise to the Coalition that rural state legislators (who are in the majority in Vermont) came to oppose Burlington's tax plea. Vermont already had its own 5 percent charge on rooms and meals; if cities could piggyback the state tax with their own levy, then state expansion in this area was increasingly foreclosed. In fact, for most Vermont communities that have few hotels and restaurants, state taxation and redistribution was the only way for them to realize any revenues from this source. Because the state and Burlington were competing for the same regressively collected tax dollar, rural state legislators and a liberal Democratic administration combined to defeat the 1985 city proposal, despite Vermont's strong tradition of local control. For those elected officials whose constituencies were beyond Burlington there was a legitimate dilemma: by keeping the rooms and meals tax exclusively for the state, there could be a progressive statewide redistribution of a regressive tax. By imposing a gross receipts tax, Burlington could redistribute the regressive tax and preserve financial autonomy. Reflecting this ambiguity, Vermont accepted Burlington's modest 1 percent gross receipts tax in 1986. Ultimately Vermont's political culture, which values local control, helped Burlington in its successful effort to convince the state legislature to pass the tax.

UTILITY EXCAVATION FEES

The Sanders administration's efforts to diversity tax revenue sources involved several major initiatives. The attempt to impose either a rental or an excavation fee on the utility companies provoked an acrimonious response. There was a firm need for such fees. Burlington's streets and sidewalks, neglected for a decade by the previous Democratic administrations, were in a serious state of disrepair. Because of increased building and hook-ups in the city, the number of utility excavations approached twelve hundred in the period 1978–82. The costs of economic development were accruing rapidly. According to Mayor Sanders, "Each one of these excavations has been patched over, some well and some not so well, but every one of them has resulted in the gradual deterioration of our streets."[70] Thus, city officials placed the primary blame for city street disrepair on the utility companies. It was estimated that Burlington's streets needed $1.2 million a year to keep them in serviceable condition. In late 1982, the Sanders administration proposed that a rent be paid by utilities for the right-of-way on city utility poles and under city streets to finance street repair. Such a fee would raise about $1 million a year according to Sanders.[71]

Whether such a fee would be legal under Vermont law was unclear. Utilities promised a long legal fight if such fees were enacted, and subsequent events proved that they were not bluffing. Assistant City Attorney John Franco claimed that the Vermont legislature granted Burlington the right to charge fees for "the use of any street or highway" and for "laying, maintaining and operating" a utility on or under such streets.[72] Lawyers for the utilities claimed Burlington had no such authority under its charter.

Utility opposition to the right-of-way fee was intense; in fact, Green Mountain Cable Television challenged the fee's legality before it was even enacted by the Board of Aldermen. Green Mountain Cable bypassed the state Public Service Board and petitioned at a top tier of the federal system, the Federal Communications Commission (FCC). Covering all bases, Robert Hart, as spokesperson for Green Mountain Cable, claimed the proposed tax was illegal under national, state, and local (the city charter) law.[73] Subsequently, the FCC dismissed the case as moot and suggested that state courts were a more appropriate forum. New England Telephone (NET) joined the fray and sent a letter to Burlington businesses claiming they would be charged the new fee. To illustrate the argument NET added a 4 percent sample surcharge to their bill.[74] NET was using its own billing system for grass-roots lobbying to counter the Sanders administration. The private utilities were united in their opposition to the rental fees.

In May 1983, while the opposition-dominated Board of Aldermen was studying utility right-of-way fees and utility arguments against them, the Progressive Coalition asked the board to levy a one-time excavation fee of twelve thousand dollars on New England Telephone. This fee was to be charged when NET moved underground wiring to make way for the Southern Connector highway. Since the connector was thoroughly bogged down with litigation, the fee was more symbol than substance. Unsurprisingly, opposition aldermen voted it down on combined Democratic/Republican partisan lines.[75] The Progressive Coalition's test of aldermanic sentiment could only have encouraged the utilities to keep fighting.

Fearing a proliferation of utility fee hikes by other communities if Burlington was successful, the utilities spared no expense to fight the Progressive Coalition initiative. Chief executives were trotted out. (At one city hearing, the vice president of NET, Deighton K. Emmons, argued against the fee.) Lawyers for the telephone, gas, and cable utilities argued that if the 4 percent fee were adopted and found legal, each utility would place a surcharge on Burlington customers' bills to pay for it. A Burlington Gas Company representative argued that the surcharge would fall heavily on the impoverished Old North End neighborhood since 50 percent of the gas company's city customers were there.[76] Interestingly, none of the utilities explained why it was so vociferously opposed to the tax if it merely planned to pass it on to its customers. Nevertheless, because the tax-free business privilege of utility line right-of-ways was being challenged by the Sanders administration, the utilities' opposition was unwavering.

Despite the phalanx of utility opposition, the Sanders administration struck back. City officials petitioned the state Public Service Board to find NET's lobbying expense to be nonreimbursable through customer charges. The Sanders administration felt that NET's anti-tax campaign should be borne by shareholders not ratepayers. As Burlington's Assistant Attorney John Franco phrased it: "The company here is not in the business of political consultation, lobbying, or propagandizing. Its business is to provide phone service."[77] Sanders was trying to use state authority to constrain NET's attack on the municipality's initiatives. The PSB consistently favored private utility interests over Burlington's interests.

In time, the Progressive Coalition strategy to thwart the utility power bloc became more sophisticated in its approach. During August 1983, Sanders dropped the utility rental fee proposal and switched to an excavation fee strategy. Instead of a blunt general tax on each utility, the excavation fee was tailored to make each utility pay for its own damages.[78] Just as utilities charge their customers higher fees according to how much use is made of the service, the Sanders administration wanted to charge an excavation fee based on the amount of pavement torn up. The voluminous testimony given by utility lawyers against a gross receipts tax to pay for rental privileges was now mostly irrelevant. By changing to a more conventional argument, Sanders hoped to pick up two opposition votes to add to the five Progressive Coalition votes on the Board of Aldermen in order to obtain a majority.

Despite the administration's change in its strategy, the utilities continued their battle against any increase in charges that was more than token. The proposed excavation fee of $10.13 a square foot would be, according to William Gilbert, a lawyer for both Green Mountain Cable and Burlington Gas, the highest in the nation. A study sponsored by the telephone company concluded that the actual cost should be $1.18 a square foot. According to city officials, the fee proposed by the Progressive Coalition would raise $500,000 a year for city streets ($360,000 from the fee itself and the rest from federal categorical grants). By comparison, the NET study determined that the fee would raise a paltry $41,000. The current fee was an insignificant $.37 a square foot. Implicitly, NET's own study proved that this fee was insufficient, but there was no offer to make up for the insufficient levels of previous years.

To the contrary, utility lawyers loudly complained that Burlington was trying to make up for ten years of municipal neglect by taxing the utilities.[79] In a *Burlington Free Press* editorial entitled, "City's Latest Street Ordinance Proposal Is Absurd," James J. Lehane, Jr., of NET succinctly argued against the Progressive Coalition's tax initiative. Lehane claimed NET had only 9 miles of underground lines in Burlington out of a total of 90 miles of streets. Furthermore, in the last six years NET excavated only 3.3 miles. Of that 3.3 miles, 2.7 were under sidewalk that it replaced. The NET spokesperson pointed out that one reason that the city proposal really irked NET (and other utilities) was that the proposed fee of $10.30 a square foot was in addition to replacement repairs provided by the utilities.[80] Even granting city officials' contention that repaired streets deteriorated at a rate 25 percent faster than that of untouched streets, Lehane's assertion that the fee was too high for replacement work was probably correct.

The real purpose of the excavation fee was the same as that of Sanders' first proposal (a rental fee for city streets and poles): to tax corporate profits to rebuild city streets. Since such a blatant assertion would result in a probable rejection by the business-minded opposition aldermen and Vermont's courts, the Sanders administration changed to a strategy camouflaged by a capitalist logic of pay for what you use while the essential goal remained the same: tax corporate profits rather than real estate for street repair.

Despite the persuasive case by the utilities, in January 1984 the Street Commission formally asked the Board of Aldermen to approve the $10.30 a-square-foot excavation fee.[81] The Sanders administration now had one ally in their fight. It was certainly in the Street Commission's bureaucratic interest to have such a fee, for they needed an estimated total of $7 million to upgrade all of Burlington's streets. However, not all city bureaucracies would profit by the excavation fee. James Howley, superintendent of water resources, claimed the fee would add $10.00 a year to residential water bills.[82] Likewise, the Burlington Electric Department would be taxed for excavations needed for downtown underground lines. The public utilities played it safe, however, despite the costs to their bureaucracies, and left the legal fight to the private utilities.

Having part of the bureaucracy, the Street Commission, solicit the rate hike from the Board of Aldermen did not disguise the fact that the excavation fee was a Progressive Coalition–sponsored initiative. To attain passage from the Board of Aldermen, Sanders offered a package deal: the mayor would support a street appropriation based on a one-year splinter tax increase of sixteen cents per hundred dollars of assessed property. Sanders would offer this ballot support only if the board would pass the Coalition's excavation fee. A mayoral veto would effectively end the splinter tax if the board declined to pass the excavation fee. The opposition made accusations of what they termed "blackmail," and in the final vote only one opposition member joined five Progressive Coalition members in favor of the measure.[83] Thus with three opposition members absent and one seat temporarily vacant, the fee passed six to three in March of 1984. Republican Alderman William Skelton called the new law "taxation without representation, a stand against democracy."[84] Now that the utilities had lost a round at the municipal level, they moved their fight one level up the federal system to the state courts.

In August 1984, a Vermont Superior Court judge ordered the Burlington Street Department to cease collecting the six-month-old excavation fee until the court could rule on the legality of the fee.[85] The state, through its courts, exercised its right to say no, at least temporarily. That same month the Public Service Board ruled that Green Mountain Cable could add a surcharge to Burlington customers' bills to pay for the excavation fee if the court accepted the legality of the fee.[86] The PSB, a state administrative agency, was acting to preserve the profitability of the companies it was charged to regulate. Not only did the PSB accommodate capitalist needs, but it acted to protect them. The state of Vermont's terrain proved hostile to city autonomy.

Continuing the erosion of Burlington's authority, Superior Court Judge Alden T. Bryan ordered, in October 1984, that there should be a hearing to decide the amount of the fee to be charged. John Franco, who had argued for the city, blasted the ruling and characterized it as a "rather astounding construction of the judicial role."[87] According to Franco, the court had chosen to become the city's legislature. Through the courts, the state of Vermont in effect expropriated Burlington's authority to set tax levels. During January 1985, the Supreme Court handed the city a minor victory: the city did have the right to tax for "all costs attributable to the maintenance, repair and deterioration" caused to city streets by utility excavations. However, the city could not charge rent for utility use of city streets. Worst of all for the Sanders administration initiative, the court ruled that "the wording (of the charter) does not permit a charge which is intended to raise general revenues for deposit in (the city's) general fund."[88] In other words, the state ruled that utilities can only be charged for actual damage to municipal property; anything above that is illegal.

To bolster their case for the $10.30 a-square-foot fee, the Sanders administration commissioned a study. Consistent with the unwritten rule that whoever pays for the study receives the conclusions they were seeking to justify, the city-sponsored study released in June 1985 found that utility patching cut a road's lifespan from a normal 18.5 years to 10.9 years (a decline of 41 percent). By these calculations, Franco claimed Burlington was asking for too small a rate increase; $14 to $15 a square foot would be more appropriate.[89] The study was prepared for a November 1985 Superior Court hearing that would accept evidence and testimony from both the city and the utilities concerning the proposed excavation fee rate.

In December 1985, the Sanders administration reached a compromise with Vermont Gas Systems and New England Telephone on the fee issue. In an out-of-court settlement, both companies agreed to pay a total of $1.76 million over a thirty-year schedule, retroactive to July 1984. This meant about $100,000 would be available right away. Sanders admitted that this settlement brought only one-half of what the city was demanding; however, it still represented a victory. City departments would be required to pay the originally proposed higher fee of $10.30 a square foot.[90] Since the imposition of the higher fee really meant a shifting of taxpayers' money to the city's general budget line from the accounts of the BED, Water Resources, and the new Public Works Department (an amalgam of the former separate Streets and Traffic commissions), there would be no net loss on the local government side. However, if the BED and Water Resources raised their rates to recover costs, homeowners and renters would end up paying more in their monthly bills.

Even after the court victory, one city business continued the litigation process. Maurice DuBois Excavating claimed that the utility fee was set arbitrarily, that the fee charged to them was incorrectly assessed, and that the city had no legal right to enact the fee in the first place. As Sanders succinctly put it: "Every one of our progressive tax initiatives has been taken to court."[91]

Thus Sanders scored a minor victory that would help repair city streets after ten years of neglect. However, the question of whether the regressive fees would be passed onto residential customers, dollar for dollar, remained open.

PROPOSED SOLUTIONS

Despite the rhetoric of the Sanders administration that the proposed excavation fee and the proposed rental fee were designed to compensate the city for road and sidewalk deterioration caused by utilities, the evidence lends itself to a conclusion that these fees were a disguised tax on utility profits. This proposed tax was a liberal reform. By collecting taxes from utility profits, the city would be able to repair Burlington's crumbling streets and sidewalks. In so doing it would be not merely providing public subsidies to facilitate capitalist growth; it would be serving the public as well.

Another benefit of taxing corporate profits to fund street repair could be either property tax relief or funds for new programs. Although a splinter tax of sixteen cents per hundred dollars of assessment was levied for street repairs, the larger share of the cost of repairs would have been funded by the excavation fee as originally proposed. Without the fee, the burden of taxation would fall upon the city's regressive property tax. Although the fee was eventually accepted by the court as legal, the amount of revenue collected by the fee that would go beyond taxing for actual deterioration caused by utility companies was modest.

Even in the unlikely case that a $10.30 per-square-foot (or higher) fee had been accepted by the state courts for both private and public utilities, the Public Service Board had already provided a precedent that could reverse the progressivity of any excavation tax. The board had given Green Mountain Cable Television the right to surcharge Burlington's customers to cover the increased costs incurred because of the excavation fee. If all the private gas, cable, and telephone utilities could pass such taxes on to the public (as they claimed they would) and if the public water and electric bureaucracies did the same, the effects would be regressive. Just how regressive would depend on the way the surcharge was imposed. If it was based on the amount of service used, businesses, which are greater users of water, gas, electricity, and telephone services than are residences, would pay a larger proportion of the cost. If it was charged as a flat fee on each gas, water, electricity, and telephone customer regardless of usage, however, homeowners and renters would bear a larger proportion of the cost. For cable television customers such a fee would inevitably be regressive since few businesses subscribe. Thus, the PSB, consistently the friend of business, had the authority to change the nature of this progressive tax, transforming a liberal reform into a reactionary reform.

Even if the state of Vermont had affirmed the higher Coalition-sponsored excavation fee, the reform proposed would still accommodate capital and would thus fall short of a democratic structural reform. Utilities are considered natural monopolies; the tremendous capital expense of creating such a facility precludes local competition. The solution for Vermont and most other states is to allow a utility monopoly under state supervision. The rate of profit is negotiated with and guaranteed by the state. Because of the symbiotic relationship between the PSB and the utilities, however, even if Burlington's excavation fee taxed utility profits, the board would compensate the utility by allowing general rate increases to maintain "acceptable" profits. These rate increases could conceivably be spread statewide, thus relieving Burlington's taxpayers, but in the larger picture this is not a democratic solution.

The rest of Vermont is even poorer than Burlington, so such a spreading of costs would inevitably be at least partially regressive, even if Vermont's industry shouldered a higher proportion of the burden. Poor, rural Vermonters, who can least afford it, would pay more. In the final analysis, the excavation fee can only be a successful liberal reform if the PSB lets it cut into utility profit rates. Unless the Progressive Coalition captures the state legislature and the governor's office, this is not likely to happen. Short of state or municipal socialization, any other reform would have to accept the capitalist requirement of minimal profitability.

ALTERNATIVE REFORMS

Transfer fees, speculation taxes, utility rental fees, gross receipt taxes, daycare assessments, tax reclassification, utility excavation fees, and property taxes on not-for-profits were all liberal reformist attempts to relieve city homeowners and renters of the regressive burden of the property tax. The record of accomplishment is very modest. Even if every proposed tax had been implemented, none would have been a democratic structural reform, that is, one providing benefits to the dominated irrespective of the needs of the predominant structures of power relations.

A local democratic structural tax reform that would replace the property tax could have two parts: (1) a strong progressive city income tax and (2) municipal ownership of essential means of production. Surprisingly, city income taxes are not unusual; in fact, in 1980 14.6 percent of all municipal revenues were raised by such taxes.[92] Bernard Sanders himself proposed (but soon abandoned) a city income tax in his 1981 electoral campaign. In 1985, echoing the early Sanders platform, Springfield, Vermont, proposed a 1 percent income surcharge tied to Vermont's state income tax.[93] Municipal income taxes are common to a few states; those that exist are not democratic structural reforms.

Existing municipal income taxes accommodate the needs of capitalism by being mildly progressive or even outright regressive. Usually they piggyback state income taxes that in turn piggyback the federal income tax with its numerous loopholes for the wealthy. An income tax that would be a democratic structural reform would be strictly progressive (taxing the upper ends of the middle class and above at a much greater rate) and would provide a floor and a ceiling for income. At a specified income level, which would be democratically determined, a threshold would be set for maximum income. Anything over the maximum would be taxed at close to 100 percent. This would be a straightforward confiscation of income for redistribution and a pure democratic structural reform. With this newly acquired revenue, the state could guarantee every citizen a minimum income, the amount democratically determined. The benefits of an income tax like this would flow to the neediest, notwithstanding the needs of capitalism and its favored classes.

A local democratic structural reform of this magnitude would be impossible to implement in a single community. Even if the state and federal governments would allow it (which they would not), capitalism would quickly negate it. Business would disinvest at a precipitous rate, and neighboring communities would welcome this fleeing capital. Not only would wealthier citizens quickly emigrate past Burlington's borders; Vermont's poor (if not the indigent of the entire United States) would rush to be Burlington's new immigrants.[94] The result would be increased demands and decreased resources, a recipe for municipal fiscal collapse.

Since a true democratic income tax is outside the realm of local possibility, could the Sanders administration have implemented a more modest proposal? Could even a progressive, liberal-reform income tax have been implemented? If we consider the fates of the transfer fee, the gross receipts tax, the anti-speculation tax, and the property tax on not-for-profits as exemplars of state response, the answer would have to be a resounding no.

Since Vermont has its own income tax, a city income tax would tax the same sources, the citizenry. In many states this would not mean an automatic veto; more likely there would be limitations placed on a city's income tax. However, Vermont's legislature explicitly rejected Burlington's property transfer tax and rooms and meals tax on gross receipts because the city was infringing on territory heretofore reserved for state taxing purposes. At least during the Sanders reign, any municipal income tax, even of a liberal reformist nature, was out of the question as long as state permission was needed. Any attempt by Sanders to redeem his 1981 election pledge for a city income tax would have been summarily dismissed by Vermont's legislature (if the opposition aldermen did not kill it first).

For a socialist city regime, municipal socialization would be a priority. Yet, municipal socialization of at least part of the means of production would have been impossible. The implementation of the excavation fee on utilities and the attempt to socialize Green Mountain Cable Television were both instructive. Vermont Gas Systems, Cox Communications, and the New England Telephone Company presented a wall of opposition to the excavation fee. Interestingly, the municipally owned Burlington Electric Department and the Department of Water Resources did not publicly oppose the fee. If Burlington had owned and City Hall had controlled the gas, telephone, and cable television utilities, the fee would not have been needed, because the profits that the fee were to tax would have been the city's to spend. Consequently, the excavation fee issue would have been moot. However, if municipal gas, telephone, and cable television were relatively autonomous city agencies, like the BED and Water Resources, the fees might be imposed.

If Burlington had indeed procured the gas, cable, and telephone franchises and added them to its existing municipally owned electricity and water utilities, the city would have owned a significant portion of the local means of production and would greatly have increased its autonomy. Revenues from such municipal industries could, if wisely managed, defray the costs of government; thus, regressive property taxes could be reduced. A most revolutionary democratic structural reform would be socialization of these industries without compensation to their owners. If the owners were compensated, investment dollars would merely perpetuate unequal relations in some new area of investment. No state or federal court, however, would ever allow socialization without compensation; nor would the Public Service Board. In fact, considering the Public Service Board's pro-business stance and that the purchase of such facilities would need a PSB imprimatur, it is almost inconceivable that the city would receive permission even to purchase the facilities at the fair market price. Municipal democratic socialization of utilities in Vermont awaits a Coalition takeover of state government.

TAKING TAX REFORM TO A HIGHER LEVEL

Although this chapter is about the attempts by the city of Burlington to increase its autonomy and implement democratic reforms through city tax initiatives, the Progressive Coalition's state initiatives must be briefly mentioned. After the almost consistent repudiation of city tax initiatives by the state, the Sanders administration proposed an elaborate tax program to be implemented statewide that would relieve the property tax burden. In September 1985 Mayor Sanders combined with the state Parent Teachers' Association and the left-leaning Rainbow Coalition of the Democratic party to present the following plan:

- decoupling the state income tax from the federal level
- removing loopholes and tax breaks from the state tax
- levying a state property tax on commercial and industrial property

- allowing communities to levy taxes other than the present property tax
  . . .
- The first $25,000 of the value of a primary residence would be granted a "homestead exemption" from municipal property taxes
- The state property tax relief program would be beefed up
- The state would pay revenue sharing to municipalities
- State aid to local education would be increased[95]

This package was a very progressive liberal reform but not a democratic structural reform. The Progressive Coalition's consistent failure to reform local taxes through local elected office helped shape this alternative strategy. The election of the Kunin administration, one reputed to be liberal by the mainstream press, did not result in the adoption of this progressive plan. Mayor Sanders, the Progressive Coalition, and other progressive state forces realized that the state level and not the local offered a sufficient degree of autonomy for enacting progressive reform.

7
Foreign Policy

To most political analysts, foreign policy is the responsibility of the national government; state and especially local government are far removed from this sphere of decision making. The Progressive Coalition challenged this model of divided federal responsibility: the Sanders administration had a foreign policy.

A top priority for the Progressive Coalition was United States cooperation with the Soviet Union to reduce the risk of nuclear war. The Coalition also favored a policy of nonintervention by the U.S. government in the domestic affairs of other countries. In fact, the Sanders administration on several occasions demonstrated solidarity with the revolutionary regime of Nicaragua. Although Burlington's foreign policy had no discernible impact on the anti-Marxist proclivity of the Reagan and Bush administrations, it was an attempt at reform.

Most observers think of political reforms as tangible redistributions of resources according to the much-blathered political science definition of "who gets what, when, how."[1] But the Sanders administration's foreign policy initiatives, instead of producing tangible benefits, were designed to change consciousness. The administration was trying to enact reform at an abstract level by offering an alternative socialization stressing the positive value of democratic cooperation with existing socialist countries and movements to replace the typical American's ingrained anticommunism. Attitudes that oppose U.S. hegemony were being fostered to supplant the anticommunist mentality. If such a critical reform of consciousness were successfully disseminated throughout the community of Burlington, it would do little to change national foreign policy. If such attitudes were spread throughout the nation, the consequences would be profound.

Since it would be difficult to measure a community's consciousness without administering opinion polls, this chapter will be confined to the brief histories of several major Sanders administration actions that attempted to further the socialization of attitudes that oppose U.S. hegemony. These actions will include the civil disobedience incident at General Electric, a proposed resolution condemning the invasion of Grenada by the United States, a proposed resolution condemning the State Department's inclusion of Burlington into an area where Soviet citizens were forbidden to travel, and the establishment of friendly relations with both Nicaragua and the Soviet Union.

CIVIL DISOBEDIENCE AT GENERAL ELECTRIC

Burlington is home to a large General Electric defense plant in the city's Lakeside neighborhood. Unlike GE's consumer products divisions, which claimed in the company's slogan to "bring good things to life," the GE Burlington plant produces Vulcan Gatling guns for the United States Department of Defense and for allied nations' military forces. These high technology, conventional weapons are required equipment on many U.S. aircraft, jeeps, and tanks.[2]

The destruction delivered by these weapons is awesome; a six-barrel model can fire an incredible six thousand rounds a minute. The AC-47 planes equipped with three such weapons were called "Puff the Magic Dragon" in Vietnam, and with good reason. The following description of a press correspondent captures the depersonalized killing ability of the Gatling-equipped AC-47: "Capable of circling long hours over a beleaguered fort or outpost, Puff can start the deadly circle quickly and in three seconds cover an area the size of a football field with at least one bullet to every square foot."[3] Used to decimate enemy villages in Vietnam, these Gatling guns have been reported to have been used in a similar fashion by the military in El Salvador.

Although GE Burlington's products could justly be accused of spreading death and destruction in Third World countries under siege by revolutionary forces, for many in the greater Burlington community the company provided positive, lucrative benefits. As the sole supplier of Gatling guns to the United States military, GE could afford to pay high, unionized wages and still post a guaranteed profit. In fact, it was rumored that GE Burlington was GE's most profitable division; however, information about profitability or anything else was scarce. In 1981, when the reformist *Vermont Vanguard Press* was doing a study on the Burlington plant, a tour, photographs, even an in-office interview with the public relations director, were refused. Normal business secretiveness combined with the veil of national security allowed GE to deflect local public scrutiny of its affairs. What was known about GE Burlington's publicly funded largesse was that it provided a yearly $50 million payroll (1981 figures) and was the second largest industrial employer in Vermont (IBM in nearby Essex Junction being first). It was a monopoly supplier, but labor tenure was sporadic because the number of employees fluctuated with military buildups and declines. During the Vietnam War year 1968, GE Burlington employed 3,484; by the détente year 1973, it employed only 1,693.[4] With the Reagan buildup, employment levels were maintained at 2,000 during the period under study. In a community of 38,000, one employer directly providing over 2,000 well-paying jobs has substantial political impact whether it chooses to exercise it or not.

GE Burlington was also a major city taxpayer. Although it was housed in a converted turn-of-the-century textile mill, the company was equipped with large quantities of the latest capital-intensive machinery; whatever was owned by GE, and not by the U.S. government, was taxable under Burlington's business inventory tax. As long as Burlington was dependent on property taxes, GE Burlington's portion was essential for holding the line on real estate taxes, a Progressive Coalition goal.

Despite the material benefits that GE Burlington brought to the community, the Burlington Peace Coalition (BPC), a regional pacifist group, opposed the plant's operation. With competent leaders such as Grace Paley, Robin Lloyd, and Dave Dellinger, all longtime peace activists, the visible local presence of the BPC placed Burlington at the forefront of anti-militarist protest in the 1980s. The ideal goal of BPC members was to have the antiquated General Electric plant converted to civilian production. Robin Lloyd pointed out the contradiction between the reality of a defense plant and the ideal of a peaceful community: "How can we condemn local violence in the streets of Chittenden County [Burlington's county], when we accept institutionalized killing as an economic support for the country?"[5] For the BPC, economic arguments that GE workers and the community were dependent on Burlington GE's defense work did not override the need to stop production of such horrific weapons.

The BPC argued that the positive example of Philadelphia's Boeing Vertol Company provided a feasible economic alternative to the continued war machine. In the Boeing Vertol case, during the late 1970s, the company, a manufacturer of military helicopters, lost its contract for the next generation of such craft. While finishing up the remainder of its helicopter orders, the company eased into the construction of electric trolleys rather than exercise the traditional option of closing the plant. In Burlington, peace activists used this example as a recommended alternative to the typically framed debate of weapons production versus shutdown. GE executives rejected the idea of conversion, saying it was neither possible nor wanted.[6] Since GE could close the plant at will, the company held an effective veto power over alternative production.

In keeping with their activist stance against weapons production, the Burlington Peace Coalition planned a July 1983 civil disobedience demonstration against Burlington GE. Grace Paley, the protest leader, said the group planned to stop trucks from picking up or delivering at the plant. She and Dellinger emphasized that GE workers were not the target of the group's protest activities. To demonstrate their lack of hostility to the plant's workers, the peace activists planned to serve refreshments, including Nicaraguan coffee, to passing employees.[7]

Although a prominent and consistent critic of U.S. foreign policy, Sanders opposed the protest. He was reputedly upset about not being apprised of the BPC's plans before their public announcement.[8] As a former Socialist Workers' party member who emphasized the primacy of the working-class struggle, Sanders was sympathetic to the unionized workers' complaint that they were helpless victims being attacked by the protesters; he had won many endorsements from union members in his 1983 reelection campaign.

Despite the BPC's assertions of amity toward the GE workers, the workers responded with hostility. At a meeting between representatives from the union and the BPC before the civil disobedience action, union leaders class-baited protesters, accusing them of being rich suburbanites threatening workers' jobs.[9]

It was true that many of the peace protesters were not from blue-collar backgrounds and had no direct link to the capitalist mode of production (if we define production as the manufacture of goods). Instead, the protesters were from postindustrial backgrounds, either comfortably middle class or countercultural, and were therefore removed from the intensity of class conflict that was manifested daily on the factory floor.[10] Thus it was not surprising that the issues with which they were most concerned were not directly tied to the struggle of blue-collar workers.

Despite the class differences between the protesters and the blue-collar workers, however, union officials, an elite of the workers, had previously given support to BPC concerns. Francis Moisan, president of Local 248 of the International Union of Electrical, Radio, and Machine Workers, and other union officials had in the past supported BPC marches against the Reagan administration's military build-up: "We marched with those people in Montpelier," he said. "We marched with them in Washington." But he believed it was wrong to attack the plant workers: "I have a family to support and everybody else there has a family to support."[11] The workers refused to accept the BPC's assertions that the proposed action was not directed at the company's rank and file.

Since many of the Burlington Peace Coalition members were also Progressive Coalition activists, Sanders was presented with a dilemma. Supporting one group meant alienating the other. Without hesitation, the mayor tilted toward the union members. He even echoed their class-baiting line:

The result of what they [the BPC] are doing is to point the finger of guilt at working people. Not everybody has the luxury of choosing where they are going to work . . . or the money not to work. . . . The answer is not to blame the workers who are trying to make a living but to change the government.[12]

The BPC accused Sanders of polarizing the situation by dividing the workers from the peace activists. Murray Bookchin, an anarchist scholar and local peace activist, argued: "The mayor is acting as a publicity man for GE, not the socialist mayor of Burlington. . . . As a progressive mayor he should function to bring both sides together."[13] Sanders did attempt to mollify both sides.

During a meeting of union leaders, protest leaders, and the mayor, the BPC, in the face of union intransigence, compromised and moved the protest to a rear gate of GE that was used primarily for deliveries and not by workers.[14] Sanders inaccurately portrayed this acrimonious meeting to the press as friendly.[15] With the BPC at odds with the mayor and union workers, General Electric's plant manager, William J. Cimonelli, acted to aggravate the split in the ranks of the opposition. Cimonelli wrote a public letter: "We believe it is unfair for local GE employees and the company to be subjected to these demonstrations. We believe we are being thrust into the nuclear disarmament controversy simply because we are a convenient target in the region."[16] Thus, by the day of the civil disobedience action, June 20, 1983, the socialist mayor, GE workers, and GE management were all on the same side.

A BPC protest march two days before the action did not include the mayor, who usually took part in such activities. Greg Guma, a local peace activist, summed up the festival atmosphere of the march: "Everyone's mellow here except for Bernie."[17] In addition, that same day Sanders asked the police chief to cancel an agreement with GE to reschedule deliveries or shipments on June 20 to avoid conflict. Both the police chief and GE spokesperson Jack Waller said they had no idea what agreement Sanders was talking about; they may have been trying to avoid an embarrassing public disclosure.

On the day of the civil disobedience action, Burlington's first ever, eighty-eight protesters were arrested for blocking GE's rear entrance; twenty-nine came back to be arrested again. A nervous Mayor Bernard Sanders stood conspicuously behind the police barricades during the first set of arrests. It all went amicably despite the police chief's order to videotape the protest against Sanders' wishes. (As an independent commission, the Police Department could legally ignore Sanders on most issues.) The protesters handed leaflets to stoical GE employees; there were virtually no verbal exchanges. Sanders later stated that he was satisfied with the conduct of everyone involved.[18]

The *Vermont Vanguard Press* editorialized that the incident went off with such quiet that it lost its meaning:

Civil disobedience is supposed to be a strong sentiment of real non-cooperation with government sanctioned atrocities. Officially sanctioned "protests" [quotation marks in original text], even with the sinister overtones provided by police videotaping, are a contradiction in terms.

The deals that the Burlington Peace Coalition struck with General Electric, Mayor Sanders, and the police limiting the demonstration and CD to a backgate should make activists question their own commitment. It is one thing to take a stand for what you believe in and accept the consequences—whatever they may be; it is another when the consequences are so sanitized as to be meaningless.[19]

Despite Sanders' commendation of city police (who did act with restraint), to call the protest "officially sanctioned" was to distort the mayor's opposition to it. A fairer judgment would be that Sanders acted to minimize the damage created by the Progressive Coalition's support of unionists against community peace activists. It was public knowledge that Sanders wanted to cancel the action.

A few days after the protest, Dellinger and Lloyd asked the mayor to create a committee to study the prospects of converting the GE plant to civilian use. Politically astute, Sanders sidestepped the demand by claiming it was too soon for him to make such a commitment. He finessed the specific demand with a platitude: "There's no question we intend to be very active in the whole question of war and peace."[20] But he confronted other foreign policy issues head on and took controversial stands.

THE GRENADA RESOLUTION AND THE STATE DEPARTMENT BAN ON SOVIETS

The months of October and November 1983 were very busy ones for U.S. foreign policy makers. In a rapid succession of events, United States troops invaded Grenada and deposed its government, and the Department of State increased to 20 percent the amount of America off-limits to Russian nationals. The Sanders administration, rejecting its limited role within the federal system, proposed resolutions to the Board of Aldermen on both issues.

The invasion of tiny Grenada by thousands of U.S. troops to depose a Marxist regime, which had established itself by a bloody coup d'etat, aroused angry emotions among Progressive Coalition activists, who could only voice opposition to the national government's action after the fact. The invasion was planned and executed under secrecy by the White House and the Department of Defense. By the time the public was aware, it was faced with a fait accompli. Since the military incursion could not be blocked, it could only be protested.

On October 31, 1985, while U.S. Army Rangers were still wiping out pockets of Grenadan resistance, the Progressive Coalition acted under the leadership of Alderman Terrill Bouricius. The Coalition sponsored a rally outside the Contois Auditorium to encourage their supporters before the evening meeting of the board. The spirited protesters then jammed into the auditorium for the meeting and heard Alderman Bouricius offer a resolution condemning the Grenadan invasion. The resolution, addressed to Congress and the President, urged that U.S. troops be immediately withdrawn from Grenada and that the United States stop hostile actions against Nicaragua. Bouricius described Burlington's citizens to the overflow crowd of three hundred as "a free, independent and moral people who oppose the imperialistic actions and domination of the weak by the strong wherever it occurs."[21]

Many supporters of the resolution, including an impassioned Mayor Sanders, spoke to the board to argue for passage. Sanders told the board that if cities had taken stands against the Vietnam War at an early stage, that tragic conflict might have been curtailed much sooner. He warned that such irresponsible actions by the U.S. could lead to military exchanges with the Soviet Union: "This is putting us on the brink of war to end all wars. And when that moment comes and you turn on the radio, and the sirens come and you wonder whether or not it was appropriate for the Burlington Board of Aldermen to speak out on it, it might be a little bit too late." More concisely, Alderman Peter Lackowski argued: "Even if the lies they're [the U.S. government] putting out were true, it still wouldn't justify what we're doing."[22] Since the crowd was dominated by Progressive Coalition supporters, response to the oratory in support of the resolution was enthusiastic.

Within the crowd, there were anticommunist dissenters to the proposed Grenada resolution. Fire Commissioner Gardner Briggs claimed that if we did not fight the communists in Grenada we would "be fighting them on the Texas border." Republican State Representative Pete Chagnon of Burlington said the proposed resolution sounded as if it had come "out of Havana, Cuba, instead of Burlington, Vermont." Republican Alderman Allen Gear defended the invasion, claiming it "was in part to rescue Americans there but it was also to stop the spread of communism."[23] The debate was more overtly ideological than most issues debated in city halls. The Progressive Coalition hoped that opposition Alderman Maurice Mahoney, a Democrat, would break ranks with the Democratic/Republican opposition and vote with the radicals. These hopes were ended, however, when Mahoney called the resolution unacceptable: "It would be easy for people to pass this tonight, go home, feel smug and self-righteous."[24] Mahoney complained that the resolution should not have been placed at the top of the council's agenda, but he did mention that he could have voted for it if the section condemning U.S. hostility to Nicaragua were deleted.

The resolution was defeated by a five-to-five tie vote: the five Progressive Coalition members voted for it, and the five Democrats and Republicans voted against it. (Two Republicans and one Democrat were missing.)

Two days after the vote, the *Burlington Free Press* Editorial Board chided the Sanders administration for wasting city time on such a debate:

What should be disturbing to the people of the city is that the aldermen spent a considerable amount of time on a foreign policy matter while legitimate city business was ignored and some important issues had to be postponed. . . . [The aldermen] need not be reminded that they were elected by the people to solve city problems, not to engage in debate on matters that really do not fall within the realm of their authority.[25]

Since Alderman Bouricius did not plan to resubmit his Grenada resolution for another vote, the issue of whether foreign affairs should be discussed at City Hall meetings was moot for the moment.

Both Burlington's radicals and its conservatives were ready for a respite from foreign policy issues when the U.S. State Department again aroused the ire of the Coalition, a few weeks after the Grenada invasion. Without warning, the State Department declared Chittenden County off-limits to Soviet journalists, diplomats, and business people. The State Department argued that the area in the U.S. forbidden to Soviet travel was being expanded to 20 percent because the U.S.S.R. excludes Americans from 20 percent of their territory. Joe Reap, a spokesperson for the U.S. State Department, tersely noted: "It's called reciprocity. They started it."[26] Another reason why a locale can be placed off-limits is if it has an important military installation or defense plant.[27] Did Chittenden County's GE, DEC, and IBM plants (the last two being overwhelmingly geared to civilian production) qualify Burlington to be in a zone of exclusion, and if so, why in November of 1983? Since the specific reason why Chittenden County was chosen was classified information, one could only speculate.

Sanders and the Coalition were angered by the State Department's decision, which was made with no consultation of local officials. The mayor quickly and publicly condemned the ban:

At a time when there is an absolute need for increased communication and understanding between the peoples of the United States and the Soviet Union, this childish and arbitrary act by the State Department seems to me to be absurd. . . . I personally resent the fact that in the "defense of freedom" [quotation marks in original text] the State Department is denying the people of our country—which includes the largest university in the state—the freedom to communicate and exchange ideas with whom they want.[28]

Some Coalition members wondered if the ban was applied for a reason other than random selection or defense considerations. Perhaps the U.S. State Department wanted to undermine Burlington city officials' "freedom to communicate and exchange ideas with whom they want." Suggesting that the State Department's choice of Burlington was political, Coalition Alderman Peter Lackowski claimed it was widely known that Burlington had been in the forefront of efforts to lessen tensions between the U.S. and the U.S.S.R.[29] After all, Chittenden was the only one of Vermont's fourteen counties in which the ban was applied.

On November 29, 1983, Alderman Terrill Bouricius offered a resolution protesting the exclusionary ban imposed by the State Department on Chittenden County. The debate began following the same ideological paths as the one several weeks before on the invasion of Grenada. This time, there was a significant twist; Republican Alderman Diane Gallagher successfully moved to end debate after only twenty-four minutes, thereby limiting debate to the aldermen. The cloture of debate forced Burlington's citizens who had come to speak on the issue to be merely passive witnesses. They left that night without ever addressing the board.

During that twenty-four-minute debate, Alderman Maurice Mahoney tried to sink the resolution with an amendment that would ask the State Department to encourage the Russians to drop their travel restrictions.[30] Mahoney's amendment was killed because most of the opposition Democrats and Republicans did not seek a compromise but wanted to defeat the measure outright. Alderman Gallagher also added a new argument to the foreign policy fray when she said that the aldermanic council was not academically qualified to make decisions on foreign policy. Democratic Alderman Linda Burns complained that the Coalition had not been outraged when the KAL airliner was shot down that summer.[31] At the end of the limited debate, the foreign policy resolution protesting the ban on Soviet visitors was defeated eight to five. With all Republicans and Democrats present and voting as a bloc, the Coalition's official protest had little chance of passing.

The opposition Democrats and Republicans carried on an extended argument that foreign policy issues have no place on the local political agenda. Alderman Allen Gear added that voters were telling him "this is a waste of time." Republican Robert Paterson argued that the proposal was "totally irrelevant as far as this city council is concerned."[32] A few days after the defeat and the opposition chiding,

Sanders publicly countered their criticisms. Uncharacteristically, he took a defensive approach initially and argued that only five issues not strictly local were discussed at the last 120 meetings. He went on to counter that communicating with the Soviets is a local issue.[33] Attempts by the opposition to prevent the Progressive Coalition from placing foreign policy issues on the local agenda were only partially and temporarily successful. Although the elected Coalition members were now slow to place resolutions in front of the Board of Aldermen after two back-to-back defeats, other Coalition members were keeping foreign policy issues in the local news and continuing the local political socialization of the citizenry against U.S. hegemony.

In March 1984, Jeanne Keller, the assistant city clerk, and Barr Swennerfelt, the assistant city treasurer, both Coalition members, were arrested in a civil disobedience action. The two Sanders appointees, with forty-three other peace activists, sat in at U.S. Senator Robert T. Stafford's offices protesting his support for Reagan administration policies in Central America. Swennerfelt defended her action on the *Burlington Free Press* editorial page, "One of our biggest accomplishments . . . was the education of hundreds of people on the situation in Central America and the United States' role in shaping its destiny."[34] Eight months later, both Swennerfelt and Keller were cleared of charges because they convinced a jury that occupying the offices was necessary to fight a greater evil, U.S. intervention in Central America.

SOLIDARITY WITH NICARAGUA: A BRIEF HISTORY

The lull in foreign policy activity at City Hall by elected Progressive Coalition members was broken in July 1984. The Sanders administration asked the Board of Aldermen to establish a sister-city relationship with a Nicaraguan city under Sandinista control, Puerto Cabezas.[35] Two months later, with three Republicans absent, the board was able to pass a Coalition-sponsored resolution. The Coalition had tried to present the resolution as nonpolitical, but its inherent political character soon brought ideological bickering to the surface. Republican Samuel Levin repeated the familiar Republican line that local issues, not foreign affairs, should occupy the board's time. Sanders angrily retorted: "The reason that property taxes are so high is that the federal government is spending more than $200 billion a year on the military. I'm tired of hearing the Republican argument because it's a cowardly argument. If you're concerned about local issues, let's stand up to the military."[36] A few days later, the influential *Burlington Free Press* castigated the Sanders administration foreign policy in familiar terms—stick to city business.[37]

The next day, September 20, in a debate entitled "Should Burlington Have a Foreign Policy?" Mayor Sanders faced two opposition foes: the conservative city Republican chair, Frederick Bailey, and the liberal city Democratic chair, Caryl Stewart. Bailey took the familiar Republican line about foreign policy not being the concern of city officials. He advised Coalition members to run for the U.S. Senate or the presidency if they were concerned about foreign policy. Stewart's argument was more complex and less predictable than Bailey's. By acting unilaterally, she argued, the city was trivializing other grassroots foreign policy initiatives such as the nuclear freeze adopted by a majority of Vermont communities. "In Burlington, we're giving up reality for the rhetoric." She went on to accuse Coalition supporters of being faddish: "There's an 'in' thing about this slightly outrageous city government we have; if you're not for it, you're a bore."[38] Although there were differences in Bailey's and Stewart's attacks, both agreed that the Sanders administration should desist from foreign-policy making.

Sanders countered vigorously, repeating his stance that military spending drains resources from localities. In apocalyptic language, he went on to say, "When Plattsburgh [an airforce base across the lake in New York] goes and when Burlington and the entire state of Vermont goes, I think that's a local issue!"[39] Sanders also claimed that provocative issues, such as those labeled foreign policy by his opposition, led to increased voter participation. On the specific issue of Puerto Cabezas, Republicans and Democrats argued that the choice of a Nicaraguan city was inappropriate because of that country's leftist government. Sanders deflated this argument by reminding the audience that eleven hundred American municipalities have sister cities in the Soviet Union. Ironically and perhaps unwittingly, Sanders' opponents undercut their own positions. By debating the mayor, Bailey and Stewart gave Sanders another local forum from which to spread his opinions on international socialist solidarity, just what they were trying to remove from the local political agenda.

Republican and Democratic aldermen realized that the Coalition's effort to change the political agenda was resulting in the dissemination of views that the major parties would rather see contained. After reluctantly accepting a diluted resolution in support of the concept of sanctuary for Guatemalan and El Salvadorian refugees (which had significant support from local clergy) by a seven-to-four vote, embarrassed opposition members maneuvered to isolate foreign policy debates at City Hall.[40]

In April 1985 opposition aldermen passed a resolution (seven to six) setting aside separate meetings for foreign affairs. Frederick Bailey, former city Republican chairman and now an alderman, claimed he did not want to demean such discussions; instead, he sought to give them more time. Considering Bailey's debating position the previous year, this new stance leant itself to being labeled hypocrisy or a blatant lie. Sanders called the new resolution an "arbitrary separation."[41] While it was true that the opposition's resolution effectively gave foreign policy issues their own agenda, it was one of tertiary importance. This was an obvious attempt at containment by trivialization. Editorial support by the conservative Burlington Free Press for the measure affirmed its reactionary nature.[42]

Meeting during an opposition-imposed special session for foreign affairs, the Coalition registered a surprising victory in May 1985. By an eight-to-three vote, with only the Republicans voting nay, the Board of Aldermen passed a resolution encouraging trade between Burlington and Nicaragua in protest of the recently imposed Reagan embargo. Alderman Terrill Bouricius introduced the resolution with Coalition backing; to everyone's surprise, the Democrats backed the measure. Sounding like a Coalition member, Democrat Paul Lafayette said: "I hope we can send a message that we do care about human beings, and maybe this can be a first step." For a change, Democrats were distancing themselves from the consistently conservative Republicans. Since two months before, the Democrats had again been humbled at the polls by Sanders, it was likely that they were changing strategies to co-opt the Progressive Coalition in a future, post-Sanders era. In addition, Alderman Paul Lafayette had his own peace credentials; he was a conscientious objector during the Vietnam War.[43] Contrasting Lafayette's remarks with those of Republican Bailey is instructive. Bailey accused the Sandinista government of having "turned their back on democracy" and of having as their objective to "spread this Marxist-Leninist government to neighboring states."[44] This was an almost verbatim repetition of the official Reagan administration position.

Following the Coalition's surprising victory, Mayor Sanders made plans to accept an official invitation (one of three hundred given to various American progressives) to visit Nicaragua on the sixth anniversary of the Sandinista revolution in July 1985. Republican Alderman William Skelton offered his ominous vision of such a trip to the *Burlington Free Press*: "It should tell people where his real interests lie. Burlington is nothing but a steppingstone in his long-range ambitions and plans."[45] The *Burlington Free Press* Editorial Board likewise castigated the mayor for his planned trip in terms that can only be described as insulting:

What is troublesome, however, is that the mayor fancies himself a budding diplomat capable of making intelligent decisions about the merits of a government on a long-distance basis. It is the classic mistake made by amateurs. . . . But one thing is certain: While Sanders is in Nicaragua, he can do little mischief in Burlington. That, in itself, might be the best—and only—argument in favor of the trip.[46]

Considering that the mayor had frequently expressed his intention to run for governor in the future, such a trip could prove politically damaging. Sanders himself said:

I suspect that there are many people in the city of Burlington who are not going to be happy about my going, who think that a mayor should stay at home and deal with what they perceive as local issues. . . . But I think the issue of war and peace is such an overwhelmingly important issue that every public official in this world has got to speak up on these things. . . . I think that in terms of my own political future, probably what I'm doing is not a very wise thing to do, but so be it.[47]

Despite almost certain negative political fall-out, Sanders went to Nicaragua accompanied by a reporter for the *Burlington Free Press*, Don Melvin, who conveyed to the paper's front pages the mayor's provocative remarks. From the beginning, Sanders claimed he would not be used as a Sandinista propaganda piece; he would study both their successes and their errors.[48] Sanders visited Puerto Cabezas; there he had an impromptu debate with U.S. news reporters, accusing them of not telling the truth. At Managua, while speaking with George Crile of CBS, he called network correspondents "worms" because of their uncritical reporting of Reagan pronouncements. He went on to say to Melvin that "one would hope that the media would analyze the positions of both nations equally" when instead they had "become spokesmen for the American government's position."[49] On July 20, 1985, Sanders met with Daniel Ortega Saveedra, the president of Nicaragua, and expressed solidarity with the Sandinista revolution. Throughout the trip, Sanders made statements opposing American intervention.[50] Sanders blasted the U.S. for opposing the latest proposal to bring peace to the area.

Although Sanders supported the Sandinistas, he was critical of them. In a closing interview with Don Melvin before returning to Burlington, Sanders questioned whether the Sandinistas had too many soldiers under arms and whether the spiraling cost of necessities was in part due to Sandinista mistakes. A victim of government harassment in the 1960s, Sanders also had misgivings about Sandinista censorship:

Obviously, as someone who has a very strong belief in civil liberties and the right of freedom of expression, it is very distasteful to me to hear of censorship in any form. My hope is that in Nicaragua in the near future, there will be total freedom of expression for all individuals. That does not exist today.[51]

As a democratic socialist, Sanders chose not to be totally uncritical of the Sandinista regime. In fact, during his visit, he met with various opposition groups. Despite the Sandinistas' "mistakes" Sanders remained committed to the revolutionary government's right to evolve and rule without U.S interference.[52] The controversial trip to Nicaragua may have hurt Sanders' political ambitions, since his comments had daily front-page exposure in the *Burlington Free Press*. Nevertheless, such a forum for socialization of radical points of view on foreign affairs is unusual if not nonexistent in most communities.

Sanders' 1985 visit to Puerto Cabezas, Burlington's Nicaraguan sister city, was paralleled in 1988 when Mayor Sanders, with Alderman Terrill Bouricius, made a visit to Burlington's newest sister city in the Soviet Union, Yaroslavl. Sanders had more than improving American-Soviet relations on his mind. Without reservation, he solicited press exposure for this trip from the state's two largest newspapers, the *Burlington Free Press* and the *Rutland Herald*. Both declined.[53] With the thaw in Soviet-American relations, Sanders had hoped that a well-publicized trip to the Soviet Union would boost his Congressional campaign. The polls showed no rise during his stay. Nonetheless, bilateral city-to-city foreign relations were established. Contacts between peoples whose governments had been waging a cold war were now warming with official friendship.

PROPOSED REFORM AND ALTERNATIVES

Unlike almost any other municipality in the United States, Burlington, Vermont, had a foreign policy. The goal of this foreign policy was neither to enact treaties nor to mediate disputes between nations. In contrast to that of nation states, the foreign policy goal of the Sanders administration was to alter the consciousness of Burlington's citizens by protesting, debating, and circumventing current U.S. foreign policy. The Progressive Coalition was opposed to U.S. hegemony, particularly in Latin America and the Caribbean. Any U.S. action to coerce Third World countries to accept American domination was resolutely opposed. Besides opposing U.S. policy in the Western Hemisphere, the Coalition members supported revolutionary regimes there, specifically in Grenada and Nicaragua, the latter being offered material support as well as verbal solidarity. Finally, the Coalition sought friendly relations with the State Department's primary adversary, the Soviet Union.

This attempt to change community anticommunist attitudes to anti-imperialist attitudes, if successful, would be a democratic structural reform. The needs of capitalism and the roles of federalism were not merely disregarded; they were attacked. By soliciting solidarity with socialist nations, the Sanders administration was attempting a reform at an abstract level. A new consciousness, if successfully accepted by the majority of Burlington's residents, could provide the base for other reforms. Once a new world view is internalized, the flaws of existing institutions become exposed to the public. By trying to change foreign policy attitudes, the Coalition challenged two power-relation structures: capitalism and federalism. Capitalism was the explicit villain that the Coalition was challenging.

Displaying solidarity with revolutionary Nicaragua was a way of fighting the capitalist system. Establishing a sister-city relationship with Puerto Cabezas despite the Reagan embargo of all but humanitarian aid shipments to Nicaragua was a defiance of capitalism's needs. Although the Reagan and Bush administrations have not invaded Nicaragua, they have made an example of the leftist government by making it hemorrhage. By imposing an economic embargo and by supporting the Contra forces, the U.S. has simultaneously reduced the Nicaraguan economy to a shambles and terrorized its citizenry. If the price of socialism is to be death and destruction, capitalism will look better to the citizens of Nicaragua and other nations. By establishing a sister-city status with Puerto Cabezas, the Sanders administration had undermined the ideological rationale for such hostile acts. Sanders' visit to Puerto Cabezas, his qualified support for the Sandinistas, and his unqualified hostility to U.S intervention was a public denial that Nicaragua deserved to be ostracized. Since Nicaragua has chosen the noncapitalist path of development despite the hostility of the U.S., the Sanders administration's support for such a regime is counter to the needs of capitalism. If Nicaragua is successful in dropping out of the capitalist system and in materially improving the well-being of its people, it will be a positive normative example that will undermine capitalism's seeming inevitability.

By showing solidarity with Grenada, the Sanders administration was trying to undermine domestic support for actions that sustain the capitalist system. The secret invasion of Grenada resulted in the successful toppling of a revolutionary regime. Unlike the gradual escalation of U.S. hostile action against Nicaragua, the surprise (to the American public) attack on the island could not be delayed by nationwide progressive efforts to curry public opinion in Grenada's favor before hostilities began. Alderman Bouricius' resolution was an attempt to make local citizens aware that the invasion was not the "rescue mission" the Reagan administration claimed and the press reported. By arguing for troop withdrawal and noninterference in other nations' affairs, the Coalition was trying to build grass-roots support against future U.S. invasions. Although there was no time for public opinion to have an effect on U.S. intervention in Grenada, public opinion throughout the U.S. has had some effect on blocking direct U.S. intervention in Nicaragua.

The failure of the Grenada resolution does not mean that the Coalition goal to change consciousness and make a public protest failed. In opposing the resolution, the *Burlington Free Press* Editorial Board and the Republican/Democratic opposition gave the issue more publicity than there might have been had it unobtrusively passed; the Coalition objection to the U.S. invasion was widely reported through local radio, television, and newspapers. This publicity in itself was a form of success, even though the attitudes of the Burlington public remained unmeasured both before and after the resolution.

The resolution opposing the ban on Soviet travel was also a qualified success despite its failure to be adopted. Coalition sources exposed the irrationality of U.S. (and U.S.S.R.) foreign policy. The arms race, a byproduct in part of the conflict between the needs of a capitalist system and the needs of a socialist system, is acknowledged as a dysfunctional and potentially deadly logic by most Vermonters.

Before the resolution, most of Vermont's communities had adopted nuclear freeze resolutions through local referenda. The exclusion of Soviet citizens from Burlington may have been a way to contain these pro-freeze attitudes. Before the State Department ban, Soviet officials espousing a nuclear freeze had visited Burlington City Hall and colleges in the area to present their positions. Whether or not it was intentional, the State Department used its authority to prevent the continued dialogue. A resistance demand was offered in the Coalition resolution asking that the ban be rescinded. The Coalition was aware that only by continuing verbal interchange could the well-socialized anticommunism of the American public be reversed. The reflexive opposition to the Coalition's resolution by Democrats and Republicans illustrates the depths of American anticommunism. Nevertheless, in many American communities, such a ban on Russian travel would bring little or no response; in Burlington, consciousness was such that it was at least on the political agenda.

The establishment of the sister city relationship with Yaroslavl in the U.S.S.R. was another attempt to break with anti-Soviet and anti-communist hysteria. By regularizing relations, Burlington's citizens received a view of the Soviets that was unmediated by State Department interpretation. If such efforts could be multiplied, Cold War tension could be defused from the bottom of the federalist system up.

The Coalition resolutions to establish a sister city in Nicaragua, protest the invasion of Grenada, demand the rescission of the ban on Soviet travel in Burlington, and establish a sister city in the Soviet Union were collectively an attempt to reverse anticommunist hostility. Not only were these resolutions inimical to the needs of the capitalist system, but they also challenged the federal system. The seldom-challenged rule is that foreign policy is a responsibility of national government exclusively. Formally, the states have no concurrent powers in foreign affairs; localities are even further removed. The Sanders administration refused, however, to accept the federal system's distribution of authority. Although Burlington was precluded from substantively changing U.S. foreign policy, the Coalition attempted to create the city's own diplomatic links. The sister city relationship with Puerto Cabezas was not a treaty, but it was diplomacy at a city-to-city level. Despite an embargo on Nicaragua enforced by the U.S. national government, city government was creating ties, not breaking them. The less successful resolutions on Grenada and the Soviet ban were also Coalition foreign policy pronouncements. The ability of the national government to speak with one voice was being undermined. Outside of a few progressive cities, such as Berkeley, Santa Monica, and Santa Cruz in California, most other cities passively accept the prevailing federal distribution of authority. Obstreperous Burlington at least debated foreign affairs policies.

The Sanders administration's treatment of the General Electric civil disobedience action was the antithesis of its other efforts at changing community consciousness to effect a profound democratic structural reform; it was reactionary, counterproductive, and a disgrace. From the beginning of the GE debacle, Mayor Sanders accepted the union's unfounded position that the workers were the target of the Burlington Peace Coalition's civil disobedience action.[54] The BPC took extraordinary precautions to allay the workers' fears, including the relocation of their protest to a rear gate. Politically, it was a no-win situation for the mayor; the resistance forces were divided into two camps: the peace activists and the unionized workers. Both groups had their share of Sanders supporters. Notwithstanding this dilemma, Sanders' reflexive support of the workers reflected his commitment to an industrially based socialism. Such a commitment could make the American left even weaker than it already is.

As manufacturing continues its decline in postindustrial America, there will be fewer and fewer blue-collar workers. Even if levels of manufacturing were to remain steady or even increase, the number of factory workers will decline over the long term. Automation is rapidly replacing and reducing the number of workers in almost all phases of manufacturing. As factory workers become a residual category of the employed, the hope that they will become a revolutionary proletariat representing the majority of the population becomes more and more absurd. Instead, their importance to the left should reflect their dwindling numbers. The demands of blue-collar workers must be ordered with the other social movements comprising America's contemporary left, including gays, blacks, ecologists, Gray Panthers, and peace activists; otherwise, giving blue-collar workers primacy will only fractionalize the diversity of resistance groups.

Regardless of the appropriate status of blue-collar workers in the ranks of the left opposition, the prohibition against the manufacture of weapons that are used indiscriminately on Third World peoples was a more important goal than that of protecting the jobs of a labor elite. Although Sanders had said, "Not everybody has the luxury of choosing where they are going to work . . . or the money not to work,"[55] it would not be realistic to view workers who make weapons used in anti-socialist struggles as merely passive victims of capitalism. For those GE workers who opposed U.S. intervention, there was other work available in Chittenden County. The other work was not as well paying and thus it was not in their material interest to change jobs, but the other work was not filled with moral ambiguity. We cannot assume, however, that all GE workers had qualms over their duties. When the *Vermont Vanguard Press* interviewed exiting GE plant workers, some of the comments suggested there were no qualms: "It doesn't bother me that [GE] makes guns. I feel the United States has to have a defense; it has to be prepared. . . . [GE] is keeping America strong."[56] "Ninety-nine point nine percent don't mind the work. We figure it's either them or us."[57] It is not known if "ninety-nine point nine percent" of GE workers were committed to the production of Gatling guns as a moral necessity; however, there was scarce evidence that they would prefer making toasters.

In contrast, the actions of the Burlington Peace Coalition were clearly progressive. Challenging GE's assertions that they were merely complying with U.S. government orders was an important attempt at undermining the amorality of capitalist logic. The supposed detachment of GE to the purposes of its products did not jibe with its company slogan about bringing "good things to life." Burlington Peace Coalition protesters were exposing this inconsistency.

The peace activists were ready with alternatives to the continued production of military weapons at the GE plant. Both GE and the *Burlington Free Press* Editorial Board denied the feasibility of converting the plant to civilian purposes. The successful renovation of a Victorian-vintage factory nearby, however, exposed this widely told generalization as inconsistent with existing local business investment patterns. A multistory brick building housing a defunct cereal business was renovated with an Urban Development Action Grant of $675,000, a state-financed revenue bond of $1,000,000, and $625,000 in private money. Subsequently, all 63,000 feet were leased by small business tenants.[58] With state and national government aid, bridges could be built from the Coalition to the small business sector if the GE plant were closed, but only if the Coalition's elected representatives were responsive to such demands.

This is not to say that the GE workers and the city workforce at large would be better off economically if the plant were closed down and the facility successfully subdivided for small business use. Most new businesses in this postindustrial city would be service industries, which are necessarily labor intensive and provide many jobs. However, the jobs created would fall into a ratio of one-third that pay well and two-thirds that pay near minimum wage and are mostly part-time.[59] Former GE workers' extensive industrial skills would make them unqualified for the management end of the service industry; thus, they would likely fall into the poorer-paying, unskilled service-sector positions.

Even if replacement of the GE plant were not possible, could the Sanders administration have implemented a democratic structural reform and closed the plant without compensation to its owner? Sanders thought so; he admitted in a private interview that GE could be hounded out, though he opposed such efforts.[60] The economic rewards GE provided to Burlington effectively stayed the mayor's hands. Sanders failed to specify what approaches could be taken if he and the Coalition were so inclined; two come to mind. Intermittent civil disobedience by groups of activists including prominent city officials such as the mayor himself could be used to convince GE to relocate; upsetting delivery and shipping schedules, for example, could create anarchic conditions for production. A more conventional approach would utilize the city's zoning power. Burlington's Municipal Development Plan could be amended to forbid the manufacturing of weapons. By progressively interpreting the present law's stated purpose of encouraging "the appropriate conservation and/or development of all land in Burlington in a manner which will promote public health, safety, morals, etc.,"[61] city officials might try to order the plant closed on almost any of these criteria. The state courts would probably overturn such efforts, but even if they did not, a moratorium on Gatling gun production would be only temporary. Upon hearing of GE's closing, hundreds, if not thousands, of communities would solicit GE to be the site of the new weapons plant.

Any effort sponsored or merely condoned by the Sanders administration to stop GE's production of Gatling guns, regardless of the outcome, would drastically lower business confidence. Any conglomerate that had defense-related production would reconsider investing in Burlington, even if the actual planned investment was the production of a good or service unrelated to defense. The possibility of impromptu disruptive demonstrations or of community dissent infecting company workers would make other areas of the nation seem more desirable. Also, local businessmen would dislike the precedent of local government's backing activities that disrupt the "apolitical" realm of the private sector. There would be unanswered questions that would threaten business confidence: Could workers be organized to demand more control over production? Could city imposed regulations on what was produced be on the future political agenda?

One other constraint on any city government sponsored attempt to close GE is the threat of electoral defection. Without doubt GE's unionized workforce and their families, tenuous Sanders supporters, would electorally defect if GE closed its plant because of City Hall hostility. Also, other blue-collar workers might interpret such activities as anti–working class, and return to their former political party, the Democrats. And perhaps the greatest threat would come from the always simmering tax revolt voters. The removal of GE from the city's Grand List would likely mean a reduction in tax revenue unless another capital intensive firm could be enticed to replace it, an unlikely scenario. Such political fodder would be well used by Sanders' opposition at election time.

Yet, even if Mayor Sanders did want the plant to remain open, he ultimately ended up on the wrong side of the police barricades. No affinity with workers' interests or support for GE's continuing presence could justify the mayor's support for GE workers over the BPC. In April 1985, fifty protesters repeated the civil disobedience action and sat at the GE rear gate from 6:00 A.M. to 5:00 P.M. one day. There were no shipments, no deliveries, and no arrests.[62] This is what would likely have happened during the 1983 action if Sanders had not interceded. In 1985, the mayor and GE union officials chose to ignore the protests, and the resulting political fall-out was inconsequential. In 1983, economic and electoral constraints had acted against the mayor's supporting the demonstrators, but such constraints did not demand his supervision of the protesters' arrests.

Unfortunately, Sanders' tolerance for civil disobedience campaigns at GE was tested again; again he was found wanting. Barr Swennerfelt, the Sanders appointee who was arrested in 1984 for participating in a Senate office sit-in, was arrested in May 1985 for placing flowers in a GE tank-mounted Gatling gun on General Electric property and again in June 1985, with her husband, for protesting at GE. This time the Swennerfelts, both Quakers, were sowing corn, symbolic seeds, to protest the Gatling guns' 6,000 discharges a minute;[63] on August 14, 1985, they were sentenced to eight days in jail. The next day Barr Swennerfelt and Sanders jointly announced her "resignation"; in truth, the mayor fired her because she refused to give up civil disobedience. As Alderman Bouricius phrased it,

Civil disobedience is not a tactic that Bernie finds fruitful, but he and Barr had come to an understanding that he would tolerate it as long as it didn't interfere with her job. It was Barr's choice, but when her activities began to affect her ability to do her job, then lines had to be drawn.[64]

Since Swennerfelt's eight days of incarceration were greater than her vacation time, Sanders claimed she would be cheating the taxpayers.[65] Thus, for an unexcused absence from her job for just over one week, the socialist mayor of Burlington, Vermont, fired a dedicated member of the Coalition. Three years later, Swennerfelt gave an interview from a Vermont jail where she had been imprisoned for yet another civil disobedience action against GE Burlington. Asked about her firing in 1986, she said, "I became a political liability for Bernie."[66]

Swennerfelt's firing is a logical consequence of Sanders' position on the first GE civil disobedience action, proving that his presence behind police barricades was no aberration. Whether or not Sanders intended to, he defended GE against the anti-militarist elements of the Coalition. Instead of being at the forefront of protest, Sanders was suppressing it, despite his assertions to the contrary and despite the intent of the Coalition's previously proposed resolution on Grenada and pronouncement of solidarity with Nicaragua. Since Barr Swennerfelt's absence (eight days) was similar in length to the mayor's trip to Nicaragua, Sanders' protests of dereliction of duty were shallow if not unfounded. Civil disobedience was a justifiable response to U.S. militarism and thus justified her absences for incarceration.

Mayor Sanders, himself, had an uneasiness with the countercultural aspects of the Burlington Peace Coalition. His working-class socialist values differed from the libertarian values of many BPC members. His ambivalence toward the left's new social movements was not limited to the BPC; Sanders was similarly estranged from Burlington's feminist community.

8

Sexual Politics

The Sanders administration was primarily concerned with economic reforms; relations between the sexes involved a different category of analysis, a different structure of power. Two of the most important Progressive Coalition initiatives on relations between the sexes fell into both the economic and the interpersonal realms. These issue areas, like structures themselves, are not strictly separate, since each structure has a relationship to the other. The two initiatives that are examined in this chapter involved attacks on the imperatives of male domination and capitalism. Nonetheless, women's issues took a back seat to other issues on the Sanders administration's agenda.

When Sanders was first elected in March 1981, feminist members of the Progressive Coalition lobbied the mayor to create a task force on women as he had on taxes and the waterfront. The feminists demanded an autonomous body that would make recommendations to the mayor while still retaining its independent status. During initial organizational meetings, the mayor opposed any autonomous status. He wanted the task force to merely offer recommendations; an autonomous status for the task force raised the possibility that the women's community would be critical of Sanders administration initiatives if they were anti-feminist or even if the administration's proposals ignored women's demands. In the end Sanders capitulated, and the task force kept itself from becoming merely an adjunct of the mayor's office. Once the Mayor's Task Force on Women was established, however, it took six weeks for the Sanders administration to find a room in Burlington's City Hall where the members might meet.[1] The San ders administration had reason to fear that the women's movement might be divisive to Progressive Coalition solidarity: there was evidence that Burlington's feminists were both vibrant and independent.

Unlike many communities in which the women's movement had waned during the 1980s, Burlington retained a small, activist feminist community. The most desired reform that liberal feminists had articulated in the 1970s, the individualistic notion of the equality of opportunity, had been enacted in the Civil Rights Act of 1964. By the late 1970s, this reform had been implemented to a significant degree and the feminist movement began to decline. Burlington has not been immune to this nationwide phenomenon. In a series of revealing articles, Leslie Brown, writing in the *Burlington Free Press*, found that young, upwardly mobile women (the population strata that furnished most feminists in the 1970s) were either unconcerned with or hostile to feminism. One young female lawyer remarked, upon being asked if she were a feminist: "Burlington is such a small community that if you get the reputation of being a bitch it can really hurt you."[2] Burlington's female high school students were also hostile: "If I'm good enough at what I do, I won't need something like the ERA." "Everyone has exactly the same opportunities. If women are worried about whether they're getting equal status, they should just work harder."[3] Also, many lower-class women were hostile to feminism.[4] Despite these ominous signs of the decline of feminism in Burlington, there remains a core of women who became feminists in the 1970s and have kept their commitment. Aligned with these feminists, who are in their thirties and forties, is a smaller group comprised of nonconforming female college students who promise to keep the local feminist resistance alive, albeit at a reduced level.[5]

Burlington's feminist groups revealed their resistance actions soon after Sanders won the mayor's office in March 1981. In a night march, hundreds of feminists protested an alleged gang rape at a Greek fraternity house and a cover-up by the University of Vermont. Brandishing signs cut in the shape of axes that read "CASTRATE," the female marchers deviated from their police-approved route and surrounded the Sigma Nu fraternity house yelling, "Surprise for you, Sigma Nu." After leaving the scene of the alleged rape, marchers stopped at the UVM president's house and taunted him to come outside. Sponsoring the march were several local feminist organizations: Women Against Rape, Burlington Women's Center, Women Helping Battered Women, and UVM's Women's Group and Referral Center. Celia Vera, a march organizer, read a manifesto of demands, which

included a city-funded home for battered women, self-defense programs for young women in city schools, and a female-staffed sex
crime unit in the Burlington Police Department.[6] (The Progressive
Coalition did eventually fulfill the first two demands.) Although the
women's movement was not being replenished by numerous new
members, its existing advocates could raise hell.

The Mayor's Task Force on Women contained volunteer representatives from women's groups ranging from the activist members of
Everywoman's Place to the elite Business and Professional Women's
Club. There was an open-door policy; the only criterion to attend
meetings was that one had to either be a resident of Burlington or
work there.[7] This voluntary task force was white and overwhelmingly middle class, as one of the members admitted with lament.[8] Ranging in their views from radical feminist to mainstream liberal feminist,
the active members who attended meetings were united by their opposition to male domination. Pornography, abortion rights, health education, nonsexist education, and safety from male violence, in addition to economic issues, were concerns of the autonomous advisory
group.

One of the demands of community feminists and the task force
was a women's shelter to provide battered women a refuge from male
violence. In April 1983, this goal was met by the Sanders administration, which allocated $80,000 from Community Development Block
Grant funds and $760,000 from the Housing and Urban Development
Department.[9] These block and categorical grants from the national
government allowed the Sanders administration to satisfy a primarily
noneconomic feminist demand. Although male violence against
women is seen as primarily a noneconomic issue, it still takes money
to buy and operate the shelter staffed by the feminist organization
Women Helping Battered Women. It was hoped that the federal funds
would make the shelter self-supporting, but such plans were at the
mercy of the national government. As federal funds for welfare uses
were incrementally pared away by the Reagan-Bush administration, it
became doubtful that the Progressive Coalition could meet feminist
demands by funding the shelter out of city-generated revenues.

The relationship of feminists to the elected representatives of the
Progressive Coalition was supportive but tentative, as evidenced by
the feminist insistence on autonomy for the Task Force on Women. In
a bid for women's support, Sanders approved a change in name from
the Task Force on Women to the Women's Council and its status from
temporary to permanent in 1983.[10] Although such a move was sym-

bolic, it represented the Progressive Coalition's electoral need to solidify feminist support. In February 1983, Bernard Sanders ran a reelection campaign advertisement in the local radical feminist monthly, *Commonwoman*, stressing a pro–women's rights platform. A "whistle-stop" campaign to prevent rape, city aid for child daycare, comparable worth for city employees, and an increase in the number of women in Burlington's government were all programs that Sanders claimed he would "work for."[11]

Although all of these programs were enacted at least in part, one was a token effort: increasing the number of women in city government. The whistle-stop campaign (intended to act as a deterrent to muggers and rapists) involved distributing loud whistles free of charge to women and the aged.[12] Despite the fact that this program originated in the Women's Council itself, as an attempted solution to male violence against women, it is difficult to discuss seriously. A small daycare program was established in the basement of a municipal building. After much pressure, Sanders, in his last year in office, attempted to impose a $600,000 tax on employers to fund daycare. Ultimately, it failed at the polls.

The other promised reform made during the 1983 campaign was a comparable worth program for female city employees; this was actually implemented in its entirety. Another reform in the area of sexual politics was enacted in 1985, a city ordinance forbidding discrimination in housing to homosexuals.

COMPARABLE WORTH

Bernard Sanders promised to try to implement "pay equity for city employees which could set an example for other employers in the area."[13] Better known as comparable worth to feminist advocates, this reform was passed with relatively little bickering by the Board of Aldermen, who were unaware of its radical nature. Comparable worth is a labor policy that goes beyond the liberal demand of equal pay for equal work. Advocates of comparable worth argue that there are whole job classifications that are demeaned by lower pay and status because they are dominated by women or other minorities. Despite these occupational inequalities, comparable worth advocates would grant that within a single job category equal pay for equal work can be enforced with some degree of effectiveness. Thus, the salary of a male secretary in Burlington's City Hall, by education and seniority, would not be more than that of a female worker with the same qualifications and in a similar position. However, comparable worth advocates argue that because secretarial work is dominated by women, the entire occupation is paid less than it would be if white men dominated its ranks. The antidote to this problem is to reevaluate job classifications by a common set of criteria that transcend specific occupations and instead compare and evaluate them.

By evaluating differing job content by uniform standards, comparable worth eliminates underpayment for jobs held by women and minorities by upgrading classification and remuneration. Conversely, it can scale down job status and payment to occupations historically dominated by white men. Occupations differing as widely as librarian and truck driver can end up with the same ranking after a comparable worth study. (Usually truck drivers make considerably more than librarians.) The general criteria used in job evaluation are "skill, effort, responsibility, and working conditions." These may be refined to more specific subcategories, such as "job-related experience, length of formal training required, frequency of work review, the number of other workers an employee is responsible for, impact on and responsibility for budget, physical stress, time spent working under deadlines, time spent in processing information," and so forth.[14] Despite the obvious appeal of comparable worth to fairness, based on bureaucratic principles of meritocracy, it has been a source of irritation to the nation's conservatives.

Clarence Pendleton, a prominent conservative, a black, and chair of the United States Civil Rights Commission appointed by President Reagan, made headlines in 1984 by calling comparable worth the "looniest idea since Looney Tunes came on the screen."[15] Many other conservatives argue that comparable worth is unneeded because the private labor market, working under the capitalist principles of supply and demand, if left unfettered would soon level any discriminatory hiring practices. The conservative argument claims that those employers who fail to hire and fairly compensate competent women or minorities are at a competitive disadvantage. The most competent women and minorities seek out the firms that do not discriminate.

Fortunately for the Progressive Coalition, this argument against comparable worth based on the capitalist logic of supply and demand was not accompanied by the well-publicized, shrill rhetoric of Pendleton and Reagan until after the Board of Aldermen had passed the new reclassification measure. Ignorant of the full implications of comparable worth, the board's Republican/Democratic majority easily approved a job reclassification resolution based upon pay equity introduced by Progressive Coalition Alderwoman Zoe Breiner. The easy passage was prompted by the fact that job reclassification was long overdue; it had not taken place in twelve years. A reclassification was conducted by a consulting firm, Labor Relations Associates, and completed in July 1983. Sanders budgeted an additional $200,000 (a considerable sum to a property-tax dependent small city) to upgrade the salaries of affected employees, mostly women, whose jobs were reclassified upward by the study.[16] New contracts with city unions were negotiated on the basis of the study's findings.

To the surprise of Mayor Sanders, his labor negotiator and personnel director, James Dunn, and the president of the local chapter of the American Federation of State, County, and Municipal Employees (AFSCME), Lindol Atkins, on October 7, 1983, the new contract was rejected by a one-vote margin (twenty-three to twenty-two). With over seventy employees absent, those who felt shortchanged by the contract dominated the vote. This was an unexpected setback for the Sanders administration, which prided itself on good labor relations. In fact, according to Sanders, this was "one of the best contracts ever negotiated for the union."[17] Passage had seemed assured to both the administration and union leaders. Both the leadership and the rank and file of all three municipal unions had overtly supported the Coalition's candidates and Sanders' reelection in March of that same year. Sanders had even pressured the board over strenuous Republican objections to include in the contract the end of a city practice of paying nonunion employees more than union employees, a union-busting technique that would remain in effect until the new contract was ratified.

Despite Atkins' enthusiastic support, the problem with the contract from the AFSCME workers' point of view was two-fold. The police, a separate union, were given raises of 5 percent greater than those of the AFSCME workers. This was to stop police trainees from leaving for better-paying suburban localities. A second problem, one germane to relations between the sexes, was that after comparable worth reclassification, many male workers were given token raises, some as little as $1.50 a week, while other workers, mostly women, received raises of up to $50 a week. Angry male workers protested such a reordering of wages the only way they could—by rejecting the contract. Both Atkins and Dunn tried to keep the press in the dark about the reasons for the defeat of the contract.[18]

The successful strategy of muffling the conflict was affirmed a

month after the initial rejection of the contract when AFSCME accepted the exact same contract in a vote of fifty-nine to five. Atkins
claimed in vague generalities that additional explanation and a greater turn-out changed the tally.[19] Details of why eighteen people who
previously had rejected the contract either changed their votes, abstained, or absented themselves were kept secret.

Despite the paucity of information, it can be concluded that there
was a split in the Progressive Coalition's support groups. Just as the
workers at General Electric reacted against a perceived threat to their
livelihood by the Burlington Peace Coalition, the mostly male AFSCME
workers initially rejected the claims by women to more pay. And like
the split between BPC and GE workers, the conflict between women's
demands and male workers' privileges was patched over but not really
resolved. Since women were demanding and receiving resources that
could be used for across-the-board increases that would disproportionately favor men under the old system, there were real winners and
losers in the adoption of comparable worth.

PROTECTING GAYS' HOUSING RIGHTS

During the period under study, the struggle for gay rights in Burlington was vocal and open. Homosexuals in Burlington organized,
demonstrated, and demanded civil rights guarantees from local government. Throughout the period under study, gay men and women
who were a faction of the Progressive Coalition, pressured City Hall
to enact a housing ordinance protecting them from discrimination; in
1984 their effort was successful.

Because of their link to the women's movement, Burlington's lesbians have been organized longer and more effectively than their
male counterparts. *Commonwoman*, a radical feminist newspaper, was
a key mode of communication between gay women as well as being
an avenue of socialization of feminist ideology. In its first issue, the
lead editorial, "Politics of Penile Penetration," took a radical lesbian
position, arguing that all conventional male/female intercourse is a
manifestation of male exploitation.[20] Alongside "Politics of Penile
Penetration" was another editorial entitled "Straight Talk," which il-
lustrated the community's gay/straight differences:

As a heterosexual woman, I have found it difficult to become an active member of Burlington's feminist community. I have felt outnumbered and intimi-
dated by the strong lesbian faction here. I have watched shyly from the side-

lines, believing that my time and energy were unwanted unless I was one of "them." [quotation marks in original][21]

Although denied by the co-chair of the Women's Council, Suzanne Gillis, there was a deep split between the straight and lesbian components of Burlington's feminist movement, which shadows such a schism in the liberal, feminist-dominated National Organization of Women.[22] The split was also in evidence at Everywoman's Place, a community meeting spot for the women of Burlington. Within the confines of Everywoman's Place there were arguments between lesbians who for the most wished to exclude men from activities and those straight women who wished to include them.[23] Despite a schism over sexual preference within the women's movement, both straight and gay women did work together on the Women's Council. Nevertheless, the potential for fracturing the local women's movement and Burlington's left resistance remained.

Paralleling other local efforts around the United States, in the spring of 1983, the homosexual community in and around Burlington planned a Lesbian and Gay Pride Day that would feature a parade throughout the city's downtown area. Since many homosexual activists were also supporters of the Progressive Coalition, the organizers of the march asked for an official proclamation of support from the Board of Aldermen. During the subsequent debate, Republican Alderman Diane Gallagher complained, "Can't you go out and have your party and enjoy yourselves and make your point without asking the city to have a proclamation?" Because two conservative opposition aldermen were absent, the Coalition managed to pass the proclamation on a partisan six-to-five vote. After the vote, both absent aldermen publicly stated that they would have voted against the measure if they had been present. Placing some distance between themselves and gay rights, even some of the Coalition members who voted for the resolution carefully announced they support civil rights, not homosexuality. Progressive Coalition Alderman Ricky Musty claimed his support did "not represent an endorsement of homosexuality. It [was] a vote to support the civil rights of an oppressed group." Sanders echoed his support cloaked in civil rights rhetoric: "In the city of Burlington and in the state of Vermont people have the right to exercise their life styles. It's an American right, anyone's right to have a march. This is a civil liberties question."[24] On the day of the march only one of the Progressive Coalition elected officials, Peter Lackowski, walked with the 350 gay and lesbian supporters.

It was not surprising that the mayor and all the Coalition aldermen but one were absent; public homophobic hostility was manifest. After passage of the resolution, Alderman Bouricius received a variety of hate mail and telephone calls.[25] The *Burlington Free Press* editor gave free reign to homophobic hate mail, effectively magnifying anti-gay hostility. Selected quotations from the editorial pages reveal the depth of unpopularity of the Progressive Coalition proposal among some members of the community:

Has the city of Burlington become a Sodom and Gomorrah? . . . I think this is an abomination to our Lord. . . . Is this what you want [Sanders] to do to your city—turn it into a side show? . . . Honoring gays by designating a day for them is about the most asinine thing the Burlington aldermen and Mayor Sanders have done to date. . . . It's also said that Burlington, "The Queen City of Vermont," may be known as "Queer City of Vermont."[26]

Lesbian activist Peggy Luhrs summed up the response of the gays to the straight backlash:

Well, the shit really hit the fan this week. The City Council proclaimed Lesbian/Gay Pride Day. The organizing committee made all the plans for a celebration. Then guess who came out of the closet . . . the homophobes. The Christians, remember those folks who gave us the Inquisition and the witch burnings. . . . They're still at it. I guess we should know who they are now.[27]

The following spring the aldermanic council was again asked to officially endorse Lesbian and Gay Pride Day. With opposition Democrats and Republicans in control, a watered-down resolution affirming the civil rights of homosexuals was passed by a slim seven-to-six vote; there was no official endorsement of the day by the Progressive Coalition.[28] Subsequently, Mayor Sanders sent a letter of support to the march leaders claiming he was "confident [their] work will result in a freer and more democratic society."[29] Despite the political setback by the board and anti-gay sentiments in the community, the Progressive Coalition decided to push for a housing ordinance that would protect homosexual renters.

In October 1984, the Progressive Coalition proposed a law that would make it illegal for landlords to discriminate against tenants because of their sexual preference. Also, landlords could be fined from $35 to $250 for refusing to rent to the physically handicapped, blind, crippled, elderly, families with children, or persons receiving public assistance.[30] The total number of people covered by an ordinance written for such a wide spectrum of minorities within the community would be a near majority of renters. The Progressive Coalition was also taking a "civil rights" approach consistent with the board's slim majority vote on that spring's Lesbian and Gay Pride March.

Various Democratic and Republican aldermen attempted to kill the resolution through amendments or other parliamentary procedures. Samuel Levin proposed a plan that would leave the matter to the Vermont legislature; Democratic Paul Lafayette proposed a new committee of landlords and tenants to study the matter further. Coalition Alderman Rick Musty recognized Lafayette's familiar maneuver: "This is merely a disguise to bury this ordinance in a committee, ladies and gentlemen."[31] It looked as if the ordinance was faced with the usual seven-to-six defeat on partisan lines, when Allen Gear, a conservative Republican who attended meetings in a wheelchair, made his support for the measure known. With the proposed ordinance's passage a certainty, the remaining opposition Democrats and Republicans reversed their positions. The housing rights ordinance passed unanimously.[32]

Perhaps only because of the affliction of one Republican opposition member, an ordinance that protected homosexuals and other minorities from housing discrimination was passed even by those who really opposed it. Republican Gear may have been further moved to vote for the measure after Progressive Coalition Alderman Peter Lackowski movingly told the board before the vote of how he was turned down by a Burlington landlord for an apartment because his wife was handicapped: "[The landlord] didn't want to talk about it; he just wanted to rent to someone else because she was handicapped."[33] Whatever the normally conservative Gear's reason for supporting the proposal, the Coalition's strategy was effective. By including the handicapped, welfare recipients, the aged, gays, and families with children (a group not usually seen as a minority), the minority resistance groups that so often oppose each other's initiatives, or are at least unconcerned with measures that do not affect them directly, were united in support. Even the recalcitrant opposition to Republicans and Democrats were embarrassed into supporting a measure that they normally would have consigned to defeat. If a gay-rights housing ordinance had been proposed as a solitary measure, its defeat would have been certain.

PROPOSED REFORM AND ALTERNATIVE REFORM

The housing ordinance that forbade landlord discrimination against gays and other groups was a liberal reform. Although on the face of it such a law was far-reaching, the housing ordinance was not a serious attempt to either undermine the dominant sexual relations in Burlington or protect the housing rights of a composite of minorities. Male dominance and enforced heterosexuality were certainly not threatened by this reformist acceptance of the civil rights of gays. The democratic intent of this measure was undermined by the fact that it proved to be very difficult to enforce, and, even if enforced, its sanctions were of little consequence.

During the debate over the proposed housing ordinance, landlords expressed fears that they would lose a traditional business privilege, the right to reject bad tenants. Sanders retorted that this was untrue, that "landlords don't have to rent to some idiot who's going to destroy their house. . . . You can interview 12 different people and choose."[34] The difference that the new ordinance mandated was that a landlord could not discriminate against gays, the aged, the handicapped, people on welfare, or people with children; other reasons for discrimination were still permissible. However, in reality, a city with a severe housing shortage such as Burlington could often have many prospective tenants attempting to rent an apartment or house. Unless the landlord was stupid enough to reveal his or her intent, discrimination against any of the above groups (particularly in the most sought-after housing) without fear of prosecution was very easy. To prove that the landlord intentionally discriminated illegally, a rejected tenant would have to have evidence of the owner's or manager's state of mind—an almost impossible task. As Stuart Bennett, representative of Apartment Owners, Inc., bluntly told the Board of Aldermen, the new ordinance would increase the expectations of prospective tenants while encouraging landlords to be dishonest or at least hide their reasons for rejecting applicants.[35]

True to Bennett's predictions, it was reported that two months after passage welfare recipients were being legally excluded under the new ordinance. One landlord maneuvered around the law by demanding $700 in deposits and rent in advance from welfare recipients. In this case, the landlord's intent was clear but legal: "We will rent (to welfare recipients) if we have to, but if we could get away with it we won't."[36] There is no reason to think that prospective gay tenants could not be similarly thwarted by frivolous or irrelevant reasons presented by landlords whose real motive was homophobia. Landlords could maintain that straight-appearing applicants were given priority because they had better references or they applied first, or for any number of reasons that beg the truth. Although such assertions could be challenged in court and Assistant City Attorney

Gretchen Bailey maintained her willingness to do so, with the burden of proof resting upon unorganized individual tenants, not many could be expected to initiate such suits. Even if the landlord were successfully prosecuted, the penalty range began at a minimal $35; the maximum fine was $250, considerably less than a month's rent.[37] The minimal deterrent value of such small amounts questions the seriousness of the authors of the ordinance.

Burlington's 1984 housing ordinance protecting the rights of homosexual and other renters was symbolic rather than substantive. If the authors of the law had claimed that it was meant to be merely symbolic, it would have been an effort at socialization of tolerance toward homosexuals and other minority groups. But because the authors acted as if this ordinance were a serious response to minority discrimination, it was only a minimally liberal reform and implicitly dishonest. The right of landlords to rent to whomever they wish, a capitalist privilege, was publicly challenged, though the ordinance's restrictions could be easily eluded. Likewise, the heterosexual values of male-dominated society were publicly challenged by a measure without practical enforcement provisions. However, the Progressive Coalition's support of Burlington's gay and lesbian communities was on record. Despite the law's ineffectiveness, it could only anger Burlington's overt homophobes.

An alternative democratic structural reform to protect housing rights for gays and other minorities might be an ordinance which would make City Hall the monopoly agent for all rentals. Under this proposal, all apartments or houses for rent would be handled by a special city agency that would regulate the rate (to prevent discrimination against low-income renters) and would give preferential treatment either to those most in need or to those who are members of groups (designated by the Board of Aldermen) historically discriminated against. Landlords would lose the pre-rental right of refusal. Such an ordinance would protect the aged, the handicapped, people on welfare, people with children, and the gay community and also give these groups first choice of available housing; this would counter the logic of capitalist refusal to rent to low-income people as a bad investment as well as the logic of other repressive value structures that foster discrimination against gays, blacks, and other oppressed peoples.

A democratic structural housing reform could never be enacted in Burlington. The best evidence is that in 1981 a public referendum to set up an innocuous fair housing commission, which would have had the power to limit excessive rents, was defeated by a crushing four-to-one margin.[38] As in many smaller urban communities, Burlington's rental units are not large apartment complexes; most are in two- and three-family houses, often owner occupied. Such landlords will fight vociferously to defend their right to rent to whomever they please. It is noteworthy that such small units are exempt from federal civil rights statutes. Also, single-family homeowners often rent rooms to students in Burlington; under a city monopoly referral service, they too would lose the right to choose from among prospective tenants. Many of these homeowners would choose not to rent at all under such regulations. Smaller landlords and single homeowners would likely organize themselves in an ad hoc coalition with the owners of large apartment complexes to defeat any referendum for a tenant referral service based in City Hall. A threat to property rights would unite these disparate realty owners. The likely result of such a democratic initiative would be a repetition of the 1981 vote.

Even if Burlington's renters united with progressive homeowners and won such a referendum, the future of the initiative would remain in doubt. Certainly, Burlington's larger apartment complex owners would appeal the measure's legality in court. Without the approval of the Vermont legislature, the new city agency would have no legal basis in Burlington's existing city charter. Considering the legislature's failure to approve various previous city proposals, the likelihood of state approval of a municipal referral agency for tenants would be negligible.

Although the chances that this hypothetical democratic structural housing reform would ever be implemented in Burlington are nil, within the boundaries of liberal reform, it falls short of representing the most that could have been done. The fines for housing discrimination should have been much higher. Except for public exposure of accused and convicted landlords, there are almost no substantive sanctions included in the ordinance that was passed. Also, the legal grounds for tenant rejection could have been detailed. Instead of giving landlords the leeway of vetoing prospective tenants for any reason except those associated with being aged, handicapped, homosexual, welfare recipients, and parents with children, a set of guidelines specifying the reasons acceptable for rejection of a tenant could effectively narrow prejudicial actions. By limiting and demanding documentation of the causes for rejection, tenants could challenge capricious or discriminatory decisions by a landlord with some hope of victory. While this would be simply a liberal reform, since the realm for discrimination by landlords would only be narrowed and not eliminated, it would be superior to the Progressive Coalition measure.

The housing rights ordinance was the most pallid of liberal reforms; the comparable-worth pay-equity program at City Hall was a much more ambitious reform. Comparable worth in its ideal form is a democratic structural reform that ignores the needs of both patriarchy (male domination) and capitalism.

Comparable worth undermines the material underpinnings of the patriarchal and capitalist systems. Because the value of work is based on four nonsexist criteria—skill, effort, responsibility, and working conditions—the occupations that are disproportionately filled by women are not monetarily devalued merely because they are peopled by women. There is a need for comparable worth because there are certain occupations that offer affective rewards that attract many women. Elementary education and childcare are two examples of the jobs that provide an emotional component not found in most other lines of work. Women, because of conscious role modeling or sublimation, have historically been attracted in large numbers to, and thus have flooded the labor market for, such positions.[39] Since women-dominated occupations are already devalued in a male society, the excess participation of women in certain job categories acts to depress the market wage rate even further. Thus, the needs of capitalism and partriarchy are in unison when women are subjugated to the capitalist need for low wages and the male need to keep women financially dependent on men.

Capitalism in its ideal form recruits labor through the system of supply and demand. When a new area of profitability is established in the economy, wages for workers who are specifically trained in occupations needed in the expanding industries rise until the demand for such workers is met. As the demand is overfilled by hopeful workers, the excess supply drives wages down. With pay cuts and vacant positions, frustrated workers will search for and train for better-paying jobs. Comparable worth derails this process. Wages are paid only by the four established criteria; increased demand for certain occupations means no rise in remuneration. Conversely, the oversupply of workers to certain occupations (even in declining industries) should not lead to wage reductions if the comparable worth formula is left untainted by market logic. Thus, on the theoretical level, supply and demand differentials are negated by comparable worth.

Nevertheless, some of the foremost advocates of comparable

worth are accommodating market ideology to facilitate the acceptance of the reform in capitalist society. Two prominent advocates have argued:

The goal of comparable worth policy is to pay a fair market wage to jobs historically done by women. . . . Comparable worth advocates seek to disentangle and remove discrimination from the market. The laissez-faire doctrine underlying the free market ideology assumes that employers and employees bargain as equals. Comparable worth policy can contribute toward a smoothly running marketplace. . . . By interfering in the free market we re-establish *laissez-faire* as the organizing principle guiding social relations in the labor market.[40]

Bending comparable worth programs to the "fair market wage" means that supply and demand must be factored into the four guiding criteria of skill, effort, responsibility, and working conditions. In and of themselves, the four criteria may or may not be correlated with supply and demand; there is no one-to-one correspondence. If there were such a congruence, the conservatives would be correct, and comparable worth would not be needed. In this accommodationist mode, the Burlington comparable worth study ultimately compared the wages of city employees after reclassification with those paid by area employers and concluded: "Salary levels for each classification are competitive with the labor market, designed to attract and retain qualified employees"; "Burlington leads the competitive marketplace in terms of hiring salaries for most of the benchmark positions selected."[41] The area market wage rate, since it was considered (even in the minds of those conducting the study) to be the legitimate standard, was a yardstick of success.

It was not surprising that Labor Relations Associates, the firm that reclassified Burlington's occupational structure, used the area wage rates as benchmarks. Although comparable worth in its uncompromising form is a democratic structural reform, the limited scope of Burlington's program was not destructive of the capitalist wage practices of the Greater Burlington area and thus marked this initiative as a liberal reform. By implementing comparable worth within the city's work force, the Sanders administration wished to set an example for area employers, though there was no reason to believe that without legal sanction any area employer would follow Burlington's lead. For Burlington, an extra $200,000 had to be appropriated for the first year of the new contract to redress wage inequities. There would be little incentive for profit-making or not-for-profit institutions to permanently increase costs by adopting comparable worth. Also by using prevailing area capitalist wage rates as a yardstick, Labor Relations Associates implicitly accepted capitalist rules of supply and demand as valid wage-setting directives. Thus the results of the study reflected the context of capitalist relations between owners and wage earners. Comparable worth, as a formula of meritocracy, should have been used to set wages purely by its own logic in which supply and demand would have been irrelevant.

For comparable worth to be the democratic structural reform it theoretically promises, it would have to have nationwide application. If the Progressive Coalition had tried to implement comparable worth on the capitalist and not-for-profit employers in Burlington, the result would have been failure. The business community would have opposed the added wage bill that comparable worth would have imposed, and Burlington's Democratic and Republican aldermen, almost always sympathetic to business, would have voted it down. If not, Vermont's courts would have voided it as a regulation not granted by the authority of the city charter. And, finally, if these avenues failed, capitalists and not-for-profit organizations, obeying market directives, would relocate and thus escape the authority of the law.

Despite the radical democratic content of comparable worth, the concept was accepted by the city without opposition from the heads of bureaucratic agencies, probably because comparable worth, as applied to the city bureaucracy, attacked male domination, not bureaucratic organization. Comparable worth is reasonably compatible with bureaucratic logic. The major organizing scheme of public bureaucracy is hierarchic; Burlington's public sector was no exception to this. Labor Relations Associates divided Burlington's employees into a hierarchy of four groups: managerial, first; professional and administrative, second; trades and services, third; and public safety, fourth. Within these groups there were four major factors surveyed: education/experience, supervisory responsibility, environmental conditions, and difficulty of work. Each of the factors was weighted by importance with a multiplier of 10, 8, 3, and 10, respectively.[42] Thus education and supervision, which favor those higher on the bureaucratic pyramid, were given multipliers of 10 and 8, respectively, while working under adverse physical conditions was given only a 3 multiplier. A value judgment was made by Labor Relations Associates that education/experience and supervision are worth 600 percent more than environmental conditions. The complexity (difficulty) of a job was worth three times more than the conditions under which that job was performed. Thus a college graduate bossing a crew would earn up to six times more than a worker picking up garbage or unblocking a clogged sewer pipe. This weighting of responsibility and education is both anti-egalitarian and anti-democratic. Thus, bureaucratic structure with its undemocratic division of responsibility and rewards is affirmed and legitimized by comparable worth.

Since comparable worth policies are compatible with hierarchic organization, the question arises about whether they really provide "comparable worth." An essential problem with the concept of comparable worth seems to be the way it disproportionately weights its categories to favor jobs that are filled by elites. For example, education and supervisory functions were given greater worth in the Labor Relations Associates study. These value judgments were imposed by outside professional elites and may well diverge from the workers' own evaluations of job characteristics. To make comparable worth truly democratic, workers of an organization would design and evaluate jobs by their own agreed-upon values. This would strengthen comparable worth as a democratic structural reform.

Considering the compatibility of comparable worth as it is commonly implemented, with bureaucratic practice and organization, it is not surprising that almost all such equity pay reforms have been implemented by government and not by the business community.[43] The logic of supply and demand, capitalism's logic, is secondary to the internal functioning of bureaucracy. Likewise, whether or not a bureaucracy's leadership and reward distribution favors men or women is secondary to a bureaucracy's operation. Bureaucratic logic and comparable worth are not inherently contradictory; in fact, they are complementary.

Since comparable worth destabilizes capitalism and patriarchy but affirms and legitimizes bureaucratic organization, can it be called a democratic structural reform under any circumstances? Yes, because comparable worth is focused toward ending wage discrimination by sex. It provides benefits to dominated women that are destabilizing to the need for men to dominate. Capitalism, although not the primary target, is similarly destabilized since comparable worth in its ideal form denies the logic of supply and demand. That comparable worth affirms another inegalitarian substructure, bureaucracy, does not deny its radical challenge to both male domination and capitalism.

BURLINGTON'S WOMEN'S AGENDA COMPARED
WITH MAYOR SANDERS' AGENDA

There were other reforms enacted in Burlington that were germane to the goal of making the relations between the sexes more equitable. Besides comparable worth and the housing ordinance, the Progressive Coalition established a shelter for battered women, a self-defense program, the whistle-stop safety campaign, and a limited daycare program with a progressive sliding fee; members of the Coalition also made a sustained effort to exclude pornography shops from Burlington and attempted to levy businesses and not-for-profits for daycare services. Together these reforms did not significantly alter the unequal relationship between males and females or gays and straights, but they provided some benefits to the dominated.

Many of these reforms emanated from the Women's Council, but none that did was a democratic structural reform. When asked what local government could do to combat patriarchy, Suzanne Gillis, co-chair of the Women's Council, replied, "Nothing."[44] The discretely private nature of relations between the sexes, which is regulated more by patriarchic ideology than law, keeps democratic structural reforms that would destabilize patriarchy from even being on the agenda. If the co-chair of the Women's Council cannot imagine a local reform that could successfully challenge patriarchy, it is difficult to criticize the Progressive Coalition for not taking the lead in proposing such reforms.

Nevertheless, even if the Women's Council had proposed such reforms, Mayor Sanders, because of his economistic orientation, would have given such reforms low priority on the local political agenda. It is surprising then that he supported comparable worth since he had previously said that he did not favor measures that would materially reward women at the expense of the male workforce. In a 1981 interview with *Commonwoman*, Sanders deftly opposed affirmative action plans for women. Asked if his administrative assistant in City Hall would be a woman, Sanders answered:

O.K. Let me deal with that. You may like it or you may not like it. I will not hire someone because she or he is a woman or a man. I'll hire somebody because they can do the job. I'm not going out of my way to hire a woman.

When pinned down by the interviewer about his position on affirmative action, Sanders answered in a politically safe and noncommittal fashion: "I would say right now you'd find very few women active in city government. I would expect the number of women to increase."[45] The number of women in city government did increase, but not nearly in keeping with their numerical majority. In fact, even the conservative *Burlington Free Press* Editorial Board chided Democrats, Republicans, and Progressive Coalition members alike for their neglect in appointing women to Burlington's ubiquitous and autonomous city commissions. Of twenty seats filled in June 1985, just three went to women.[46] In Burlington's Fire Department, of eighty-four fire fighters, eighty-four were men. Although Peter Clavelle, personnel director, had the department advertise to attract female recruits, quotas that would ensure female representation were not proposed.[47] Such a proposal would have undoubtedly angered the male preserve of firemen, who on and off supported Sanders.

The Sanders administration's lack of concern for sexual oppression did not stop at opposition to affirmative action. Using words that would be contradicted by his later support for a housing ordinance which protected gay rights, Sanders went on to argue that "sexual freedom" was already guaranteed by the First Amendment to the Constitution.

INTERVIEWER: If there was a gay rights proposal for job discrimination, general harassment, would you support it?

SANDERS: Probably not. When you're dealing with priorities—there are hundreds and hundreds of young kids in the city whose lives are being destroyed—have no place to go. They can't go to school—they're going into the army—that's my priority. I think the First Amendment is very clear on protecting people's rights to sexual freedom. I know in many communities gay rights is a big thing. To me it's a civil liberties matter. I believe very strongly in civil liberties. If people tell me they're in a bar and they're being harassed because they're gay—tell me about it and I'll do something about it as I will if someone has a religious belief. They have the right to practice freely. I will support that. I will not make it a major priority.[48]

Sanders' blunt answer revealed his priorities; gay liberation clearly was not one of them. His administration's subsequent support for Lesbian and Gay Pride Day can be discounted as political posturing. The Sanders administration's support for a housing bill guaranteeing the rights of homosexuals to rent appears to be equally motivated by short-term electoral goals. This attitude no doubt contributed to the loose wording of the measure and the minimal penalties that make the ordinance almost empty of substance.

It can be safely concluded that the Sanders administration's reforms attempting to make relations between the sexes more equitable were not originated at City Hall. The amorphous and democratic organization of the Women's Council allowed the gay, lesbian, and women's groups in the city to place measures on the political agenda that the administration would otherwise have ignored. Even if the administration had actively sought democratic structural reform of the relations between the sexes, it would likely have failed. However, such a commitment would have led to more effective liberal reforms. With all its flaws, comparable worth was the most important reform challenging the existing relations between the sexes passed during the period under study.

This review and analysis of the Progressive Coalition's reforms in the area of sexual politics concludes the last of the four empirical case studies. The next chapter will sum up the empirical findings and discuss the theoretical implications that follow from those findings.

9
On the Question of Reform and Local Autonomy

The administration of Bernard Sanders, the socialist mayor of Burlington, could not implement a wide-ranging series of democratic structural reforms. A few liberal reforms were passed, and most reactionary reforms were either thwarted or delayed.

Clearly, the unmitigated exploitation of the waterfront by private developers was prevented by the Sanders administration. After considerable bargaining, the Sanders administration backed the Alden Plan, an attempted liberal progrowth reform that failed (even though a majority of those voting in a referendum approved it) because the city charter stipulated a two-thirds margin for passage. Conservatives and ecologists opposed it for cross purposes. Working-class voters rejected the plan because the resulting benefits would go mainly to the upper classes. In the end, stalemate prevailed. Like the initial plans for waterfront development, the Southern Connector highway proposal, as planned before Sanders won the mayoral seat, was a blueprint for a reactionary reform. Sanders thwarted this proposal and substituted a liberal, pro-neighborhood version. Because of ambiguous language in the final agreement, however, this may yet turn out to be a reactionary reform. The final results of waterfront and highway development in Burlington remain to be seen. As of this writing, the only conclusion that can be reached is that these reactionary reforms were delayed. A third issue of economic development—whether Burlington should have municipally owned cable television—was resolved as a liberal reform. The skillful use of the federal

198

system by the Sanders administration after the state Public Service Board had thwarted the initial, ambitious attempt at democratic structural reform, forced both Cox Communications and the new owners of the franchise to make liberal concessions to both the city government and cable customers. The final tally for the three cases of economic development is two reactionary reforms blocked and one liberal reform secured.

The outcomes of the tax issues were similarly muddled. There was only one reform proposed that even approached being democratic structural in nature, a municipal income tax restricted to upper-income households. This proposal never made it past the rhetorical agenda of the first mayoral campaign. Many liberal tax reforms were proposed; the daycare levy, excavation fee, antispeculation tax, tax reclassification, property transfer fee, and not-for-profit property tax all fall into this category. The property transfer fee and the anti-speculation tax (which gained the favor of the voters only in a weakened form) were unambiguously defeated in the state legislature. Tax reclassification, after being passed by Burlington's voters, was vetoed by the state legislature. Later, Vermont's legislators finally accepted a business-backed compromise that allowed this tax increase on the profit-making sector. Unlike those liberal reforms, the utility excavation fee was enacted by the Sanders administration with permission from the state judiciary. However, the proposed rate of the tax was halved. If this tax is eventually passed on to residential customers as a flat-rate increase, it will lose its liberal rating and become decidedly reactionary. The state courts totally rejected the business-backed property tax levy on the not-for-profit sector. The daycare levy that was transformed to serve suburban needs was voted down by Burlingtonions.

The rooms and meals tax, a reactionary reform, was first turned down by the voters and then accepted, only to be vetoed by the state. In a watered down form, it was finally accepted by both after business gave its blessing. The same business-dominated commission that advocated the rooms and meals receipts tax (as a temporary measure), made the repeal of the inventory tax on business the quid pro quo. A reactionary reform was traded away for a slightly less reactionary reform and a liberal reform (tax reclassification). Finally, property reappraisal, as homeowners consistently suspected, was a reactionary reform that was partially offset by tax reclassification. The final tally for the tax issues is two liberal reforms implemented, four liberal reforms defeated, and three reactionary reforms enacted.

The foreign policy reforms are not so easily summarized. Since there was a series of measures designed to socialize a new consciousness, legislative enactments and defeats cannot measure success. Two resolutions were defeated, but sister-city relationships were established with communities in Nicaragua and the Soviet Union. Nevertheless, even the defeats stirred debate and furthered the cause of the Sanders administration. Also, the mayor's trips furthered thinking about the relationship of the United States to both of these socialist regimes. Only the mayor's reactionary responses to civil disobedience detracted from the effort to alter political consciousness toward a progressive foreign policy. The sum of actions had the potential to be a democratic structural reform: altering a community's political thinking from complacency in foreign affairs to an active opposition to American hegemony. Without sophisticated opinion polls to measure the changes, we must list the sum of these measures as a "potential" democratic structural reform on our scoreboard.

The last two reforms, those dealing with relations between the sexes, were both enacted. Comparable worth as a reform that would have been an unambiguously democratic structural measure if it had not been weakened by its modest scope. Still, it was the most successful legislative enactment of a democratic structural reform in Burlington. The renters' rights bill, designed to protect homosexuals and a panoply of other tenant groups which were discriminated against, was a symbolic liberal reform (though it was not billed that way); the problems of enforcement and the minimal fines prescribed by the measure could hardly be expected to deter any potentially bigoted landlord. Under the category of sexual politics, the final tally is one liberal reform bordering on being democratic structural and one pallid liberal reform.

If the reforms are divided into those primarily economic and those more clearly associated with the demands of the new social movements, the difference in the rate of success is apparent. The capitalist State, as neo-Marxists theorize it, clearly checkmated most of the Sanders administration economic initiatives. The successes were watered-down compromises and the failures at least balanced those modest enactments. The economic development and tax reforms that were implemented seldom resembled those that were originally proposed.

The new social movement issues fared somewhat better. Foreign policy resolutions failed to pass the Board of Aldermen two times in a row. However, if the ultimate goal was to change consciousness, defeat was at times as rewarding as success. Since the issues were perceived as more symbolic than material, there were few constraints enforced on the debate by the capitalist and federalist systems. Local business was not threatened in any immediate sense, and the national government could afford to overlook this isolated, obstreperous challenge to its monopoly on foreign affairs (although the State Department travel ban might have been a deliberate effort to upset Burlington's foreign policy).

The sexual politics reforms were both successful. The renters' rights turned from near defeat to unanimity because of the vote of one handicapped Republican. Although this reform was also economic and thus bore the enmity of landlords, it passed the Board of Aldermen by lumping the interests of gays with those of various other sectors of the community. Comparable worth was implemented practically without comment (until male members of the city workforce realized its redistributive potential), and this was a dramatic reform. The outcomes suggest that the demands of the new social movements may find a better response within the capitalist State than purely class-based demands will. Unfortunately, this success may really symbolize a greater failure. Many of the most fundamental demands of the new social movements may not be effectively dealt with by legislative solutions. Patriarchy, compulsory heterosexuality, and even militarism have societal roots that run so deep that although they may be clipped back by legislative approaches, they will still thrive. Even if government nudges society toward change, the underlying relations of inequality may still be faithfully reproduced. The anti-sexist provisions of the Civil Rights Act of 1964 have not significantly ended the dominant position of men in Burlington or elsewhere. Even so, those demands of the new social movements which are not redistributive in nature may find more acceptance than left economic reforms.

INTERPRETIVE LACUNAE AND POST-MARXISM

The shortcomings of American urban political economic theory become readily apparent when those theories are applied to Burlington's politics. Although post-Marxist theorists have not yet elaborated an urban politics theory, the general framework that analyzes non-economic struggles as equally legitimate as class struggles provides a needed supplement to neo-Marxist theorizing. Mainstream approaches such as those of Paul Peterson and the public choice school do not even consider the issue of such struggles as important enough to warrant their analysis.

Paul Peterson's economic determinism in *City Limits* is no more acceptable than neo-Marxist economic determinism.[1] Peterson's predictions about local state policy and the actions of local political elites are, for the most part, contrary to events in Burlington. Although the Sanders administration did at times pursue pro-business economic initiatives, it did not do so either willingly or under the trickle-down assumptions that Peterson claimed should have been at work. When Sanders worked with the Alden Corporation to facilitate the largest development project ever proposed in Vermont, it was preceded by hundreds, if not thousands, of hours of strategy sessions and negotiations with Alden to extract the most possible public benefits. Although a great part of the Progressives' working-class constituency judged that the negative consequences would be greater than the benefits, Sanders' public statements indicate that he believed that he won for them the best possible benefits. In any event, Sanders' delaying of the Southern Connector and his many attempts to redistribute the tax burden onto business do not in any way conform to Peterson's model of how city political elites promote pro-business developmental policies.

Peterson's generalizations that city elites easily contain dissident movements are wrong on two counts as applied to Burlington.[2] First, the economic dissidents elected important city leaders. They controlled the mayor's office, a plurality of the Board of Aldermen, and eventually a few of the influential city commissions. Second, the ecological left in Burlington was not effectively contained by the Sanders administration. With almost no funding, the ecologists united with tax-protest conservatives and defeated the Sanders-Alden proposal at the polls. According to *City Limits,* this would be impossible.

Second, Peterson's categories of analysis are purely economic and thus could not be used to evaluate new social movement demands such as sister-city relations with socialist nations or protests against State Department bans on travel. Since Peterson's concern is not with these noneconomic issues, it was reasonable that he created a policy framework that excluded them. Nonetheless, such exclusion was really a way of devaluing such policy concerns.

The public choice school, on which Peterson so heavily relies, can tell us little about which proposals the Sanders administration attempted. If the social service mix was the key to explaining city politics, how does a political economist find consistency with Sanders' frequent referenda defeats (Alden Plan, renter's arbitration board, rooms and meals tax, anti-speculation tax, and the daycare levy) and his reelection by increasing pluralities? Was this not proof that city politics cannot be reduced to the simple formula of finding the correct mix of services? Also, there was no noticeable influx or outflow of citizens looking for that ideal service package; Burlington's population remained a stagnant thirty-eight thousand. Even more important, the public choice school can tell us little about the formidable constraints to increasing city services, constraints having nothing to do with public opinion. Municipal cable television was thwarted by Cox Communications and the Public Service Board. Consumer sovereignty was surely an illusion since no city in Vermont offered this service to its citizenry. Finally, even if citizens were primarily motivated by the availability of city services, the one-quarter of Burlington's population near or below the poverty line had no money to shop for a nicer package in the suburbs.

If the narrow economism of service delivery politics is inappropriate for evaluating Burlington's politics, the much wider net of urban neo-Marxist theorizing also fails to cover the range of possibilities. Although neo-Marxism has well analyzed the relationship of capital and the national state to the local state, it has mostly ignored the crucial middle-level of federalism. The state of Vermont had greater direct effect on almost all of Burlington's tax initiatives and two of the three economic development projects discussed here than did capital or the national government in their more distant directives. Although most of the state's actions were conditioned by capital, the mediating effect of the state had its own independent influence as well. Vermont's judiciary sustained both the excavation tax and the public uses doctrine after qualifying them. Since prominent business elites unequivocally opposed the city's position in both cases, any orthodox Marxist notion that state government was merely a committee for the ruling class cannot be affirmed. The resulting decisions represented some degree of victory for the Sanders administration. In the final analysis, it must be concluded that the state as a semi-autonomous part of the federalist system had tremendous leverage over any city policy initiative.

Neo-Marxists have done little analysis of the states, but even more surprising has been the lack of a framework to systematically analyze the content of reform legislation. No doubt, this is the legacy of orthodox Marxian theorizing that devalues any reform less than revolutionary. With revolution being a romantic and most unlikely solution in contemporary America, a scale to evaluate left legislative reform is needed, and this work has moved toward that end.

Although there is no neo-Marxian framework for policy analysis, the relationship of outside developers to the city is overstated. Burlington's experience with developers cannot be reduced to an outside intrusion of capital over an unsympathetic public. Pro-growth values were almost ubiquitous in Burlington as they have been in most of America. Sanders' support for the Alden Plan contradicts any romantic notion that Burlington's local reformers opposed growth and were defeated by the ruthless onslaught of capital. Growth was not forced on unwilling Progressives. Instead, they sought to shape it to provide the greatest degree of public benefits they could extract. By 1989, the local Greens were running their own mayoral candidate against all of Burlington's pro-growth political parties. Neo-Marxism's economistic world view actually helped shape the consciousness (and thus the policy choices) of Progressive Coalition activists.

While the elected elite of the Progressive Coalition were mostly united by a common economistic world view, the rest of Burlington's diverse left had a varied and contradictory agenda that proved to be a constraint on the Sanders administration. Homosexuals, women, ecologists, and peace activists were all separately organized and not reticent about making demands in return for their support. The demands of each new social movement grouping had economic consequences, but their demands were not derived from class conflict.

American urban neo-Marxist theorists have grappled with the new social movements, but little has been done to demonstrate their differences from the traditional class-based left. It is in the arena of struggle that is not class generated that post-Marxist theorizing becomes useful. Burlington's experience proved that coalitions between the class-based left and the new-social-movement left could successfully elect local officials. Once the objective that had united them had been achieved, the basic contradictions and differing priorities rose to the surface. Neo-Marxist theorists and activists have not sufficiently valued the changes that have been wrought by the transformation to postindustrial society. Noneconomic demands from the new social movements are now competing with class-based struggles on the urban terrain.

In Burlington the consequence of these left divisions was an additional constraint on city reform possibilities. The Vermont Greens helped kill the Alden Plan because economic growth as proposed, socialist or capitalist, contradicted their view of the good. Likewise the Burlington Peace Coalition's priorities clashed with those of the blue-collar workers at GE. Mayor Sanders, with little hesitation, chose the working class over the new social movements. The autonomous Women's Council did not challenge the Sanders administration so directly, but friction was noticeable. It was as if the materially derived social relations of the last century were sparring with the ideologically derived social relations of this century.

The salience of ideology is key to the emerging post-Marxist (postmaterialist) paradigm. The demands of Burlington's ecologists, feminists, peace activists, and gay activists, even when economic, were not strictly (if at all) derived from the mode of production. Most of the Progressive Coalition were sympathetic to their demands; the mix of policy initiatives proved this. However, when the volume of attempted Progressive reforms and the effort spent on them is calculated, the economic priorities dwarf those of the new social movements. Only with an understanding of the ideology of the Progressive Coalition members can their priorities be explained. Their class proclivities are not revealed by their class backgrounds; Progressives and members of new social movements were often quite similarly situated. The most doctrinaire Coalition Marxist, Terrill Bouricius, worked at the semicommunal Green River Co-op market with countercultural lesbians. To some extent, each chose his or her battle. Unequal relations were the common denominator and a given; the selection of which system of oppression to confront provided for some element of free will. Ideology had its own explanatory effects in Burlington. Post-Marxism emphasizes the ideological over the material; just the reverse of traditional Marxist analysis.

It should be emphasized that the ideological divisions between class-oriented and new-social-movement activists were paralleled by collaborative efforts. Peace activists and Progressives were united in their support for socialist sister-city relations and Sanders' official visits. Also, comparable worth and the late but innovative attempt to provide partially socialized daycare were welcomed by feminists. Sanders even attempted to electorally court the Vermont Greens by promising that if he were elected governor he would shut down Vermont's only atomic power plant (provided he could find a substitute power source).[3] Only by paying heed to the struggles of the non-Marxist left could class-based activists hope to gain sufficient electoral support for their own initiatives. Using the post-Marxist inclusive approach to study Burlington's politics not only remedies neo-Marxist theorizing, but also suggests the only viable route of success for left activists. Burlington's pluralistic left often cleaved to or were cleaved by the issues, very much in the contradictory meanings of that word. With left cohesion, the autonomy of Burlington's political leadership increased; with division, it decreased.

BURLINGTON'S AUTONOMY

Since Burlington's government in the 1980s was the fortuitous beneficiary of a robust winner-city economy, the constraints imposed by capital on its autonomy were not as severe as those faced by this city and other urban municipalities during the 1970s. Most reactionary reforms that would have aided capital were prevented or at least slowed. Some liberal reforms were passed, but no democratic structural reforms that directly challenged capital were enacted.

As a system, capitalism paradoxically both limited Burlington's leaders and provided them the wherewithal to bargain for benefits. The business climate in Burlington revived quickly after the recession years of 1981 and 1982. Business confidence in the Burlington economy was healthy for reasons that had little to do with political elites. Investors clearly wanted to be part of the postindustrial boom. This gave the Sanders administration a bargaining leverage that the mayor of Gary, Indiana, could only dream about. Nonetheless, there were clear limits to autonomy even in the best of business climates.

Business confidence did not represent an inelastic demand to do business in Burlington. Neighboring municipalities were ready to welcome any business defectors; the telephone company migrated to South Burlington. Manufacturers were footloose throughout postindustrial New England. Local developers were seeking to build or expand suburban malls with ample free parking, unlike downtown Burlington where there was a charge for city streets and garages. In the last two years of the Sanders' regime, a giant mall was proposed by the Pyramid Corporation in the nearby town of Williston. Utilizing state environmental impact ordinances. Sanders fought its construction in the same way his predecessor, Gordon Pacquette, had done ten years before.[4] Not only did the Sanders administration act to protect the business climate of the downtown business community, but the local left even subsidized new small business ventures. The demands for business confidence helped shape the left agenda and not only in terms of resistance.

Business confidence was a state of mind, dependent on the expectation of profit. As long as it remained strong, the Progressives could have an agenda that demanded more public benefits. The economic base was strong enough that socialist rhetoric, liberal reforms, and even proposed democratic structural reforms did not erode it. The ideology of capitalism could be challenged on many fronts, from foreign policy to land use, without dissipating business confidence. Profit was not immediately threatened. And when specific sectors were threatened, capital investment was neither halted nor withdrawn by other sectors. By pursuing the public trust doctrine in the courts, the Sanders administration was arguing the radical case for municipal confiscation without compensation. Such a bold move against the almost unquestioned belief in property rights inhibited capital investment along the waterfront, but there was no economic crisis in the neighboring downtown. Business confidence was dependent on the sum of material factors that result in an environment conducive to capital. The Sanders administration did little to foster those material factors, and its radical actions did little to diminish them. Any solidarity among local capitalists against so-called Progressive Coalition socialism was undermined by those who would break ranks to make a buck. Winner-city status was exploited by the Sanders administration with little apparent blackmail from local business. It was in the federalist system that business fought its battles; any threatened retribution such as disinvestment was not credible.

Notwithstanding the Sanders administration's pro-growth policies, the Progressive Coalition was not a local committee of the ruling class. Capital was both resisted and shaped by the radicals in Burlington, even while capital was shaping the agenda of the Progressive Coalition. With business confidence high, the Sanders administration took the offensive. It was usually frustrated by Vermont's judiciary, legislature, or bureaucracy. The sum of failures was not as surprising as the modicum of success demonstrated by the Sanders administration's deft maneuvering through the federalist system.

The veto opportunities within the federalist system were used extensively by the Sanders administration. Incredibly, on the economic front, the Progressives fought a *Fortune* 500 company, a development corporation with national capital backing, and the state of Vermont over the issue of municipal cable. Although the Sanders administration did not reach its goal, it extracted some impressive concessions. However, in this and the other cases of city victories, it cannot be said that the Sanders administration unequivocally achieved its objectives. Paradoxically, the conservative bias of the federalist system was used by Progressives to extract concessions. By using the negative institutional bias of the state courts, the state bureaucracy, and mayoral vetoes, the Progressives could, and did, partially jam federalism's labyrinthine mechanism. The federalist structure of overlapping jurisdictions was manipulated by actors at the weakest level of the structure to create a slightly larger sphere of autonomy for Burlington.

Autonomy was both facilitated and limited by the federalist system because federalism was less than a complete structure of power. By contrast, actions of capital were much more decisive than those of the State: Alden Corporation bought land while the Board of Aldermen debated, and Cox proceeded with its rebuilding program while the Sanders administration could not even arrange a hearing in front of the Public Service Board for its proposal.

Certainly, capital had its divisions. After GE's agent in government, William Aswad, planned the connector route to avoid the parking lot, a local bottler whose plant would be razed by the proposed route went to court and beat the corporate giant. Even more divisive, some local capitalist renegade developers worked with the Sanders administration to build moderate-income housing. Nevertheless, the swamp of interbusiness conflicts could not compare with the flood of interfederal warfare waged over Progressive Coalition legislation.

The institutional hurdles that had to be surmounted within the federalist system were clearly daunting. On the entry level, the Progressive Coalition's failure to control the Board of Aldermen prevented some proposals. This could be countered by obtaining a petition securing the requisite number of citizen signatures, thereby placing the measure on the ballot for voter approval. Using democratic theory as a standard, this tapping of direct authority, receiving the permission of the sovereign people, should have been the most fundamental base for local authority. Repeatedly, the results of this litmus test of democratic will demonstrated that local sovereignty did not remain with the local populace. The gross receipts tax on rooms and meals to aid the schools was easily passed by the voters and just as easily denied by the Vermont legislature. Only when business gave its imprimatur could the will of the people of Burlington prevail in the state legislature.

In addition to the constraints imposed by state elected officials, unelected local state officials used bureaucratic authority to frustrate the directives of elected leaders and those of the citizens. The Burlington Electric Department helped sabotage municipal cable and the

Planning Commission competed with elected officials to control waterfront development until much of their authority was redirected to the mayor's office. Since each bureaucracy had its own agenda, the bureaucrats were useful allies in the quest for more political autonomy only when their agenda coincided with that of the elected officials.

Besides the intralocal state challenge, there was an always present interlocal governmental challenge. The surrounding communities, seeking to enhance their own autonomy, could influence Burlington's actions. Repealing inventory taxes and offering relocation subsidies to business were both suburban ploys that could be used to woo fleeing Burlington capital. Pressure at this level of the federalist system created an equilibrium of competitive business incentives. If the Progressives upset the equilibrium too greatly, the best option for many Burlington businesses was to leave the city. However, most measures that were forceful enough to upset the equilibrium were out of the city's hands.

Unlike the more manageable local hurdles, the state hurdles were large indeed. Once a piece of legislation involving any city charter change passed, the Vermont legislature could exercise its veto. And even if the state legislature was not involved in a city policy, the executive bureaucracy and the courts each could, and often did, act to limit Burlington's authority. In contrast, the state level could also enhance local autonomy. Increased funds, court decisions, or bureaucratic rulings, when in harmony with the positions of local state elected officials or citizens (as expressed in referenda), all increased local autonomy, though instances of such harmony were rare.

By contrast, the national government's approval was seldom needed. National government influence usually took the more remote form of shaping the playing field. For example, the Southern Connector was possible only because of national funding. Also, the search for progressive taxes was exacerbated by revenue cutbacks. Despite these examples, once in a while the national government could put up direct obstacles to local state policy: the EPA effectively rerouted the Southern Connector (endangering a fragile state–local state compromise), and the State Department banned Soviet visitors from Chittenden County with no input from local officials.

The national government's greatest contribution to Burlington's authority, however, was in its grants. For the local state, getting the grant was the first step, one that confounded the Alden Plan. When grant money was received for projects that were in harmony with the wishes of elected officials or referenda, city autonomy was increased. This situation reversed itself when local official attitudes changed after grants were received or the strings attached to the grants became too onerous. Autonomy actually did decrease in Burlington because of changed local attitudes to a received grant. Completion of the Southern Connector, for example, was contingent on national financing formulae. Once Burlington committed itself to the project, Vermont's Transportation Agency chose the route and the dimensions of the project. Changes proposed by the Sanders administration were resisted; local state autonomy was compromised. By contrast, if relatively string-free general revenue sharing were to reappear or community block development grant funding were to increase, local state policy options would increase in proportion to the funding available.

The stratified but overlapping structure of federalism caused both successes and failures in the attempt by the Progressive Coalition to expand local state authority. Clearly, there are limits to reform that undermine majority rule at the local level. Finding those exact limits and codifying them into exact formulas are impossible. The independent effects of personality, economic prosperity, left unity, state and national government response, and even chance prevent any specific threshold from being identified. Nonetheless, the formidable reality of constraints to reform and the vast directives that shape and guide the local agenda exist and are in basic contradiction to the concept of majority rule at the most basic unit of democracy, the local state.

10

Prescription: A State-Based Strategy for the Left

Urban neo-Marxist analysts have offered few prescriptions to remedy the plight of the local state. In light of the almost universal conclusion of these left theorists that the local state is ill-equipped to meet the needs of its citizens because of the constraints of capital, their failure to specify remedies strongly implies that the analysts believe the problem is virtually insurmountable.[1] Taken at face value, the experience of Burlington bears out this pessimistic view. Despite modest successes, most initiatives were either defeated outright or adopted in a watered-down form. A closer look suggests a prescription that would have sustained most of the Progressive Coalition's attempted reforms: left capture of the state of Vermont's electoral machinery.

If the Progressive Coalition had controlled the governorship, the legislature, the state bureaucracy, and the courts, almost all the reforms that were approved by the Board of Aldermen and the citizenry through referenda could have been adopted and implemented. The most consistent set of obstacles to local reform in Burlington was not the direct interference of the business community or the national government; it was the state of Vermont in its multiple forms. In the area of economic development, the waterfront could have been purchased by the state and turned over to Burlington (or in an even more radical move, a state court could have awarded title of the disputed property to the city or the state). In fact, in 1986, sometime liberal Democratic Governor Madeleine Kunin did consider the possibility of buying the land and turning it into a park. No doubt, Sanders' gubernatorial challenge that year placed the proposal on the agenda for consideration. Also, since the size, design, and route of the Southern Connector were all largely determined by the state Transportation Agency left control could have meant an entirely different set of options. Finally, the proposed municipalization of the cable television franchise (the most radical economic development reform) would have been ensured by either Progressive Coalition control of the Public Service Board or devolution of control to the Board of Aldermen and mayor.

Progressive Coalition tax policy proposals would similarly have benefitted from favorable state action. The (unfortunately regressive) room and meals tax, the transfer fee proposal, the anti-speculation tax, tax assessments on not-for-profit corporations, and even a local municipal income tax would all have been feasible. Any proposed utility excavation fee could have been made relatively immune from state court challenge. More important, economic development programs considered too radical to place on the local state agenda could have been considered.

The demands of the new social movements outside the economic sphere could have been addressed. A Progressive Vermont might facilitate pacifist consciousness by subsidizing anti-militarist training in the schools. In the area of sexual politics, comparable worth (no doubt in a watered-down form) might be incrementally expanded to the private sector. Liberal reform would be the norm, and democratic structural reform would be possible at times. The entire spectrum would move sharply to the left.

However, though left capture of Vermont is desirable, it is not likely. Even in Burlington, the only city in the state where the left held office, the radicals could not take control of the City Council. Sanders' run for the governor's seat was quite ineffective before and while he was the mayor of the state's largest city. Any left strategy to capture local or state government must deal with the consistent problem of too few votes for left candidates or initiatives.

The solution to this problem lies in counteracting both the dispersion of America's left and the left's fantasy of a mass movement. Even the size of the left remains a mystery. Any calculation of the committed gay, black, Latino, feminist, ecological, union, socialist, and gray activists (though orthodox Marxists would not accept most of these groups as the left) is difficult, if not impossible, since the numbers fluctuate greatly. At any given time, the left is a minority within almost any given community.

Much of the problem is due to geographic dispersion. The local left has few concentrations; most concentrations usually surround institutions of higher learning. Significant numbers of the left live in San Francisco, New York, and Boston, and in the smaller communities of Berkeley, Santa Cruz, and Burlington. Unfortunately, most of the left are in states large enough that those committed to democratic structural reform are a distinct minority bloc of voters. California, New York, and Massachusetts, where much of the American left resides, have masses well socialized to be either hostile to or at least uninterested in socialism and most other types of democratic socialist reform. Even smaller states, such as Vermont and Connecticut, have majorities that are unsympathetic to such reform.

To achieve left control of a state's elected offices in an environment hostile to democratic structural reform requires an unorthodox solution. Even the most optimistic and sympathetic left analyst must concede that the traditional solution of radicalizing the American masses has proven to have a transitory effect at best. Historically, the left has placed an emphasis on educating the public to left views. For the time and effort spent (with the important exceptions of those who have never voted), this has been and will continue to be a waste of time. Even during the greatest crisis to American capitalism, the Great Depression of the 1930s, most voters kept their old party loyalties, including most Republicans![2] Burlington's politics offer further evidence of this pattern of established voter loyalty. The Progressive Coalition's most active members were either leftists who came from out of state or native Vermonters who came of voting age during the turbulent Vietnam era. If Vermont's population were not one-third flatlanders (the uncomplimentary term that natives use for nonnative Vermonters), there would not have been any significant left constituency in Burlington or anywhere else in the state. Even with this in-migration, local public opinion polling shows that of the three parties in Burlington, the Progressive Coalition has the least support by far.[3] More important, Progressive Coalition victories in Burlington have not been duplicated anywhere else in the state.

The unorthodox solution to this problem is a future relocation of the left to Vermont or a state that has a similar sparse population and an existing left presence.[4] By relocating in sufficient numbers to a state such as Vermont, the existing left could capture the state's elective offices in relatively few years. Vermont, with its left base in Burlington and low population, is the best candidate on the East Coast for a left migration; it could rapidly have a majority left electorate with the in-migration of tens of thousands of feminists, ecologists, socialists, gay activists, gray activists, left academics, and civil rights activists.

The key to success is timing. Arthur Schlesinger, Jr. (no friend of the radical left), has documented the reform cycle in American history and found that it has a generational basis. About every thirty years a reform generation comes to maturity (voting age), and the priorities of "public purpose" displace those of private purpose.[5] Although Schlesinger is self-deceptive about how much public purpose has displaced private purpose in American society, the rhythm of reform has been borne out. For the left, this means that the radicals of the 1960s have parented a generation of red-diaper babies that will create the next college-generation left in the 1990s. Schlesinger argues that the last publically interested generation began with the 1961 administration of John Kennedy. Thus he finds the next reform generation making its political presence known around 1990.[6] If he is correct, the emergence of radical college-age youth should appear somewhat after this period. Radicalism among students did not spread out of the prestige universities to the other institutions of higher learning until the second half of the 1960s. A possible delaying factor for the next left is that the baby boomers of the late 1960s utilized the increased availability of contraceptive devices and delayed having their children until they were in their thirties. The next left generation will likely make its debut as a mass movement in the mid to late 1990s at the earliest.[7] With few family responsibilities and a renewed sense of idealism, this new generation could be the one that relocates to Vermont and establishes a normative model of left state government. The present academic left needs to establish blueprints for the coming generation to facilitate an American journey toward a more democratic society.

Capture by the left of the elected offices of state government would not be enough to ensure democratic socialist reform at the local level. To reconstitute the state government in such a way as to maximize local government's ability to institute democratic structural reform would have to be a clear priority.

TOWARD A MORE DEMOCRATIC LOCAL STATE

If the left were to populate and capture a state electorally, the problem would remain of how to increase local autonomy to the point at which democratic structural reform, or at least liberal reform (which approaches being democratic structural reform), is encouraged. A state government dedicated to both democratic structural reform and maximum autonomy of local government would cede most authority to the local level. In certain areas, however, it would reduce local authority to enhance those prospects of reform that challenge the dominant structures in our society. Thus, in certain policy areas, the prescriptions are seemingly paradoxical: to increase local autonomy, it must be reduced.

Tax policy is one such area. A progressive, liberal-reform state income tax could be used to replace most local taxes. A state income tax is desirable even though Burlington's attempts to find a progressive tax and Vermont's repeated actions to prevent or limit such efforts seem to argue the opposite approach: letting local government raise its own revenue with a minimum of state constraints. However, the situation would change dramatically with a new majority; there should be little similarity between the actions of Vermont of the early 1980s and those of a progressive state electorally controlled by the next left. This sweeping expansion of state authority through the imposition of a dominant state-collected tax would be necessary to prevent the suburban escape from taxation.

To replace most local taxation by a state income tax is to recognize how severely limited local taxation efforts are because of the potential outflow of more affluent citizens and capital investment. A progressive income tax, if implemented, would increase the cost of migration; one would have to cross state lines rather than merely relocate across a town boundary. (To prevent interstate capital flight, tough laws against plant closings would be needed.) The tax revenue collected could be redistributed by a formula that stresses need; however, all allotments would be sufficient to fund an entire municipal budget. All communities would be allowed to tax beyond their state allocations if they wished to expand services.[8] If all or most funding were provided from the state treasury, the ruinous competition among localities over tax rates would be alleviated. To prevent the state from managing every administrative detail of local programs, the state would leave implementation to local authorities.

Besides removing much of community tax authority by imposing an almost unitary state tax, to maximize the possibility of democratic reform, the state would forbid all gratuitous subsidies to business by government. Unless an equity portion of the business were offered to the state or local government equal in dollar value to any subsidy provided (thus there being, in effect, no subsidy), no government funds could be expended or tax breaks given to help any business not worker owned. To prevent the competition among local governments for business investment that results in the public subsidy of capitalism, the central authority of the state government would be increased to forbid such giveaways by local (and state) governments.

To combat other structures such as sexism, racism, and ageism, state government would also infringe on local authority. In the state constitution there would be provisions to protect women, blacks, Latinos, homosexuals, the elderly, and the handicapped. There would be a provision allowing the state legislature to identify an oppressed group and give it compensatory privileges so that it could combat its subordinate status. This would legitimize the much-besieged remedy of affirmative action. Such a state constitutional provision is necessary to prevent community majorities from discriminating against local minorities. Just as the campaign for states' rights in the South in the 1960s was an attempt to preserve forced black segregation and the domination of whites in the guise of decentralization, so too could the development of plenary state authority foster local discriminatory policy. The national government, which overrode de jure racial segregation in the South and helped to override patriarchal segregation of occupations nationwide, retreated from these positions in the Reagan years. State government can legislate to reverse this passive acceptance by the national government of domination that is not economically determined. A state constitutional amendment designed to combat one of the most virulent forms of sexism, the denial of sexual preference, would be a priority. However, these liberating state laws would necessarily come at the expense of local state authority.

With the exceptions made, the vast majority of other areas of state authority should be devolved through the state constitution to the local state, which would become the site of original decision making. To make sure that state government did not go beyond its primary role as a conduit of funds for local government and a protector of minority rights, a detailed enumeration of local powers would have to be included in the state constitution. Any general provision should be avoided. The fate of the Tenth Amendment to the Constitution is instructive here: "The powers not delegated to the United States by the Constitution, not prohibited by it to the States are reserved to the States respectively, or to the people." This provision, which retains most governing authority for the states and gives only "delegated" authority to the national government, has been widely violated in the latter's favor.[9] To prevent a parallel state incursion into local authority,

the following areas of authority would have to be specifically delegated to local government:

1. fire and police protection (including trial courts)
2. education
3. welfare
4. ecology and public health
5. utility regulation
6. regulation of private property (planning and zoning)
7. eminent domain (without restriction)

Such a compilation of local power would effectively nullify the tyran-
ny of Dillon's Rule.

It should be recognized that local practice, no matter how democratic, can have deleterious effects on the whole. To remedy local
obstructionism, a state constitutional provision that would allow the
state to intercede by a two-thirds vote of the state legislature in any
specific locality where there is abuse of authority would be a necessary safeguard. The two-thirds threshold would prevent state incursion in all but the most outrageous local actions. Also, by relegating
any state incursion to specific communities, the scope of state intervention would remain severely circumscribed.

With state government's authority severely limited and local government's authority proportionately increased, local government itself must be thoroughly democratized. In its present institutional
form, the local state's fragmented organization acts as an internal limitation of authority. To remedy this ill, a two-level community government is necessary, with the neighborhood assembly being the primary decision-making authority. Burlington has experimented with a
direct democracy format in its neighborhood planning assemblies
(NPAs). Their role has mostly been that of a sounding board on city
development programs. The observations of Michael Monte, the may-
or's liaison to the NPAs, are summarized by Pierre Clavel (who is
sympathetic to Monte's ideas):

[Monte] thought the assemblies were developing as viable organizations under the rather loose rein the city gave them, but he had no illusions about
their being autonomous. He still controlled their checkbooks, for example; he
could negotiate each meeting. He called them a "hybrid between the centralized planning structure and a process whereby . . . critical issues in a
ward are raised."[10]

This truncated role of the NPAs has been criticized by Burlington activist and scholar Murray Bookchin. Bookchin argues that Mayor Sanders has gone on public record opposing town-meeting (direct democracy government) and that the neighborhood planning assemblies "have essentially been permitted to languish in an atmosphere of benign neglect."[11] Burlington's NPA experience demonstrates a mistrust of pure democracy. The relegation of pure democracy to a rhetorical function allows special interests institutional avenues by which to penetrate the representative and bureaucratic aspects of local government. By being removed from the democratic process, Burlington's Planning Commission defended the interests of business without fear of recall.

By delegating the primary functions of the newly empowered local state to neighborhood assemblies, niches of bureaucratic institutional power or sites of government authority exercised by other structures of power are put at a disadvantage. With public decision-making an exercise in pure democracy, other interests in society would have to react to policies made directly by citizens. As it now stands, representatives and bureaucratic institutions removed from direct public input are the initiators of public policy; citizen input, whether outrage or support, comes second. Such hands-on democracy by neighborhood assemblies would make unnecessary most city bureaucracies, unless the assemblies chose to maintain them. Initial policy options in the areas of fire, police, welfare, ecology, education, utility regulation, and the regulation of private property specific to neighborhood boundaries would all be subject to the authority of neighborhood government. Neighborhoods could contract out police, fire, and educational responsibilities, or they could create their own bureaucracy subject to being abolished by fiat of the local majority.[12] Some work assignments might be portioned out to citizens, or volunteerist efforts might blossom. No matter what option was taken, the goal of ultimate community control would be enhanced.

In the crucial area of land use, business would have to approach neighborhood assemblies for any new project, expansion of an existing project, or relocation away from the neighborhood.[13] A majority vote could reject or accept a business proposal or a state-sponsored project just as representative legislative bodies are free to approve or disapprove proposed legislation. Zoning boards would be superfluous and henceforth abolished. In sum, without delving into endless details of specific examples that would fall short of the variety of local problems, under assembly government the policy process would begin at the neighborhood level.

Before elaborating on when a neighborhood decision would become subject to review by citywide government, a few paragraphs on the format of local direct democracy are in order.[14] A pure democratic form of neighborhood democracy would have a permanent site large enough to accommodate all citizens. Citizens would be allowed to speak for limited periods and a limited number of times to avoid monopolization of debate by the more articulate and extroverted. A chair, the elected representative to the citywide common council, would make procedural rulings in such matters. Thus discourse would be both open and ordered in neighborhood assemblies.

Every citizen in the assembly jurisdiction (not merely the citizens in attendance) would have a single vote on all issues. Two-way cable (preferably municipally owned) would be installed so that citizens could both discuss and vote on matters from their homes. Question-and-answer periods with elected representatives on all issues would be established and the times published before any meetings. Meetings would have regular and convenient times set by the majority to facilitate maximum attendance. And to prevent the problem of a controlled agenda in these neighborhood assemblies (a technique often used to suppress conflict in representative bodies), periods of open, unguided discussion at each meeting would have to be prescribed.[15] With these ground rules, the basis for a more democratic local state would be set.

Yet, no matter how democratic the nature of neighborhood government, there will be projects (such as an uninterrupted bike path) desired by an overwhelming majority of city dwellers that could be obstructed by a single neighborhood; also there are likely to be disputes between adjoining neighborhoods (for example, whether to license a noisy bar on an adjacent border). To coordinate citywide projects, the Common Council could only override a specific neighborhood assembly's vote by a two-thirds majority. This two-thirds threshold would protect the primacy of direct democracy at the neighborhood level and would limit citywide intrusion on pure local democracy in the affected neighborhoods.

The above scheme would not be another fragmentation of government authority because internal cohesion would be fostered by an overlapping neighborhood-based representation. To counteract potential political fragmentation, the preferred form of representation

on the Common Council would be a combination of elected representatives and an equal number of randomly picked representatives all
selected from each neighborhood. The elected representatives would
be in regular communication with their constituents since they would
chair the neighborhood assemblies and regularly interact in question-
and-answer sessions. Representatives would be elected yearly and
would be subject to recall at any time by an assembly no-confidence
vote. Sortition would randomly give representation to all classes and
all kinds of people, especially those politically handicapped by being
poor or inarticulate. The randomly selected, untutored members of
the Common Council would have equal voting rights and most often
act as a jury over the proposals of their elected colleagues. By unifying neighborhood leaders and even the most reticent citizens in the
Common Council, any local government's constitutional fragmentation should be overridden by a community-based general will.

Despite this democratization of policy making and representation, the likelihood that neighborhood assemblies would choose to
keep citywide bureaucratic services because of the inertia of past practice or because centralized delivery service might prove more cost-
effective must not be overlooked. If the need for a limited number of
city commissions is perceived and the commissions are democratically chosen by all or even several neighborhoods that would pay for
them out of their state-allotted funds, a similar but slightly different
form of representation than the common council would be in order.
One quarter of citywide commission members would be chosen by
the council itself. Another quarter would be chosen by secret ballot by
the employees of the particular department or departments under the
commission's authority, since only inclusion of the bureaucracy in the
democratic process can temper its anti-democratic proclivities. The
remaining half of the commission representatives would be chosen by
sortition, each neighborhood represented equally. Again, this is an
attempt to overcome municipal fragmentation by democratization,
thereby creating, through articulation, a general will.

As important as this restructuring of the local state is, it is not
sufficient for the creation of a democratic society. Successful relocation of enough left-minded citizens to create a large numerical majority would certainly cause the state and local state governments to be
reconstructed to reflect this growth of the resistance to both class and
other forms of domination. Yet if the greater private world that is now
legally protected from the democratic process is left intact, it is likely
that dominating structures will not be seriously challenged.

The essential problem is that both business interests and the organized groups that defend inegalitarian cultural practices can penetrate and malignly influence democratic government. The antidote to this private system of structural domination, however, is the democratization of institutions and relations outside the traditional purview of government. A top priority would be the creation of worker-owned industries that could be widely sponsored and subsidized by state and local governments and that would be exempt from the state no-subsidy rule. However, to avoid the fate of one failed experiment, the Vermont Asbestos Group, whose workers sold their shares to an outside entrepreneur, rules that allow only one vote per share and one nontransferable share per worker would have to be enacted to prevent creeping capitalism.[16] In addition to worker-owned enterprises, local food and health cooperatives would be established, thereby creating a tightly webbed network of local left interdependence sufficient to counter the disaggregating effects that occur within the left plural resistance to dominating structures.

To foster the efforts of the plural non-class resistance, new social movements should be allowed to voluntarily segregate and create their own neighborhood communities. Oppressed groups recognized by the left-controlled state legislature might prefer to create extended communal living arrangements. Many gay, black, Latino, and feminist activists and writers have expressed this interest at one time or another. In our own time, people of retirement age have created such exclusive communities in Florida and Arizona without the stigma of enforced segregation. However, in a democratic state, more-privileged groups, especially business people, would have to obey equal-opportunity laws. Treating less-than-equal groups in a juridically equal fashion at best provides an equality before the law and obfuscates the deeper structural causes and effects of inequality. However, making favored groups obey equal-opportunity laws undermines their dominance. Giving special privileges based on living arrangements to groups that are traditionally discriminated against fosters much-needed solidarity for their struggle for equality.

Inevitably, the voluntary segregation and subsequent cohesion of specific left resistance groups can only aggravate the problems of left conflict that were so pronounced in the struggle by the Burlington left for gay rights, demilitarization, and ecological preservation. At present, there are no concrete institutional forms that will eliminate the differences that divide gays, feminists, ecologists, socialists, labor, and peace activists. Notwithstanding, one improvement would be open-ended dialogue (that would not suppress conflict) shared in the neighborhood assemblies and common council. Since conflict often has to be increased before it can be resolved, it may be beneficial to let it run its course. This is the essence of struggle. In addition to respecting the grievances of others, the establishment of voluntarily segregated communities could help accommodate left differences by creating new micro-societies that would be directed at fighting specific structures of oppression. It is uncertain what new democratic institutions (with possible applicability to other communities) might evolve in the context of voluntary segregation. At the very least, it would provide an escape option for oppressed groups from inegalitarian cultural practice.

However, the most important glue with which to bind the plural left would be local control of the means of socialization. Neighborhood schools, local electronic media, and a daily newspaper would be the most important conduits of a left consciousness that could combat class, sexual, racial, and other inegalitarian relations. Neighborhood schools controlled by left democratic assemblies could socialize and emphasize egalitarian values to children from nursery school through high school. Likewise, free-wheeling debates in a community-owned newspaper and on community-owned radio and cable television could sharpen the focus of the issues and might also provide heretofore unimagined egalitarian prescriptions. These institutions of socialization combined with the pure democracy of neighborhood assemblies can foster the challenge of democratic structural reform.

CONCLUSION

The prescriptions offered are merely a starting point for creating a truly democratic society, a process without end. Even if these prescriptions were strictly followed, it is likely that mostly reformist reform would predominate. Socialism and thorough democratic reform are impossible in just one city as in just one state or nation. For example, a left city or state government could perhaps trap existing capital investment within territorial borders, but it could not force new investment from private actors or corporations. State and local investment policies would have to compensate, a formidable problem for small, left-dominated communities in competition with capitalism. And if business in itself is not a sufficiently difficult adversary, the

United States government acting in the interests of capital or other structures is powerful enough to move the locus of authority on any given issue to the national level. When the United States abolished state rate-regulation over cable television, it was a case of business using a higher level of federal authority for its own advantage. Thus a more autonomous local state cannot individually slay structures of domination but can only challenge them.

Yet local autonomy under a left aegis would push reform to its limits of possibility. If an entire state of left communities could collectively offer a qualitatively superior alternative society to the American public, it would go a long way toward legitimizing left reform. A compilation of left-most liberal reforms and a smaller number of democratic structural reforms would offer an example of progressive achievement the left could call its own, something the left now lacks.

Notes

CHAPTER 1

1. Greg Guma, "Eight Years That Shook Vermont," *Vermont Vanguard Press*, March 16–23, 1989, p. 9.

2. Louis Berney, "Sanders on Sanders: Meet the Mayor," *Vermont Vanguard Press*, March 13–20, 1981, pp. 12–13.

3. Interview with Bernard Sanders quoted from Steven Soifer, "Electoral Politics and Social Change: The Case of Burlington, Vermont" (Ph.D. diss., Brandeis University, 1988), p. 61.

4. Berney, "Sanders on Sanders."

5. Soifer, "Electoral Politics," pp. 62–63.

6. Dirk Van Susteren, "Liberty Union Leaders Quit," *Burlington Free Press* (hereafter cited as *BFP*), October 12, 1977.

7. Soifer, "Electoral Politics," pp. 63–64.

8. Ibid., pp. 73–74.

9. Ibid., p. 66.

10. Greg Guma, "Changing of the Guard; or, How Burlington Got a Radical Mayor," *Vermont Vanguard Press*, March 13–20, 1981, p. 10.

11. All of the following reasons for Sanders' victory come from Soifer, "Electoral Politics," pp. 71–81.

12. On the destruction of low-income neighborhoods as a byproduct of urban renewal see Martin Anderson, *The Urban Bulldozer* (New York: McGraw-Hill, 1964).

13. Soifer, "Electoral Politics," p. 54.

14. The works of Saul D. Alinsky have become the bibles for grassroots organizing techniques. See his *Rules for Radicals: A Practical Primer for Realistic*

Radicals (New York: Vintage Books, 1972) and *Reveille for Radicals* (New York: Vintage Books, 1969).

15. Soifer, "Electoral Politics," pp. 74–76.

16. Alan Abbey, "Mayor Bombarded at Candidates Forum," *BFP*, February 26, 1981, p. 10.

17. Industrial Cooperative Association, *Jobs and People: A Strategic Analysis of the Greater Burlington Economy*, December 1984.

18. Soifer, "Electoral Politics," p. 59.

19. Peter Freyne quoted from Soifer, "Electoral Politics," p. 79.

20. Ibid., p. 81.

21. In 1986, this ad hoc group formally became a political party while still lacking most of the formal procedures of the other two established parties. Peter Freyne, "Life After Bernie?" *Vermont Vanguard Press*, June 29–July 6, 1986, pp. 1, 7.

22. Although Sanders' electoral machinery in Burlington was almost wholly composed of Progressive Coalition members, he always ran as an independent.

23. Tom W. Rice provides empirical evidence demonstrating the breadth of Sanders' electoral coalition in "Who Votes for a Socialist Mayor? The Case of Burlington, Vermont," *Polity* 17 (Summer 1985): 795–801.

24. In the first few years the local press often referred to the Progressive Coalition as "the Coalition"; after several years the name "Progressives" appeared in its place. Both terms will be used here synonymously.

25. Greg Guma, "Changing of the Guard," pp. 1, 10–11.

26. Alan Abbey, "Mayor Reaches Compromise with Aldermen About Aide," *BFP*, April 15, 1981, pp. 1B–2B.

27. Louis Berney, "Judge: FBI Embarrassed the Mayor," *BFP*, April 15, 1981, pp. 1B–2B.

28. Interestingly, these editors (who wrote the *BFP*'s editorials throughout the period under study): Richard M. Bottorf, Daniel W. Costello, and Leo J. O'Connor preferred a quiet inquiry. "FBI's Sanders Probe Went Too Far," *BFP*, April 16, 1981, p. 10A.

29. Scott Mackay, "Democrats Swept off City Board by Sanders' Supporters, Republicans," *BFP*, March 4, 1982, pp. 1B, 7B.

30. Advertisement entitled "WARNING!" *BFP*, February 24, 1983, p. 10A.

31. Advertisement entitled "Burlington Business Provides," *BFP*, February 27, 1983, p. 5A.

32. Scott Mackay, "Gear Won't Let Mayor Speak About Connector," *BFP*, April 21, 1983, pp. 1B, 4B.

33. Scott Mackay, "Sanders Is Victor; All Top City Aides Are Reappointed," *BFP*, June 7, 1983, pp. 1B–2B.

34. Don Melvin, "Council Approves Sanders' $14.7 Million Budget," *BFP*, June 28, 1983, pp. 1B–2B.

35. Don Melvin, "Sanders Fails to Get Control," *BFP*, March 7, 1984, pp. 1B, 10B.

36. Don Melvin, "Linda Burns Quits City Council," *BFP*, March 13, 1984, pp. 1B, 3B.

37. Don Melvin, "Aldermen Pass Street Excavation Fee," *BFP*, March 20, 1984, pp. 1B, 4B.

38. Don Melvin, "Democratic Victory Leaves Mayor Short of Board Majority," *BFP*, March 16, 1985, pp. 1A, 9A.

39. Don Melvin, "Sanders Outdistancing Opponents, Poll Shows," *BFP*, February 2, 1985, pp. 1A, 8A.

40. Don Melvin, "Sanders Easily Wins Re-Election," *BFP*, March 6, 1985, pp. 1A, 4A.

41. Don Melvin, "Skelton Wins Board Election," *BFP*, April 2, 1985, pp. 1B–2B.

42. Don Melvin, "City Council Takes Single Voice Vote to Fill 20 Positions," *BFP*, June 4, 1985, pp. 1B, 6B.

43. Soifer, "Electoral Politics," pp. 128–30. Much of the following information on the 1986 and 1987 elections comes from this source.

44. Christopher Graff, "Poll Finds Statewide Support for Sanders," *BFP*, January 23, 1985, p. 1A.

45. Soifer, "Electoral Politics," p. 143.

46. Debbie Bookchin, "How Socialist Is Bernard Sanders?" *Rutland Herald-Times-Argus Sunday Magazine*, June 1, 1986, p. 12.

47. Peter Freyne, "Inside Track," *Vermont Vanguard Press*, December 14–21, 1986, p. 9.

48. Peter Freyne, "Inside Track," *Vermont Vanguard Press*, January 18–25, 1987, pp. 8–9.

49. See Soifer, "Electoral Politics," pp. 149–54, and Peter Freyne, "Inside Track," *Vermont Vanguard Press*, March 8–15, 1987, p. 9.

50. Mark Johnson, "Feds Hatch Mahnke Probe," *Vermont Vanguard Press*, March 3–10, 1988, pp. 1, 5, 7. Mark Johnson, "Mahnke Gets Hatched," *Vermont Vanguard Press*, May 19–26, 1988, p. 8.

51. Kevin J. Kelley, "Close but No Cigar," *Vermont Vanguard Press*, November 10–17, 1988, p. 5.

52. Soifer, "Electoral Politics," p. 159.

53. One Progressive alderman spoke to me in confidence of Sanders' role as a leader: "Never again."

54. At an April 1986 meeting of the Socialist Scholars' Conference in New York City, this charge was leveled by some in the audience during a panel discussion of Burlington's politics organized by Steven Soifer.

55. Quoted from Soifer, "Electoral Politics," p. 169. See Soifer's comments and interviews on pp. 168–82 on the potential demise of the Progressives without Sanders.

56. Tom W. Rice, "Identity Crisis," *Vermont Vanguard Press*, March 22–29, 1987, pp. 11–12.

57. Kevin J. Kelley, "Progs Face Future Shock," *Vermont Vanguard Press*, June 23–30, 1988, p. 5.

58. Kevin E. Kelley, "Clavelle to Get Progressive Nod," *Vermont Vanguard Press*, December 8–15, 1988, pp. 5, 8.

59. Guma, "Eight Years," p. 9.

60. See Robert Dahl, *Who Governs? Democracy and Power in an American City* (New Haven: Yale University Press, 1961).

CHAPTER 2

1. Throughout this book, "State" with a capital *S* will mean the totality of American government as it is commonly recognized; "state" with a lower-case *s* will designate one of the fifty states of the United States or will follow important descriptive adjectives such as nation or local.

2. Paul E. Peterson, *City Limits* (Chicago: University of Chicago Press, 1981), pp. 25–29.

3. See Paul Kantor with Stephen David, *The Dependent City: The Changing Political Economy of Urban America* (Boston: Scott, Foresman, 1988), pp. 13–14.

4. Celia Cockburn popularized this term among left academics in *The Local State* (London: Pluto Press, 1977). I will use it synonymously with local government in the traditional meaning of that term.

5. Peterson, *City Limits*. An excellent critique of Peterson's book can be found in Todd Swanstrom, "Semisovereign Cities: The Political Logic of Urban Development" (Paper presented at the 1986 Annual Meeting of the American Political Science Association, Washington, D.C., August 1986).

6. Peterson, *City Limits*, p. 41.

7. On the problems with Peterson's typologies see Robert J. Waste, *The Ecology of City Policymaking* (New York: Oxford University Press, 1989), pp. 73–80.

8. Ibid., pp. 175–78.

9. See James Weinstein, *The Decline of Socialism in America: 1912–1925* (New York: Random House, 1967), for documentation of the Socialist party's early popularity and subsequent failure.

10. Peterson, *City Limits*, pp. xi–xii.

11. Charles M. Tiebout, "A Pure Theory of Local Expenditures," *Journal of Political Economy* 64 (1956): 416–24.

12. To see the failure to come to terms with urban unrest in public choice analysis read the following books on urban service delivery: Robert L. Bish and Vincent Ostrom, *Understanding Urban Government* (Washington, D.C.: American Enterprise Institute, 1973), and Elinor Ostrom, *The Delivery of Urban Services* (Beverly Hills, Calif.: Sage Publications, 1976).

13. Kantor with David, *Dependent City*, p. 8.

14. James O'Connor, *The Fiscal Crisis of the State*, (New York: St. Martin's Press, 1973).

15. Norman I. Fainstein and Susan S. Fainstein, "New Haven: The Limits of the Local State," in *Restructuring the City*, by Susan S. Fainstein et al. (New York: Longman, 1983). Also see, from the same volume, Dennis R. Judd, "From Cowtown to Sunbelt City: Boosterism and Economic Growth in Denver," and Michael Peter Smith and Marlene Keller, "Managed Growth and the Politics of Uneven Development in New Orleans." William K. Tabb, *The Long Default: New York City and the Urban Fiscal Crisis* (New York: Monthly Review Press, 1982); Todd Swanstrom, *Growth Politics;* and Edward Greer, *Big Steel: Black Politics and Corporate Power in Gary, Indiana* (New York: Monthly Review Press, 1979).

16. Fainstein et al., *Restructuring the City*, is very good on the role of the national government in urban renewal.

17. Dennis R. Judd, *The Politics of American Cities: Private Power and Public Policy*, 2d ed. (Boston: Little, Brown, 1984), is an exception to this generalization.

18. Although most of the urban neo-Marxist writing is without prescriptions, there are exceptions. See Tabb, *The Long Default*, and also by the same author, "A Pro-People Urban Policy," in *Marxism and the Metropolis*, ed. William K. Tabb and Larry Sawers, 2d ed. (New York: Oxford University Press, 1984).

19. Peterson, *City Limits*, pp. 216–17.

20. Pierre Clavel's *The Progressive City: Planning and Participation, 1969–1984* (New Brunswick, N.J.: Rutgers University Press, 1986) does chronicle the attempts at reform by cities that have elected left officials. From a participant's point of view, see the very important but seldom cited book by the Community Ownership Organizing Project, *The Cities' Wealth* (Washington, D.C.: Conference/Alternative State and Local Public Policies, 1976), which systematically lays out a left urban agenda.

21. Werner Sombart, *Why Is there No Socialism in the United States?* trans. Patricia M. Hocking and C.T. Husbands, with a Foreword by Michael Harrington (Tubingen, Germany: Verlag von J.C.B. Mohr, 1906; reprint ed., White Plains, N.Y.: M.E. Sharpe, 1976).

22. The most insightful work on the populists is Lawrence Goodwyn's *The Populist Moment: A Short History of the Agrarian Revolt in America* (New York: Oxford University Press, 1978).

23. The ambiguous social reformer/businessman coalition of the Progressives is demonstrated by their range of reforms from the democratic, direct primary to the corporate, manager/council form of government. Howard L. Reiter takes the Progressives to task for their elite dominance in *Parties and Elections in Corporate America* (New York: St. Martin's Press, 1987), pp. 115–16.

24. See Mike Davis, "The Lesser Evil? The Left and the Democratic Par-

ty," *New Left Review* 155 (March–April 1986): 5–36, for a devastating critique of the Harrington strategy.

25. Weinstein, *The Decline of Socialism*, pp. 93, 103.

26. John H. Mollenkopf, *The Contested City* (Princeton, N.J.: Princeton University Press, 1983), p. 9.

27. Karl Marx and Frederick Engels, *Selected Correspondence* (Moscow: Foreign Languages Publishing House, n.d.), quoted in Barry Hindess, *Politics and Class Analysis* (New York: Basil Blackwell, 1987), p. 87.

28. Hindess, *Politics and Class Analysis*, pp. 87–88.

29. Louis Althusser and Etienne Balibar, *Reading Capital*, trans. Ben Brewster (London: Verso, 1979), p. 319.

30. Michael Albert and Robin Hahnel, *Unorthodox Marxism: An Essay on Capitalism, Socialism, and Revolution* (Boston: South End Press, 1978).

31. William K. Tabb, *The Political Economy of the Black Ghetto* (New York: W.W. Norton, 1970). It should be kept in mind that this was an early neo-Marxist study that was focused on challenging mainstream interpretations of black poverty.

32. To their credit, Norman I. Fainstein and Susan S. Fainstein in their book *Urban Political Movements: The Search for Power by Minority Groups in American Cities* (Englewood Cliffs, N.J.: Prentice-Hall, 1974) deviated from other neo-Marxists by deemphasizing class and emphasizing other factors.

33. See Frances Fox Piven and Richard A. Cloward, *Regulating the Poor: The Functions of Public Welfare* (New York: Vintage Books, 1971), and by the same authors, *Poor People's Movements: Why They Succeed, How They Fail* (New York: Vintage Books, 1979).

34. Cornel West argues that in three of the four categories of Marxist literature on race he has surveyed, racist attitudes are not analyzed as having "a life and logic of their own, dependent upon psychological factors and cultural practices." The fourth category did explore racism from this angle in addition to class. If we follow Althusser's boundary line for Marxist analysis, that all social relations in the last instance are determined by the organization of the economy, then this last category is not Marxist. See Cornel West, *Toward a Socialist Theory of Racism* (New York: Institute for Democratic Socialism and the Socialist Scholars' Conference, n.d.), p. 3.

35. As this new paradigm takes shape, more orthodox Marxists are stepping up the attack on those who stray from the basic assumption that the economic is primary. See Milton Fisk, "Why the Anti-Marxists Are Wrong," *Monthly Review* 38 (March 1987), and Norman Geras, "Post-Marxism?" *New Left Review* 163 (May/June 1987), for unsympathetic critiques of post-Marxism.

36. See Zillah Eisenstein, *Capitalist Patriarchy and the Case for Socialist-Feminism* (New York: Monthly Review Press, 1979), and Lydia Sargent, ed., *Women and Revolution: A Discussion of the Unhappy Marriage of Marxism and Feminism* (Boston: South End Press, 1981), for two important collections of articles on socialist-feminism.

37. Examples of each category are Alvin W. Gouldner, *The Future of Intellectuals and the Rise of the New Class* (New York: Continuum, 1979); Shulamith Firestone, *The Dialectic of Sex: The Case for Feminist Revolution* (New York: Bantam Books, 1971); and Murray Bookchin, *Toward an Ecological Society* (Montreal: Black Rose Books, 1980).

38. See Alan Sheridan, *The Will to Truth* (New York: Tavistock Publications, 1980), for a comprehensive summary of Foucault's work. For a more specific look at Foucault's work in relation to Marxism see Mark Poster, *Foucault, Marxism and History: Mode of Production versus Mode of Information* (Cambridge, England: Polity Press, 1984).

39. See Michel Foucault, *The History of Sexuality, vol. 1, An Introduction,* trans. Robert Hurley (New York: Vintage Books, 1980); Michel Foucault, *Mental Illness and Psychology,* trans. Alan Sheridan (New York: Harper & Row, 1976); and Michel Foucault, *Discipline and Punishment: The Birth of a Prison,* trans. Alan Sheridan (New York: Vintage Books, 1979).

40. Erik Olin Wright, *Class Crisis and the State* (London: Verso, 1979), pp. 55–57.

41. Of all the post-Marxists, Ernesto Laclau and Chantal Mouffe have gone the farthest in questioning historical materialism. In fact, they make the case that history is "unsutured," a direct contradiction of Marxian historical materialism. See their *Hegemony and Socialist Strategy: Toward a Radical Democratic Politics* (London: Verso, 1985).

42. The best single volume on this problem is Pat Walker, ed., *Between Labor and Capital* (Boston: South End Press, 1979).

43. See Ronald Inglehart, *The Silent Revolution: Changing Values and Political Styles Among Western Publics* (Princeton, N.J.: Princeton University Press, 1977), and Claus Offe, "New Social Movements: Challenging the Boundaries of Institutional Politics," *Social Research* 52 (Winter 1985): 833–38.

44. Offe, "Challenging the Boundaries," p. 833.

45. On the self-definition of social movements see Alain Touraine, *The Self-Production of Society,* trans. Derek Coltman (Chicago: University of Chicago Press, 1977), and by the same author, *The Voice and the Eye: An Analysis of Social Movements,* trans. Alan Duff, with a foreward by Richard Sennett (New York: Cambridge University Press, 1981).

CHAPTER 3

1. For the mainstream opinion, see Paul E. Peterson, *City Limits* (Chicago: University of Chicago Press, 1981). For the left view, see Harvey Molotch, "The City as a Growth Machine," *American Journal of Sociology* 82 (September 1976): 309–30.

2. See Robert L. Cook Benjamin, "From Waterways to Waterfronts:

Public Investment for Cities, 1815–1890," in *Urban Economic Development*, ed. Richard D. Bingham and John P. Blair (Beverly Hills, Calif.: Sage Publications, 1984), pp. 23–45; Andrew Kirby, "Nine Fallacies of Local Economic Change," *Urban Affairs Quarterly* 21 (December 1985): 208.

3. David Gordon, "Capitalist Development and the History of American Cities," in *Marxism and the Metropolis*, ed. William K. Tabb and Larry Sawers (New York: Oxford University Press, 1978), pp. 25–63.

4. The number of studies on communities competing for industrial relocations is vast. An eclectic sampling of the literature might include: Robert Goodman, *The Last Entrepreneurs* (Boston: South End Press, 1979); Richard Child Hill, "Economic Crisis and Political Response in the Motor City," in *Sunbelt/Snowbelt*, ed. Larry Sawers and William K. Tabb (New York: Oxford University Press, 1984), pp. 313–38; Ann O'M. Bowman, "Intrastate Warfare: Inner-City Revitalization in Three Cities" (Paper presented at the 1984 Annual Meeting of the American Political Science Association, Washington, D.C., August 1984).

5. Case studies on the negative consequences of economic growth are cited and summarized in Molotch's seminal article, "The City as a Growth Machine." Also, see Barry Bluestone and Bennett Harrison, *The Deindustrialization of America: Plant Closings, Community Abandonment, and the Dismantling of Basic Industry* (New York: Basic Books, 1982), pp. 86–92. Joe R. Feagin has published a Sunbelt city case study on this topic, "The Social Costs of Houston's Growth," *International Journal of Urban and Regional Research* 9 (June 1985): 164–85.

6. Robert Friedland, *Power and the Crisis in the City* (London: Macmillan, 1982).

7. This is changing, although it is much too early to estimate how widespread the new antigrowth social movements are. Measures to curtail (but not eliminate) economic development have been passed in San Diego and San Francisco. Even in conservative Orange County, California, an antigrowth referendum measure lost while garnering a respectable number of votes. Whether the thrust of these actions is merely the familiar "not in my backyard" syndrome or a new consciousness that intuits there are definite limits to economic development remains unclear.

8. Alan Wolfe, *America's Impasse* (New York: Pantheon Books, 1981), p. 238.

9. John Mollenkopf, *The Contested City* (Princeton, N.J.: Princeton University Press, 1983).

10. Mark Johnson, "West Coast Mayor Tells of Successes on City Tax Levies," *Burlington Free Press* (hereafter cited as *BFP*), December 14, 1985, pp. 1B–2B.

11. Fred Block has written a seminal article on business confidence, "The Ruling Class Does Not Rule," *Socialist Revolution* 7 (May–June 1977).

Also see Charles Lindblom, *Politics and Markets* (New York: Basic Books, 1977), chapter 13.

12. The business relocation literature is vast but mind-numbingly repetitive. Sources used for this list are Edward Humberger, *Business Location Decisions and Cities* (Washington, D.C.: Public Technology, 1983); Leonard C. Yaseen, *Plant Location* (New York: American Research Council, 1960); Jon E. Browning, *How to Select a Business Site* (New York: McGraw-Hill, 1980); and Eva Mueller and James N. Morgan, "Locational Decisions of Manufacturers" in *Locational Analysis for Manufacturing*, ed. R. Koraska and D. Bramhall (Cambridge, Mass.: M.I.T. Press, 1969), pp. 459–502.

Other volumes useful to this extended discussion on business confidence were Richard D. Bingham and John P. Blair, eds., *Urban Economic Development* (Beverly Hills, Calif.: Sage Publications, 1984); Allan Pred, *City-Systems in Advanced Economies* (New York: Jon Wiley & Sons, 1977); and Thierry J. Noyelle and Thomas M. Stanback, Jr., *The Economic Transformation of American Cities* (Totowa, N.J.: Rowman & Allanheld, 1983).

13. Humberger, *Business Location Decisions*, p. 27.

14. "Vt. Forecast: Steady Employment but Manufacturing Sector Decline," *BFP*, November 28, 1985, p. 6C.

15. Peter Carlough, *Bygone Burlington* (Burlington, Vt.: By the Author and Marcia Marshall, 1976).

16. Don Melvin, "Sanders Wants to Appeal BED Rate Decision," *BFP*, November 1, 1985, pp. 1B–2B.

17. See Dowell Myers, "Community-Relevant Measurement of Quality of Life: A Focus on Local Trends," *Urban Affairs Quarterly* 23 (September 1987): 108–25, for an attempt to find a community-based approach to measuring a city's livability.

18. Murray Bookchin, "The Bernie Sanders Paradox: When Socialism Grows Old," *Socialist Review* 90 (November–December 1986): 60.

19. N.B. Wish, "Are We Really Measuring the Quality of Life?" *American Journal of Economics and Sociology* 45 (January 1986): 93–99.

20. See chapter 3 of Roy C. Haupt, "The Power to Promote Growth: Business and the Making of Local Economic Development Policy" (Ph.D. diss., Cornell University, 1980).

21. Work and DeLouise, "Cities Where Business Is Best," p. 62.

22. H.V. Savitch, *Urban Policy and the Exterior City* (New York: Pergamon Press, 1979), p. 251.

23. Margaret McCahill and Kirk Glaser, "Nurturing Business in Burlington," *BFP*, April 29, 1984, 1E, 7E.

24. George Gilder, *Wealth and Poverty* (New York: Basic Books, 1981), pp. 99–100.

25. For certain types of entrepreneurs property taxes play a larger role in investment decisions. Office-complex developers would likely be more con-

cerned about such costs than manufacturers since such a tax is real estate specific. The Florida manufacturer survey can be found in Melvin L. Greenhut and Marshall R. Colberg, "Factors in the Location of Florida Industry," *Locational Analysis for Manufacturing*, ed. R. Koraska and D. Bramhall (Cambridge, Mass.: M.I.T. Press, 1969), p. 451.

26. On this point see Irene S. Rubin and Herbert J. Rubin, "Economic Development Incentives: The Poor (Cities) Pay More," *Urban Affairs Quarterly* 23 (September 1987): 37–57.

27. John Logan and Todd Swanstrom challenge the concept that capital is infinitely mobile, in "A Tiger by the Tail" (Paper presented at a conference of the same name, State University at Albany, N.Y., April 1989). Although the literature does overstate capital's ability to move, in a postindustrial society where the communication of information is available from every telephone connection, it seems that the mobility of advanced capital is increasing and not the reverse.

28. Alain Touraine first used the phrase "postindustrial society." See Richard Sennett's Foreword to Alain Touraine, *The Voice and the Eye: An Analysis of Social Movements* (New York: Cambridge University Press, 1981), p. ix. While Touraine was developing his thesis, Daniel Bell was doing his own work on the topic, which is more directed toward the American development of postindustrialism. See Daniel Bell, *The Coming of Post-Industrial Society* (New York: Basic Books, 1976). I have borrowed liberally from Bell's conceptualizations, yet I have also transformed them for my analytic purposes.

29. For this dire view see George Sternlieb, "The City as a Box," *The Public Interest* 25 (Autumn 1971): 14–21. Revisionist views can be found in M. Gottdiener, "Whatever Happened to the Urban Crisis?" *Urban Affairs Quarterly* 20 (June 1985): 421–27, and Alexander Ganz, "Where Has the Urban Crisis Gone?" *Urban Affairs Quarterly* 20 (June 1985): 449–65.

30. Alan J. Abramson and Lester M. Soloman, *The Nonprofit Sector and the New Federal Budget* (Washington, D.C.: Urban Institute Press, 1986), demonstrates the fiscal dependency of the not-for-profit sector on the national government.

31. See Harvey Molotch and John R. Logan, "Urban Dependencies: New Forms of Use and Exchange in U.S. Cities," *Urban Affairs Quarterly* 21 (December 1985): 148–50, on headquarter cities. However, their analysis ignores the impact of regional offices. The city's place in the international framework of capitalism is argued from a structuralist and world-system approach in Christopher Chase-Dunn, "Urbanization in the World-System," in *Cities in Transformation*, ed. Michael Peter Smith (Beverly Hills, Calif.: Sage Publications, 1984), pp. 111–20.

32. Bennett Harrison, "Regional Restructuring and Good Business Climates," in *Sunbelt/Snowbelt*, ed. Larry Sawers and William K. Tabb (New York: Oxford University Press, 1984), p. 64.

33. Robert Kuttner, "Will Unions Organize Again?" *Dissent* (Winter 1987): 53–54.

34. See Erik Olin Wright, *Class, Crisis and the State* (London: Verso, 1979) on class contradictory positions.

CHAPTER 4

1. For this study, "State" and the federalist system will be synonymous. Many neo-Marxist theorists go beyond government to define the scope of the State. The media, religious institutions, and nonprofit corporations are often considered extensions of State power. Such a loose interpretation is misleading in the context of the United States where the ideological emphasis on the superiority of the private sector sharply distinguishes the latter from the pro-capitalist government.

2. Concerning such direct orders, see Advisory Council on Intergovernmental Relations, *The Federal Role and the Federal System: The Dynamics of Growth*, A-77 (Washington, D.C.: Government Printing Office, 1980).

3. General revenue sharing was defunded by Congress in 1986.

4. Carl W. Stenberg, "Federalism in Transition, 1959–79," *Intergovernmental Perspective* 6 (Winter 1980): 118–31.

5. Don Melvin, "Board Rescinds Vote on Airport Funds," *Burlington Free Press* (hereafter cited as *BFP*), June 19, 1984, pp. 1B, 3B.

6. James Q. Wilson, *American Government: Institutions and Policies*, 3d ed. (Lexington, Mass.: D.C. Heath, 1986), p. 62.

7. Pierre Clavel, *The Progressive City: Planning and Participation, 1969–1984* (New Brunswick, N.J.: Rutgers University Press, 1986), pp. 172–73.

8. Paul R. Dommel and Associates, *Decentralizing Urban Policy: Case Studies in Community Development* (Washington, D.C.: Brookings Institution, 1982), p. 252.

9. *New York Times*, November 30, 1986, p. 16.

10. Susan Youngwood, "Leopold Says City to Be Awash in Red Ink," *BFP*, October 8, 1985, pp. 1B–2B. The entire 1985 tax income for Burlington was $19.3 million.

11. Wilson, *American Government*, pp. 62–63.

12. This entire summary is from Deil S. Wright, *Understanding Intergovernmental Relations*, 2d ed., (Monterey, Calif.: Brooks/Cole, 1982), p. 30. The last seven words are quoted from City of Clinton v. Cedar Rapids and Missouri River Railroad, 24 Iowa 455 (1868). All of this section on state/local relations is informed by Wright's discussion.

13. Wright, *Intergovernmental Relations*, p. 356.

14. Ibid., pp. 358–60.

15. Fred Teitelbaum, "The Relative Responsiveness of State and Federal Aid to Distressed Cities," *Policy Studies Review* (November 1981): 58–72.

16. Wright, *Intergovernmental Relations*, pp. 364–69.

17. Paul E. Peterson, *City Limits* (Chicago: University of Chicago Press, 1981), pp. 25–29.

18. For a good discussion of this problem see Dennis R. Judd and David Brian Robertson, "Urban Revitalization in the United States: Prisoner of the Federal System" (Paper presented at Fulbright Colloquium 1986, Liverpool, England, September 28–30, 1986).

19. Greg Guma, "Complex Political Systems Badly Needed an Overhaul," *BFP*, May 31, 1983, p. 12A.

20. Much of the following discussion on Burlington's government is based on the official city charter unless otherwise noted. Burlington, Vermont, *Code of Ordinances* (Tallahassee, Fla.: Municipal Code Corporation, 1973).

21. Greg Guma, Citizens' Panel Welcomes Views on City's Form of Government," *BFP*, March 12, 1986, p. 6A. When the word "Council" is used without the adjective "City," it refers to the Board of Aldermen only.

22. Scott Mackay, "Commissioners Don't Represent Wards Equally," *BFP*, October 3, 1982, pp. 1A, 12A.

23. For a typical perspective by acclaimed experts in American political participation, see Kenneth Prewitt and Sidney Verba, *An Introduction to American Government*, 4th ed. (New York: Harper & Row, 1983), p. 188.

24. "Where Are the Women?" *BFP*, June 7, 1985, p. 14A.

25. Burlington, Vermont, *Code of Ordinances*, p. 15.

26. For a dissenting left view see Norman I. Fainstein and Susan S. Fainstein, "Is State Planning Necessary for Capital? The U.S. Case," *International Journal of Urban and Regional Research* 9 (December 1985): 485–507.

27. Nicos Poulantzas, *Classes in Contemporary Capitalism*, trans. David Fernbach (London: Verso, 1978), pp. 24–28.

28. Nicos Poulantzas, *State, Power, Socialism*, trans. Patrick Camiller (London: Verso, 1980), p. 138.

29. Andre Gorz, *Strategy for Labor: A Radical Proposal*, trans. Martin A. Nicolaus and Victoria Ortiz (Boston: Beacon Press, 1967), pp. 7–9. Gorz uses the terms "nonreformist reform" for democratic socialist reform and "reformist reform" for merely reformist proposals that do not challenge the hegemony of capitalism. My comparable terms are "democratic structural reform" and "liberal reform," respectively.

30. See Steven Soifer, "Electoral Politics and Social Change: The Case of Burlington, Vermont" (Ph.D. diss., Brandeis University, 1988), pp. 222–35.

31. The classic case for evolutionary socialism comes from Edward Bernstein, *Evolutionary Socialism*, trans. Edith C. Harvey (New York: Schocken Books, 1961).

CHAPTER 5

1. The economic history of the local waterfront is traced in Alexandra Marks, "The Elusive Waterfront Dreams," *Vermont Vanguard Press*, August 13–20, 1982, pp. 1, 9; also see Peter Carlough, *Bygone Burlington* (Burlington, Vt.: By the Author and Marcia Marshall, 1976).

2. Jodie Peck, "New Proposal Offered for 11 Acres Along Burlington Waterfront," *Burlington Free Press* (hereafter cited as *BFP*), March 6, 1981, p. 2B.

3. Alan Abbey, "Pomerleau, Mayor Walk Side by Side," *BFP*, May 3, 1981, p. 3B.

4. Alan Abbey, "Mayor Appoints Waterfront Task Force," *BFP*, May 18, 1981, pp. 1B–2B.

5. Rick Sharp, "Public Access to Waterfront Should be Protected," *BFP*, July 29, 1981, p. 14A.

6. Joe Mahoney, "Pomerleau Envisions Condos Rising 22 Stories," *BFP*, September 25, 1981, p. 8B.

7. Scott Mackay, "Sanders Advances New Panel to Study Waterfront Planning," *BFP*, April 21, 1982, p. 2B.

8. Scott Mackay, "Mayor, Aswad Clash on Plans for Waterfront," *BFP*, July 29, 1982, pp. 1B, 8B.

9. Bernard Sanders, interview with author, Burlington, Vt., December 1983.

10. Scott Mackay, "Pomerleau Puts Waterfront Condo Plan on Hold," *BFP*, November 9, 1982, p. 1B.

11. Scott Mackay, "Waterfront Protection Plan Aired," *BFP*, December 2, 1982, p. 1B.

12. Scott Mackay, "Request for Interim Zoning at Shore Renews Arguments on Development," *BFP*, December 19, 1982, p. 3B.

13. Scott Mackay, "Board Rejects Interim Waterfront Zoning," *BFP*, January 11, 1983, pp. 1B–2B.

14. Scott Mackay, "Stephany Outlines City Waterfront Development Plan," *BFP*, February 1, 1983, pp. 1B–2B.

15. Scott Mackay, "Stephany Walks a Political Tightrope," *BFP*, February 13, 1983, p. 2B.

16. See editorial by Richard E. Fletcher, vice president of Chittenden Trust Company, "Uncertain Business Environment Fostered by City Administration," *BFP*, May 7, 1983, p. 14A. Also, the editorial board faithfully harassed Sanders and the Coalition, "Cooperation Needed to Attract Business to City," *BFP*, May 15, 1983, p. 10A.

17. Scott Mackay, "Boston Architect Hired by Investors in Waterfront Plan," *BFP*, June 15, 1983, p. 1A.

18. Bernard Sanders interview.

19. Scott Mackay, "Waterfront Zoning Proposal Tries to Please All," *BFP*, June 23, 1983, p. 1B.

20. Scott Mackay, "City Officials Still Stymied on Waterfront Zoning," *BFP*, August 9, 1983, pp. 1B, 4B.

21. Scott Mackay, "Interim Zoning Is Turned Down for Waterfront," *BFP*, August 25, 1983, pp. 1B, 8B.

22. Scott Mackay, "Aldermen Say No to Sanders on GMP Bids," *BFP*, October 14, 1983, pp. 1B–2B.

23. Scott Mackay, "Alden Corp. Buying Up City's Waterfront," *BFP*, September 17, 1983, p. 1B.

24. Scott Mackay, "Waterfront Group Chairman Slams Secrecy Project," *BFP*, October 21, 1983, pp. 1B–2B.

25. Rob Eley, "Alden Investor Is Dow Jones Heiress," *BFP*, March 2, 1984, pp. 1A, 7A.

26. Scott Mackay, "Waterfront Feud Lights Up Again," *BFP*, October 26, 1983, p. 3B.

27. Don Melvin, "$100 Million Waterfront Plan Unveiled," *BFP*, January 27, 1984, pp. 1A, 9A.

28. Don Melvin, "City May Get Right to Buy Back Property," *BFP*, January 8, 1984, pp. 1B, 5B.

29. John Donnelly, "Sanders Sees City Profit in Waterfront Plan," *BFP*, January 16, 1984, pp. 1A, 7A.

30. Don Melvin, "Council Asks for Action on Waterfront Zoning," *BFP*, February 15, 1984, pp. 1B–2B.

31. Don Melvin, "Coalition Forms to Fight Alden Waterfront Plan," *BFP*, February 10, 1984, pp. 1B–2B.

32. Ethan Schwartz, "Waterfront Group Gathers Alternatives, Plans Resistance," *BFP*, June 27, 1984, p. 3B.

33. Later the Sanders administration did sue for title to the filled-in land and lost in the state courts. The court ruled that use of the land had to be in the "public interest." What that meant exactly was not specified.

34. See Don Melvin, "State Ties Up Waterfront with Connector," *BFP*, January 28, 1984, p. 1B, for the first argument. See Doug Ireland, "Traffic May Be Waterfront Plan's Major Drawback," *BFP*, July 24, 1985, p. 3B, for the opposing argument.

35. Don Melvin, "Aldermen Approve Waterfront Plan," *BFP*, June 12, 1984, p. 5B.

36. Don Melvin, "City Waterfront Developers Pin Hopes on Federal Grant," *BFP*, January 30, 1985, p. 2B.

37. On the disappearance of moderately priced housing, see Murray Bookchin, "The Bernie Sanders Paradox: When Socialism Grows Old," *Socialist Review* 90 (November–December 1986): 60–61. On the scale-down in size, see Don Melvin, "Current Alden Plan Scaled-Down Version," *BFP*, December 1, 1985, pp. 1A, 19A.

38. Don Melvin, "Chances Dim for Lakeside Development Grant," *BFP*, March 28, 1985, p. 1B.

39. Don Melvin, "Waterfront Setback Defeated," *BFP*, June 12, 1985, pp. 1B, 3B.

40. Mark Johnson, "Waterfront Pact Finally Finished," *BFP*, October 31, 1985, pp. 1B, 4B.

41. Michael Powell, "School Board Meets Today to Consider Lakefront Pact," *BFP*, November 14, 1985, p. 1B; Don Melvin, "Democrats Take Firm Stand Against Bond for Waterfront," *BFP*, October 22, 1985, p. 1B.

42. Don Melvin, "School Board Delays Waterfront Decision," *BFP*, November 15, 1985, p. 1B.

43. Mark Johnson, "School Board Says No to Waterfront Pact," *BFP*, November 22, 1985, pp. 1B, 6B.

44. Byran B. Higgins, "Dilemmas of Urban Socialism on the West Coast of New England," *Socialist Review* 90 (November–December 1986): 64–65.

45. Mark Johnson, "Sanders Denies Sellout to Alden on Waterfront," *BFP*, November 26, 1985, p. 4B.

46. Michael Powell, "The Battle for Burlington's Waterfront Heats Up," *BFP*, November 25, 1985, pp. 1B, 3B, and "Burlington's Waterfront Plan Deserves Support," *BFP*, December 2, 1985, p. 12A.

47. Mark Johnson, "Waterfront Plan Goes Down to Defeat," *BFP*, December 11, 1985, pp. 1A, 12A.

48. Mark Johnson, "Alden Throws in Towel After Voters Say No," *BFP*, December 11, 1985, pp. 1A, 12A.

49. Peter Freyne, "Inside Track," *Vermont Vanguard Press*, February 2–9, 1986, p. 9.

50. Mark Johnson, "City, Railroad Reopen Talks on Trust Doctrine," *BFP*, October 14, 1986, p. 1B. Peter Freyne, "Waterfront Dealing," *Vermont Vanguard Press*, October 19–26, 1986, pp. 1, 6, 7.

51. Peter Freyne, "Scope," *Vermont Vanguard Press*, October 5–12, 1986, p. 5.

52. Soifer, "Electoral Politics," pp. 312–16.

53. Mark Johnson, "Waterfront Truce Disintegrates," *Vermont Vanguard Press*, October 29–November 5, 1987, p. 5.

54. U.S. Department of Commerce, Bureau of the Census, 1980 Census of Burlington, Vermont, p. 9.

55. Hollis Hope, "Who'll Stop the Squeeze?" *Vermont Vanguard Press*, May 20–27, 1984, p. 11.

56. Nelson Hockert-Lotz, "Beyond the Waterfront," *Vermont Vanguard Press*, January 29–February 5, 1984, p. 11.

57. Diana Greene, "Whatever Happened to the Tenants' Rights Movement?" *Vermont Vanguard Press*, May 7–14, 1982, p. 15.

58. Susan Youngwood, "28 Waterfront Condos Sell Before Construction Begins," *BFP*, September 10, 1986, p. 4C.

59. Hockert-Lotz, "Beyond the Waterfront," p. 1.

60. Ibid.

61. Michael Powell, "Tax District Plan May Spur Waterfront Development," *BFP*, July 19, 1985, p. 1B.

62. Eric Lipton, "Bacteria Bay," *Vermont Vanguard Press*, June 7–14, 1987, pp. 1, 5.

63. Don Melvin, "State Tells City to Dump Excess Sewage in Lake," *BFP*, April 24, 1984, p. 6B.

64. Michael Powell, "Sewer Bond Termed as Crucial," *BFP*, October 18, 1984, p. 12B.

65. "Sewage Problems Should Be Remedied Soon," *BFP*, April 20, 1984, p. 12A.

66. Powell, "Sewer Bond Vote Termed as Crucial," p. 12B.

67. Don Melvin, "Report Sends Trash Burner to Scrapheap," *BFP*, December 7, 1983, pp. 1A, 9A.

68. Don Melvin, "Aldermen, Sanders Agree; Trash Burner Gets Dumped," *BFP*, December 13, 1983, p. 6B. Before making this decision, the mayor had vetoed construction of the plant until its economic feasibility could be studied. See John Feffer, "Trash Palace," *Vermont Vanguard Press*, June 19–26, 1983, pp. 1, 10, on the Burlington Environmental Alliance's efforts.

69. Antonio Pomerleau, Kendrick Bellows, and Michael D. Flynn, "Resource Recovery Facility Study" (Burlington, Vermont, December 2, 1983, Mimeographed), p. 4.

70. Don Melvin, "Burlington Might Improve Its Landfill Rather than Junk It," *BFP*, September 18, 1984, p. 1B.

71. Of all the female members of the Board of Aldermen, only Zoe Briener adopted the title of "alderwoman," and thus only when I speak of her in particular will I use that title.

72. Don Melvin, "Current Alden Plan Scaled-Down Version," *BFP*, December 1, 1985, pp. 1A, 19A.

73. Greg Guma, "Highway Robbery?" *Vermont Vanguard Press*, October 9–16, 1981, pp. 1, 10.

74. Michael Powell, "Strengths, Weaknesses Listed in Study of Burlington Economy," *BFP*, January 27, 1985, pp. 1E, 5E.

75. William Aswad, "Connector: Let's Get On with It," *BFP*, February 2, 1984, p. 6A. Greg Guma, "Highway Robbery?" pp. 1, 10.

76. Jo Schneiderman, "Neighborhood Power," *Vermont Vanguard Press*, May 8–15, 1981, p. 9.

77. John Steinbreder, "Some Welcome Southern Connector," *BFP*, June 22, 1981, pp. 1B–2B.

78. Terrill Bouricius, interview with author, Burlington, Vt., December 1983.

79. Rob Eley, "Connector Opponents Contest Funding," *BFP*, October 10, 1981, p. 1B.

80. Alan Abbey, "Barge Canal Listed as Hazardous Site," *BFP*, October 24, 1981, pp. 1A, 4A. Later it was discovered that other still-functioning enterprises also dumped toxic wastes in the canal.

81. "Canal Problems Could Delay Southern Connector," *BFP*, August 4, 1982, p. 8A.

82. Scott Mackay, "Planning Chairman Reprimanded for Allowing Connector Studies," *BFP*, October 19, 1982, p. 3B.

83. Don Melvin, "GE's Aswad Accused of Conflict of Interest," *BFP*, July 30, 1984, pp. 1B–2B.

84. Peggy Grodinsky, "Planning Chairman Resigns, Says Frustration Is a 'Factor,'" *BFP*, May 5, 1985, pp. 1B–2B.

85. Scott Mackay, "Sanders Delaying Connector Road, Gilson Charges," *BFP*, January 5, 1983, p. 1B.

86. Joan Beauchemin, interview with author, Burlington, Vt., December 1983.

87. Scott Mackay, "Sanders Won't Block Connector Land Transfer," *BFP*, February 15, 1983, p. 1B.

88. Scott Mackay, "Politics Could Dig Potholes in Southern Connector Plan," *BFP*, February 7, 1983, pp. 1B, 3B.

89. Deborah Sline, "I Can't Change Connector, Snelling Tells Sanders," *BFP*, February 10, 1983, pp. 1A, 12A.

90. Candace Page, "Connector Bills Soar but City's Share Declines," *BFP*, April 11, 1983, pp. 1B–2B.

91. "Southern Connector Project Has Been Studied to Death," *BFP*, July 15, 1983, p. 10A.

92. "Connector is Key to Further Development," *BFP*, October 26, 1983, p. 8A.

93. Samuel Sampson, "An Investigation May Be Necessary," *BFP*, February 4, 1984, p. 6A; Armand Beliveau, "Connector, If Built as Designed, May Not Do Anybody Any Good," *BFP*, January 25, 1984, p. 12A.

94. Don Melvin, "Tie Vote Defeats New Sanders' Connector Study," *BFP*, July 19, 1984, pp. 1B, 7B; William H. Brown, "Connector Change Would Be Costly in Time, Money," *BFP*, November 30, 1984, pp. 1B–2B.

95. Don Melvin, "Aldermen Switch, Will Consider 'Pine Parkway,'" *BFP*, July 24, 1984, p. 1B.

96. Don Melvin, "Court Says Connector Necessary," *BFP*, September 1, 1984, pp. 1B–2B.

97. Mark Johnson. "Opponents: Connector Faces Bumps," *BFP*, December 16, 1984, pp. 1B, 11B.

98. William H. Brown, "Federal Agency Allots $400,000 for Barge Canal," *BFP*, March 9, 1985, p. 1B.

99. Don Melvin, "Burlington Weighing 95-for-1 Land Swap," *BFP*, September 7, 1985, pp. 1B, 3B.

100. Don Melvin, "Sanders Eying Two-Lane Connector Plan," *BFP*, May 16, 1985, pp. 1B, 6B.

101. Don Melvin, "Breakthrough in Connector Case Seen," *BFP*, August 1, 1985, p. 1B.

102. Leslie Brown, "Crampton, Sanders Fail to Agree," *BFP*, August 9, 1985, pp. 1B–2B.

103. See Sarah Wilson, "EPA Completes Initial Cleanup of Barge Canal," *BFP*, December 6, 1985, p. 10B, and William R. Braun, "Burlington Barge Canal Cleanup About to Begin," *BFP*, December 2, 1985, p. 1B.

104. Don Melvin, "Crampton: City May Lose Connector Funds," *BFP*, October 29, 1985, pp. 1B–2B.

105. Susan Youngwood, "Businessmen, Mayor Collide on Connector," *BFP*, November 8, 1985, pp. 1B, 4B.

106. Christopher Graff, "City, State Put Pen to Accord for Connector," *BFP*, November 16, 1985, pp. 1B–2B.

107. Joan Beauchemin, "Sanders Helped in Reaching Sensible Connector Compromise," *BFP*, December 4, 1985, p. 8A.

108. Soiffer, "Electoral Politics," pp. 401–3.

109. Much of the following analysis is based on Greg Guma, "Southern Connector Would Do More Harm Than Good," *BFP*, February 3, 1983, p. 8A.

110. Michael Harrington and Mark Levinson, "The Perils of a Dual Economy," *Dissent* (Fall 1985): 417–26.

111. Caryl Stewart, in her 1987 bid for the Democratic mayoral nomination, suggested an electric trolley only to be embarrassed when she could not provide data on the cost. Peter Freyne, "Scope," *Vermont Vanguard Press*, January 11–18, 1987, p. 5.

112. "Subway Aids Buffalo Rebirth," *New York Times*, August 29, 1982, p. 38; Jane Perlez, "U.S. Study Finds Flaws in Rail System Being Built in Buffalo," *New York Times*, February 9, 1984, sec. B.

113. Scott Mackay, "Cable TV Committee to Study Burlington Service," *BFP*, May 5, 1983, p. 1B.

114. Private interviews by the author with Bernard Sanders, Peter Lackowski, Terrill Bouricius, and Greg Guma confirm that all of the above were socialists except Guma. All interviews held in Burlington, Vt., December 1983.

115. "Committee Should Stick to Issue of Cable TV Quality," *BFP*, May 6, 1983, p. 10A.

116. Scott Mackay, "Cable TV Committee to Study Burlington Service," *BFP*, May 5, 1983, p. 1B.

117. Scott Mackay, "Panel, Cable Firm View Different Channels," *BFP*, June 11, 1983, p. 2B.

118. Scott Mackay, "Cable TV Takeover Pondered," *BFP*, July 22, 1983, pp. 1A, 8A.

119. Scott Mackay, "Sanders Urges Burlington Utility to Study Cable TV," *BFP*, July 26, 1983, p. 5C.

120. Timothy S. Cronin, "Utility Not Interested in Cable Takeover," *BFP*, July 27, 1983, p. 10A.

121. Scott Mackay, "TV Panel Recommends 55-Channel City Cable," *BFP*, July 29, 1983, pp. 1B, 3B.

122. Rob Eley, "Cox Asks to Increase Rate, Cable Channels," *BFP*, September 14, 1983, pp. 1A, 5A.

123. Jim Cheng, "Cox Spokesman Hart Disputes Cable Study," *BFP*, January 14, 1984, p. 2B.

124. Rob Eley, "Cable TV Firm May Fight to Get BED Report," *BFP*, February 14, 1984, p. 5B.

125. Leslie Brown, "City Can Participate in Cox TV Case," *BFP*, March 6, 1984, pp. 1B–2B.

126. Brown is quoted in Don Melvin, "Cox Cable Unwraps Plans for Burlington's Public Access Channel," *BFP*, March 29, 1984, pp. 1B, 3B.

127. Mo Shafroth, "City to Prepare Cable TV Application," *BFP*, April 10, 1984, p. 2B.

128. Don Melvin, "Deal Drafted Between City and Cox Cable," *BFP*, June 27, 1984, pp. 1B, 3B.

129. Don Melvin, "City Considering Building Its Own Cable TV System," *BFP*, August 30, 1984, pp. 1B, 4B.

130. Don Melvin, "Sanders, Electric Panel Part Company over Cable," *BFP*, September 6, 1984, p. 1B.

131. Don Melvin, "Cox Cable Agreement Rejected by Aldermen," *BFP*, September 18, 1984, pp. 1B, 4B.

132. Don Melvin, "Aldermen Reject City Cable Idea," *BFP*, September 25, 1984, pp. 1B, 10B.

133. Michael Powell, "Public Service Board Hears City's Cable Request," *BFP*, September 26, 1984, p. 1B.

134. Jim Cheng, "PSB Sides with Cox Cable on Rates; Mayor Livid," *BFP*, October 20, 1984, p. 1B.

135. Jim Cheng, "Cox Cable Sells 3 Vt. Franchises," *BFP*, February 2, 1985, pp. 1A, 14A.

136. Michael Powell, "Aldermen May Stall Cox Pole Pact," *BFP*, February 18, 1985, p. 1B.

137. Jim Cheng, "City to Appeal City TV Ruling to High Court," *BFP*, February 20, 1985, p. 1B.

138. See Don Melvin, "Legality Snags City Cable TV System," *BFP*, October 11, 1984, p. 1B.

139. William Doyle, "New Charter Law Was Necessary," *BFP*, June 3, 1984, p. 12A.

140. Jim Cheng, "Cable Fight Goes to High Court," *BFP*, March 9, 1984, p. 3B.

141. Don Melvin, "City Will Get $1 Million in Cable TV Deal," *BFP*, March 30, 1985, pp. 1A, 15A.

142. David Hench, "Aldermen Unanimously Approve Cable Television Deal," *BFP*, April 3, 1985, p. 5B.

143. "Cable Television Agreement a Coup for Mayor Sanders," *BFP*, April 2, 1985, p. 6A.

144. Peter Freyne, "Cable TV," *Vermont Vanguard Press*, February 15–22, 1987, pp. 1, 10–11.

145. Mark Johnson, "Cable TV Rates to Skyrocket?" *Vermont Vanguard Press*, September 24–October 1, 1987, p. 5.

146. "Committee Should Stick to Issue of Cable TV Quality," p. 10A.

147. "Little Justification for City-Owned Cable TV," *BFP*, September 19, 1983, p. 8A.

CHAPTER 6

1. Debbie Bookchin, "Decaying Dynasty: Paquette Faces Dissent and Three Challengers," *Vermont Vanguard Press*, February 20–27, 1981, p. 1.

2. Ibid., p. 10.

3. Ibid.

4. Ibid.

5. Alberta M. Sbragia, "The 1970s: A Decade of Change in Local Government Finance," in *The Municipal Money Chase,* ed. Alberta M. Sbragia (Boulder, Colo.: Westview Press, 1983), p. 13. On circuit breakers also see J. Richard Aronson and John L. Hilley, *Financing State and Local Governments*, 4th ed. (Washington, D.C.: Brookings Institution, 1986), pp. 138–39.

6. "Burlington Should Consider Ending Inventory Tax," *Burlington Free Press* (hereafter cited as *BFP*), July 3, 1982, p. 11 A.

7. "22 Towns Repealed Business Inventory Tax," *BFP*, March 5, 1981, p. 7B.

8. Alan Abbey, "Board Cuts Tax Assessment of Burlington Square Mall," *BFP*, August 11, 1981, p. 1B.

9. U.S. Census figures quoted in Fox Butterfield, "2 Neighbors in New England More Than a Border Apart," *New York Times*, October 8, 1984, sec. A.

10. Scott Mackay, "Aldermen Accept Reappraisal Proposal," *BFP*, March 25, 1982, p. 1B.

11. Scott Mackay, "Unlike Some State Universities, UVM Rides Free," *BFP*, December 13, 1981, pp. 1B–2B.

12. Scott Mackay, "Study Says UVM Pays $1.8 Million Indirectly to City," *BFP*, October 12, 1982, pp. 1B–2B.

13. Scott Mackay, "Sanders Blasts UVM Study on Services," *BFP*, October 30, 1982, p. 1B.

14. The dynamics of the not-for-profit sector have not been sufficiently theorized as of this writing. Urban scholars in particular need to spend more time on this burgeoning sector of the economy and its effects on the autonomy of the local state.

15. Peter Letzelter-Smith, "UVM Under the Campaign Gun," *Vermont Vanguard Press*, February 9–16, 1986, pp 5–6.

16. Peter Freyne, "UVM Stoops to Conquer," *Vermont Vanguard Press*, August 3–10, 1986, p. 5.

17. Amy Schlegel and Peter Freyne, "City vs MCHV," *Vermont Vanguard Press*, August 6–13, 1987, pp. 1, 6.

18. Mark Johnson, "Medical Center Beats Bernie," *Vermont Vanguard Press*, September 24–October 1, 1987, p. 5; Steven Soifer, "Electoral Politics and Social Change," (Ph.D. diss., Brandeis University, 1988), pp. 379–81.

19. Ted Teaford, "Stephany Proposes Repeal of Inventory Tax," *BFP*, February 16, 1983, p. 1B.

20. Scott Mackay, "Vt. Must Shift Property Tax Burden, Forum Told," *BFP*, November 3, 1983, pp. 1B, 7B.

21. Don Melvin, "Sanders Seeking Alternative to Increase in Property Tax," *BFP*, January 16, 1985, pp. 1B–2B.

22. Richard D. Bingham, *State Government in an Urban Society* (New York: Random House, 1986), p. 308.

23. William J. Donovan, "Sanders, Jeffrey Join Attack on Tax," *BFP*, October 7, 1985, p. 4B.

24. Don Melvin, "Sanders, Burns Offer Property Tax Alternatives," *BFP*, January 17, 1985, p. 6B.

25. Ibid.

26. Don Melvin, "Officials Lobby for New Taxes," *BFP*, March 15, 1985, pp. 1B, 8B.

27. Sarah Wilson, "House Committee Rejects New Burlington Taxes," *BFP*, March 30, 1985, p. 1B.

28. Don Melvin and Michael Powell, "Burlington Charter Changes Defeated," *BFP*, April 17, 1985, pp. 1A, 11A.

29. Michael Powell, "School Tax Increase Goes Down to Defeat," *BFP*, June 12, 1985, pp. 1A, 12A.

30. Don Melvin, "GE Asking Further Cut in Tax Bill," *BFP*, June 15, 1985, pp. 1B, 4B.

31. Don Melvin, "Sanders Calls on GE to Drop Tax Appeal," *BFP*, June 18, 1985, p. 2B.

32. Jonathan Leopold, "State's Inaction Puts Tax Burden in Wrong Place," *BFP*, October 16, 1986, p. 10A.

33. Melvin, "GE Asking Further Cut in Tax Bill," p. 4B.

34. David Gram, "Municipalities Stymied by Reappraisal Woes," *BFP*, July 27, 1985, pp. 1B–2B.

35. Soifer, "Electoral Politics," pp. 376–78.

36. Ibid., pp. 250–53.

37. Ibid.

38. Kevin J. Kelley, "Bernie's Daycare Dilemma," *Vermont Vanguard Press*, October 1–8, 1987, p. 6; Kevin J. Kelley, "Bernie Boosts Daycare," *Vermont Vanguard Press*, October 8–15, 1987, p. 5.

39. Mark Johnson, "Battle over the Ballot," *Vermont Vanguard Press*, June 21–28, 1988, p. 8.

40. Clemens P. Work and Richard L. DeLouise, "Cities Where Business Is Best," *U.S. News and World Report*, November 11, 1985, p. 65.

41. "Abolishing Inventory Tax Would Boost Development," *BFP*, June 19, 1984, p. 13A.

42. Gram, "Municipalities Stymied by Reappraisal Woes," pp. 1B–2B.

43. "Coalition Aldermen Unduly Scaring Homeowners," *BFP*, March 23, 1985, p. 14A.

44. Peter Freyne, "Inside Track," *Vermont Vanguard Press*, September 17–24, 1987, p. 8.

45. According to the city clerk and the city attorney, the city charter allowed for a city gross receipts tax, which is a tax on the establishment offering those services. A rooms and meals tax would be a state sales tax charged directly to the customer; it would need state legislative approval. Since the former tax was disallowed at one point by the state legislature, the distinction became moot. See City Clerk Jim Rader's comments on Soifer, "Electoral Politics," p. 363.

46. Scott Mackay, "Reappraisal, Bars, UVM Are Stumbling Blocks for Sanders' Tax Plan," *BFP*, December 11, 1981, pp. 1B, 4B.

47. Scott Mackay, "Sanders Seeks City Tax on Bed, Bread, Beverage," *BFP*, December 19, 1981, pp. 1B–2B.

48. John L. Franco, "Tax Proposals Deserve More than 'Simple-minded' Protests," *BFP*, January 12, 1982, p. 12A.

49. Louis Berney, "Plan Would Raise Rooms, Meals Tax," *BFP*, April 25, 1981, pp. 1B–2B.

50. Scott Mackay, "Sanders Fails to Generate Backing for Tax Proposal," *BFP*, January 28, 1982, p. 1B.

51. Neil Davis, "Snelling Scolds Burlington for City Tax Proposal," *BFP*, January 29, 1982, pp. 1B–2B.

52. Deborah Sline, "Burlington Wins Its Battle over Taxation Rights," *BFP*, February 26, 1982, pp. 1A, 6A.

53. Alan Abbey, "Housing Commission Plans Crushed," *BFP*, April 22, 1981, pp. 1A, 10A.

54. Diane Mueller, "Opposition Grows to Rooms and Meals Tax," *Vermont Vanguard Press*, March 5–12, 1982, p. 8.

55. Jodie Peck, "Tax Opponents Using Misleading Tactics, Proponents Claim," *BFP*, June 6, 1982, p. 1B.

56. Scott Mackay, "Mayor Says He'll Veto Property Tax Vote," *BFP*, May 11, 1982, pp. 1B–2B.

57. Scott Mackay, "Mayor Sanders Taking Gamble on Acceptance of Meals Tax," *BFP*, May 30, 1982, pp. 1B, 3B.

58. Scott Mackay, "Burlington's Voters Say No to All Three Tax Proposals," *BFP*, June 9, 1982, pp. 1A, 8A.

59. Scott Mackay, "Sanders to Do Battle for His Tax Plan," *BFP*, June 10, 1982, p. 1B.

60. Susan Youngwood, "School Panel Recommends Substitute Tax," *BFP*, January 17, 1985, p. 1B.

61. Susan Youngwood, "City Rooms, Meals Tax Passes First Hurdle," *BFP*, January 18, 1985, pp. 1B, 5B.

62. "Rooms and Meals Tax Not the Answer for Schools," *BFP*, January 19, 1985, p. 12A.

63. Jim Cheng, "Restaurateurs Divided over City Tax Proposal," *BFP*, January 18, 1985, p. 5B.

64. Michael Powell, "Rooms and Meals Tax Approved by Majority," *BFP*, March 6, 1985, p. 7B.

65. "Sanders Urges Speaker to Back City Taxes," *BFP*, March 21, 1985, p. 4B.

66. Sarah Wilson, "House Won't Yield State Powers," *BFP*, April 17, 1985, pp. 1A, 11A.

67. All of this occurred after the research for this study was completed. See Soifer, "Electoral Politics," pp. 372–76.

68. Joshua Mamis, "Taking It to the Courts," *Vermont Vanguard Press*, May 17–24, 1987, pp. 1, 6–7.

69. Howard Dean, "Local Taxes Wouldn't Help All in Vt.," *BFP*, February 1, 1985, p. 12A.

70. Scott Mackay, "Sanders Wants to Institute New Tax on Utilities," *BFP*, November 11, 1982, p. 1B.

71. Candace Page, "Sanders Insists Fee Proposal Nothing New," *BFP*, November 18, 1982, p. 1B.

72. Scott Mackay, "Right-of-Ways Fees Face Legal Battles," *BFP*, March 16, 1983, pp. 1B–2B.

73. Alexandra Marks and Scott Mackay, "Cox Asks FCC to Bar City Cable Fee," *BFP*, April 29, 1983, p. 5B.

74. Scott Mackay, "NET Says Business Will Bear Sanders' Fee," *BFP*, June 1, 1985, pp. 1B, 3B.

75. Scott Mackay, "City Won't Charge Utility for Cost of Street Repairs," *BFP*, May 3, 1983, p. 5B.

76. Scott Mackay, "Utilities Argue Against Street Rents," *BFP*, June 2, 1983, pp. 1B–2B.

77. Scott Mackay, "City Asks PSB to Make Utility Pay for Lobbying," *BFP*, June 3, 1983, p. 1B.

78. Scott Mackay, "Sanders Proposes Fee for Excavation" *BFP*, August 10, 1983, p. 1A.

79. Scott Mackay, "Utilities Aim Guns at Excavation Fee," *BFP*, November 4, 1983, p. 5B.

80. James J. Lehane, Sr., "City's Latest Street Ordinance Is Absurd," *BFP*, November 17, 1983, p. 14A.

81. Don Melvin, "Street Commission to Ask for $10.30 Excavation Fee," *BFP*, January 4, 1984, pp. 1B–2B.

82. "Aldermen Should Reject Proposed Street Repair Fees," *BFP*, October 21, 1983, p. 10A.

83. Don Melvin, "Sanders Links Tax Support to Excavation Fee Approval," *BFP*, January 6, 1984, p. 2B.

84. Don Melvin, "Aldermen Pass Street Excavation Fee," *BFP*, March 20, 1984, pp. 1B, 4B.

85. Ted Teaford, "Excavation Fee Put on Hold While Court Weighs Dispute," *BFP*, August 3, 1984, p. 1B.

86. Don Melvin, "Burlington Protests Levying of Surcharge Cable TV," *BFP*, September 1, 1984, p. 1B.

87. Don Melvin, "City Excavation Fee Back at Ground Level," *BFP*, October 10, 1984, p. 1B.

88. Don Melvin, "Excavation Fee OK'd: Question: How Much?" *BFP*, January 23, 1985, pp. 1B–2B. Parentheses were used in the Melvin article.

89. Mike Donoghue, "Report Cites Case for Higher Excavation Fee," *BFP*, June 15, 1985, p. 1B.

90. Mark Johnson, "1.76 Million Payment OK'd for Excavations," *BFP*, December 16, 1985, pp. 1B, 5B.

91. Mamis, "Taking It to the Courts," pp. 1, 6–7.

92. "City Income Tax," *BFP*, January 2, 1982, p. 12A.

93. Steve Rosenfeld, "State, Municipalities at Odds over Charter," *BFP*, March 18, 1985, pp. 1B, 4B.

94. Paul Peterson has made the point that cities cannot juridically control the emigration of people or capital in *City Limits* (Chicago: University of Chicago Press, 1981), pp. 25–28.

95. Neil Davis, "Coalition Unwraps Tax Reform Plan, Sees Income Hike," *BFP*, September 14, 1985, p. 1B.

CHAPTER 7

1. Harold D. Lasswell, *Who Gets What, When, How?* (New York: Macmillan, 1936).

2. Debbie Bookchin, "Fastest Guns in the West," *Vermont Vanguard Press*, July 17–24, 1981, pp. 1, 10–12.

3. Ibid., p. 11. The original source was unattributed.

4. Ibid., p. 10.

5. Ibid., p. 11.

6. Ibid.

7. Neil Davis, "Arms Demonstrators Target GE Property," *Burlington Free Press* (hereafter cited as *BFP*), June 7, 1983, p. 6B.

8. Greg Guma, interview with author, Burlington, Vt., December 1983.

9. Ibid.

10. See Kathy E. Ferguson, *The Feminist Case Against Bureaucracy* (Philadelphia: Temple University Press, 1984), pp. 112–16, on this point.

11. Scott Mackay, "GE Union, Sanders Join Forces to Protest Blockade," *BFP*, July 10, 1983, p. 1B.

12. Ibid.

13. Scott Mackay, "Peace Activists Upset with Sanders," *BFP*, June 12, 1983, p. 5B.

14. Hilary Scott, "General Electric Protesters Agree to Limited Sit-In," *BFP*, June 17, 1983, p. 1B.

15. Greg Guma interview.

16. Scott, "General Electric Protesters Agree to Limited Sit-In," p. 1B.

17. Mike Donoghue, "Hundreds March as Mayor Deals with Other Items," *BFP*, June 19, 1983, pp. 1B–2B.

18. Mike Donoghue, "Despite 88 Arrests, Protest at GE Plant Is Calm, Amicable," *BFP*, June 21, 1983, pp. 1A, 16A; Chris Fleary and Eric Sorenson, "Delaying the War Back Home," *Vermont Vanguard Press*, June 26–July 3, 1983, p. 3.

19. "An All-Too Civil Disobedience," *Vermont Vanguard Press*, June 26–July 3, 1983, p. 3.

20. Don Melvin, "Police Search for Nameless GE Protesters," *BFP*, June 22, 1983, p. 1B.

21. Deborah Schoch, "Council Votes 5–5 on Grenada," *BFP*, November 1, 1983, pp. 1B–2B.

22. Sara Elinoff, "Grenada Resolution: Tie Score, No Overtime," *Vermont Vanguard Press*, November 6–13, 1983, pp. 5–6.

23. Sara Elinoff, "Grenada Resolution," p. 6.

24. Schoch, "Council Votes 5–5 on Grenada," pp. 1B–2B.

25. "Debate Made Officials Ignore City Business," *BFP*, November 2, 1983, p. 10A.

26. "Closing Areas to Foreigners Is Ridiculous," *BFP*, November 23, 1983, p. 12A.

27. Carol Conragen, "The Russians Aren't Coming! The Russians Aren't Coming!" *Vermont Vanguard Press*, December 4–11, 1983, pp. 5–6.

28. Steve Farnsworth, "Ban on Russians Scalds Sanders," *BFP*, November 25, 1983, p. 4B.

29. John Goodrow and Steve Farnsworth, "Travel Ban Protest Rejected," *BFP*, November 29, 1983, pp. 1B, 5B.

250 Notes to Chapter 7

31. Conragen, "The Russians Aren't Coming!" pp. 5–6.

32. Goodrow and Farnsworth, "Travel Ban Protest Rejected," pp. 1B, 5B.

33. Don Melvin, "Sanders Defends His Stance on National, World Issues," *BFP*, December 2, 1983, p. 6B.

34. Barr Swennerfelt, "Recent Sit-In Came at the Right Time," *BFP*, March 31, 1984, p. 8A.

35. Ted Teaford, "Burlington May Get Sister City in Nicaragua," *BFP*, July 28, 1984, p. 1B.

36. Don Melvin, "Burlington Approves Sister City," *BFP*, September 18, 1984, pp. 1B, 4B.

37. "City Hall Should First Deal with City's Problems," *BFP*, September 19, 1984, p. 10A.

38. William H. Braun, "Sanders Defends Time Spent on World Policies," *BFP*, September 21, 1984, p. 10B.

39. Ibid.

40. Deborah Schoch, "City's Aldermen Tiptoe Around Sanctuary Issue," *BFP*, April 16, 1985, pp. 1A, 9A.

41. Don Melvin, "Global Issues Won't Be Heard on Aldermen's Regular Agenda," *BFP*, April 23, 1985, p. 1B.

42. "Separate Meetings for Global Issues: A Worthwhile Idea," *BFP*, April 24, 1985, p. 10A.

43. Peter Freyne, "Inside Track," *Vermont Vanguard Press*, January 18–25, 1987, pp. 8–9.

44. Don Melvin, "Aldermen OK Encouraging Nicaraguan Trade Despite Embargo," *BFP*, May 22, 1985, p. 1B.

45. Michael Powell, "Mayor Sanders Planning to Go to Nicaragua," *BFP*, July 8, 1985, pp. 1B, 3B.

46. "Is Mayor's Excursion to Nicaragua Necessary?" *BFP*, July 11, 1985, p. 12A.

47. Don Melvin, "Nicaraguan Trip Could Hurt Mayor," *BFP*, July 14, 1985, pp. 1A, 7A.

48. Don Melvin, "Sanders Begins Nicaraguan Visit," *BFP*, July 19, 1985, pp. 1A, 5A.

49. Don Melvin, "Ortega Meeting Set for Today," *BFP*, July 19, 1985, pp. 1A, 8A.

50. Don Melvin, "Mayor Sanders Meets with Ortega," *BFP*, July 21, 1985, pp. 1A, 6A.

51. Don Melvin, "Sanders Says Nicaragua Is Not a Military Threat to Any Nation," *BFP*, July 22, 1985, pp. 1A, 6A.

52. Diane Kearns, "Sanders Praises Nicaragua's Style of Government," *BFP*, August 2, 1985, p. 1B.

53. Peter Freyne, "Inside Track," *Vermont Vanguard Press*, April 14–21, 1988, p. 9.

54. Mackay, "GE Union, Sanders Join Forces to Protest Blockade," p. 1B. The mayor reiterated this position to me in a personal interview. Bernard Sanders, interview with author, Burlington, Vt., December 1983.

55. Mackay, "G.E. Union, Sanders Join Forces to Protest Blockade," p. 1B.

56. Mann, "Under the Gun," p. 9.

57. Bookchin, "Fastest Guns in the West," p. 11.

58. Susan Youngwood, "Renovated Maltex Building: An 'Incubator of Businesses,'" BFP, May 14, 1985, p. 4C.

59. Lecture by Robert Lekachman, Socialist Scholars' Conference, New York, April 1986.

60. Bernard Sanders interview.

61. Mann, "Under the Gun," p. 9.

62. Mark Johnson, "Fewer Protesters than Expected Demonstrate Against U.S. Policy," BFP, April 30, 1985, p. 1B.

63. William H. Braun and Ted Teaford, "24 Arrested for Trespassing in Central American Protests," BFP, June 13, 1985, pp. 1A, 9A.

64. Jim Cheng and William H. Braun, "Assistant City Treasurer Swennerfelt Resigns," BFP, August 16, 1985, pp. 1B, 8B.

65. Don Melvin, "Mayor Explains Policy Concerning Protesting," BFP, August 20, 1985, p. 4B.

66. Kevin J. Kelley, "A Woman Behind Bars," Vermont Vanguard Press, September 29–October 6, 1988, p. 5.

CHAPTER 8

1. The information on the six-week delay came from: Amy Magdoff, co-chair of the Mayor's Task Force on Women, interview with author, Burlington, Vt., December 1983. On the independent status of the Task Force on Women, see Joy Livingston, "Mayor's Task Force," Commonwoman, August 1981, pp. 4–5.

2. Leslie Brown, "For Young Women, Feminism Doesn't Seem Germane," Burlington Free Press (hereafter cited as BFP), March 6, 1984, pp. 1D, 6D.

3. Leslie Brown, "Teen-Age Girls Take Equality for Granted," BFP, March 7, 1984, pp. 1D, 5D. (Note that the latter comment is also consistent with capitalist ideology.)

4. Leslie Brown, "For Young Women, Feminism Doesn't Seem Germane," p. 6D.

5. The reduced numbers of feminists may prove to be analogous to the left's experience during the McCarthy era. The rediscovery of the left during the cultural upheaval of the 1960s may prefigure a future rebirth of feminism as a mass movement after a productive period of theoretical inquiry.

6. John Reilly, "Angry Women Storm Sigma Nu Fraternity," *BFP*, March 15, 1981, pp. 1B–2B.

7. Linda Comito, "Task Force on Women," *Commonwoman*, April–May 1983, p. 4.

8. Livingston, "Mayor's Task Force," pp. 4–5. Since the number of blacks in Burlington, as in Vermont as a whole, is less than 1 percent, the lack of black participation was, practically speaking, a foregone conclusion.

9. Rob Eley, "Burlington Zoners OK Plans for Battered Women's Shelter," *BFP*, June 4, 1982, 3B; Alexandra Marks, "Battered Women's Shelter Opens Up in Burlington," *BFP*, April 9, 1983, pp. 1B–2B.

10. Linda Comito, "Task Force on Women," p. 4.

11. Advertisement for Bernard Sanders, *Commonwoman*, February 1983, p. 11.

12. Linda Comito, "Task Force on Women," p. 4.

13. Advertisement, p. 11.

14. Ronnie J. Steinberg, "A Want of Harmony: Perspectives on Wage Discrimination and Comparable Worth," *Comparable Worth and Wage Discrimination*, ed. Helen Remick (Philadelphia: Temple University Press, 1984), p. 19.

15. "Concept of Pay Based on Worth Is the 'Looniest,' Rights Chief Says," *New York Times*, November 17, 1984, sec. A.

16. James J. Dunn, "City Is Tying 'Equal Pay' to 'Comparable Worth,'" *BFP*, January 28, 1984, p. 8A.

17. John Goodrow, "City Employees Reject Contract," *BFP*, October 8, 1983, pp. 1B–2B.

18. Ibid.

19. Steve Farnsworth, "Burlington City Workers OK Contract by 59–5 Vote," *BFP*, November 11, 1983, p. 5B.

20. Vicki Smith, "The Politics of Penile Penetration," *Commonwoman*, August 1978, pp. 4, 15.

21. Debi Ennis, "Straight Talk," *Commonwoman*, August 1978, pp. 4, 11.

22. Suzanne Gillis, interview with author, Burlington, Vt., December 1983.

23. Dian Mueller, "Everywoman's Place: In the Heart of the Women's Community," *Vermont Vanguard Press*, February 26–March 5, 1982, pp. 18–19.

24. Scott Mackay, "Gays' Day is Endorsed By Council," *BFP*, June 15, 1983, pp. 1B, 4B.

25. Terrill Bouricius, interview with author, Burlington, Vt., December 1983.

26. Several letters were printed under the title "Homosexual, Lesbian Pride Day 'An Abomination to Our Lord,'" *BFP*, June 24, 1983, p. 12A.

27. Peggy Luhrs, "Lesbian/Gay Pride/Promise," *Commonwoman*, August 1983, p. 1.

28. Don Melvin, "Aldermen Sidestep Proclamation for Gay Day," *BFP*, May 22, 1984, p. 3B.

29. Michael Powell, "Gays Hold Celebration in Burlington," *BFP*, June 17, 1984, p. 1B.

30. Aileen Lachs, "Housing Code Sidestepped," *Vermont Vanguard Press*, December 9–16, 1984, pp. 6, 8.

31. Don Melvin, "Aldermen OK Housing Ordinance," *BFP*, October 10, 1984, p. 6B.

32. "Housing: Justice at Last," *Vermont Vanguard Press*, October 14–21, 1984, p. 3.

33. Melvin, "Aldermen OK Housing Ordinance," p. 6B.

34. Ibid.

35. Ibid.

36. Lachs, "Housing Code Sidestepped," p. 8.

37. Ibid.

38. Alan Abbey, "Housing Commission Plans Crushed," *BFP*, April 22, 1981, pp. 1A, 10A.

39. Two works that emphasize the conscious role-modeling approach are Cynthia Fuchs Epstein, *Woman's Place: Options and Limits in Professional Careers* (Berkeley: University of California Press, 1971), and Elizabeth Janaway, *Man's World, Woman's Place* (New York: Dell, 1971). Two books that take a neo-Freudian sublimation approach are Dorothy Dinnerstein, *The Mermaid and the Minotaur* (New York: Harper Colophon, 1977), and Nancy Chodorow, *The Reproduction of Mothering* (Berkeley: University of California Press, 1978).

40. Helen Remick and Ronnie J. Steinberg, "Technical Possibilities and Political Realities," *Comparable Worth and Wage Discrimination*, ed. Helen Remick (Philadelphia: Temple University Press, 1984), p. 289.

41. Robert S. Babcock, Jr., *A Reclassification and Compensation Plan for the City of Burlington* (Montpelier, Vt.: Labor Relations Associates, [1983]), pp. 3, 10.

42. Ibid., p. 6.

43. Steinberg, "A Want of Harmony," p. 21.

44. Suzanne Gillis interview.

45. Linda Wittenberg and Carol Cohen, "CW Speaks with Bernie Sanders," *Commonwoman*, May 1981, pp. 1, 15.

46. "Where Are the Women?" *BFP*, June 7, 1985, p. 14A.

47. Don Melvin, "Clavelle Wants to Spark Interest in Firewomen," *BFP*, May 22, 1983, pp. 1B–2B.

48. Wittenberg and Cohen, "CW Speaks with Bernie Sanders," p. 15.

CHAPTER 9

1. Paul E. Peterson, *City Limits* (Chicago: Chicago University Press, 1981).

2. Ibid., pp. 175–78.

3. "Editorial," *Vermont Vanguard Press*, October 12–19, 1986, p. 3.

4. Sally Johnson, "Vermonters Battle Mall's Developer," *New York Times*, January 8, 1989, sec. A.

CHAPTER 10

1. William K. Tabb has broken ground by offering some neo-Marxian prescriptions for the local state. Outside of the concrete suggestions for a community development corporation and a new liberal-labor coalition, there is little here that has not been tried under the Johnson administration's War on Poverty. See William K. Tabb, "A Pro-People Urban Policy," in *Marxism and the Metropolis*, 2d ed., ed. William K. Tabb and Larry Sawers (New York: Oxford University Press, 1984).

2. See Kristi Anderson, "Generation, Partisan Shift, and Realignment: A Glance Back to the New Deal," in *The Changing American Voter*, enlarged ed., by Norman H. Nie, Sidney Verba, and John R. Petrocik (Cambridge, Mass.: Harvard University Press, 1979).

3. Tom W. Rice, "Identity Crisis," *Vermont Vanguard Press*, March 22–29, 1987, pp. 11–12.

4. It should be noted that this prescription was made in my dissertation: William Jon Conroy, "The Limits and Directions of a Radical City Regime: The Case of Burlington, Vermont" (Ph.D. diss., Fordham University, 1987). Every reader who has commented on my prescription has done so negatively. Until it is tried and has failed or some other solution is tried that succeeds, I stand by my comments.

5. Arthur M. Schlesinger, Jr., *The Cycles of American History* (Boston: Houghton-Mifflin, 1986).

6. Ibid., p. 47.

7. Michael Harrington has predicted a left resurgence by 1991. Michael Harrington, *The Next Left: The History of a Future* (New York: Henry Holt, 1986), p. 1.

8. This income tax transfer plan is inspired by the one presented in Samuel Bowles, David M. Gordon, and Thomas E. Weisskopf, *Beyond the Waste Land: A Democratic Alternative to Economic Decline* (Garden City, N.Y.: Anchor Press/Doubleday, 1983), pp. 374–76. I have changed the proposal of Bowles et al. from a national to state and local government transfer to a state to local government redistribution because I do not believe the American left can capture the national government in the foreseeable future.

9. On the encroachment of the national government on the states, see Michael D. Reagan, *The New Federalism* (New York: Oxford University Press, 1972).

10. Pierre Clavel, *The Progressive City: Planning and Participation, 1969–1984* (New Brunswick, N.J.: Rutgers University Press, 1986), p. 180.

11. Murray Bookchin, "The Bernie Sanders Paradox: When Socialism Grows Old," *Socialist Review* 90 (November–December 1986): 56–58.

12. The left should not automatically reject such proposals as capitalistic. Worker-owned sanitation businesses run by community residents are just one progressive possibility.

13. The United States Supreme Court has delivered an opinion restricting local land use controls where a "burden results from governmental action that amounted to a taking; the just compensation clause of the Fifth Amendment requires that the government pay the landowner for the value of the use of the land during this period." Justice William H. Rehnquist, First English Evangelical Lutheran Church of Glendate v. County of Los Angeles, No. 85-1199, quoted in Stuart Taylor, Jr., *New York Times*, June 10, 1987, p. 26. Some migration of authority to the national government could be expected if the left captured a state government. Whether this decision would invalidate an expansion of authority over land use by local government will not be known until the threshold of "burden" is elaborated.

14. Although my reconstruction of local government to a more radical democratic participatory form does not follow any one thinker's writings, the most important has been Benjamin Barber, *Strong Democracy: Participatory Politics for a New Age* (Los Angeles: University of California Press, 1984), pp. 261–93.

15. On "nondecision making" (keeping items off the agenda), see Peter Bachrach and Morton S. Baratz, *Power and Poverty: Theory and Practice* (New York: Oxford University Press, 1970), Chapter 1, "Two Faces of Power."

16. See Martin Carnoy and Derek Shearer, *Economic Democracy: The Challenge of the 1980s* (Armonk, N.Y.: M.E. Sharpe, 1980), pp. 152–57. Carnoy and Shearer, to their credit, and unlike most left authors, have written a book that is explicitly prescriptive. However, they optimistically assume a national left movement will come to control the national as well as state and local governments.

Index

Please remember that this is a library book,
and that it belongs only temporarily to each
person who uses it. Be considerate. Do
not write in this, or any, library book.